BUILDING TOGETHER

Case Studies in Participatory Planning
and Community Building

Roger Katan

with

Ronald Shiffman

New Village Press, New York

Published in the United States by
New Village Press
@ Centre for Social Innovation
601 West 26th Street, Suite 325-11
New York, NY 10001
bookorders@newvillagepress.net
www.newvillagepress.net

New Village Press is a public-benefit, not-for-profit publishing venture of Architects/Designers/Planners for Social Responsibility.

Grateful acknowledgment is made to the Graham Foundation for funding the translation of *Bâtir Ensemble*, the French publication on which this book is based, and for funding the updating and expansion of that original work.

In support of the Greenpress Initiative, New Village Press is committed to the preservation of endangered forests globally and advancing best practices within the book and paper industries. The printing papers used in this book are 100% recycled fiber, acid-free (Process Chlorine Free), and have been certified with the Forest Stewardship Council (FSC).

Original paperback ISBN 9781613320167

Publication Date: October 2014

FIRST EDITION

Library of Congress Cataloging-in-Publication Data

Katan, Roger.
    Building together : case studies in participatory planning and community building / Roger Katan with Ronald Shiffman. — First edition.
        pages cm
    Includes bibliographical references and index.
    1. City planning — Citizen participation — Case studies. 2. Community development — Case studies. I. Shiffman, Ron. II. Title.
    HT166.K3598 2014
    307.1'216 — dc23   2014029928

Front cover design: Robert Crumb

Cover photograph: Construction of a squatter settlement, Bogota, Colombia, circa 1970, courtesy Faculty of Architecture, Los Andes University

Interior design and composition: Leigh McLellan Design

BUILDING TOGETHER

Contents

Foreword

Dore Ashton

was first introduced to the work of Roger Katan in the late 1960s while researching my book for the World Cultural Guides series— *New York: Architecture, Sculpture, Painting*. What strange calling, I wondered, should draw a Mediterranean architect—born in Morocco, educated in the Beaux Arts School in Paris—from the elite Philadelphia office of Louis Kahn to the grit of Harlem poverty?

Many young architects at that time rebelled against the ideal concepts propounded by older architects. Philosophical resistance to luxury builders and their idea of urban embellishment was epitomized by those who called themselves *advocate planners*. Like Roger Katan, these planners insisted that architects can function only if they are prepared to extend themselves to activities previously considered beyond their realm of competence. Katan's attitude was a long way from the aristocratic distance of an H. H. Richardson, whose clients took his word for law, and were always rich. Katan's clients were the community as a whole, mostly the very poor in the ghettoes of Harlem, who shared with him the planner's task.

According to Katan, the only way to realize the human needs of urban citizenry is to work from every possible vantage point. He himself lived in East Harlem, had an open house system in which his neighborhood clients were free to drop in, and spent a great deal of his time teaching these neighbors the principles of planning and design. By helping them organize themselves and state their needs coherently, Katan was able to develop plans that made sense.

He also recognized the necessity of learning the intricacies of city bureaucracy and how to deal with the political aspects of each citizen's existence. Over the ten years he spent in Harlem, Katan developed a number of alternative plans for rehabilitation and rebuilding in his neighborhood. These plans showed visual imagination and indicated his close understanding of the lives of the residents in East Harlem.

Katan proposed housing for the sites to incorporate the old housing projects and be built on a prefabricated shelf system with individuals buying or leasing lots in the sky. He defended the right of the community to look forward to economic amelioration and the possibility for each individual to make a better home without leaving the neighborhood. In Katan's words, "The determination of an individual's dwelling lies, as it has with residential housing throughout human history, on his financial means, technical know-how, and personal whim. Only in this way can we be open to the essential quality of organic diversity within the urban environment, which has been the natural outcome of human settlement in the past. This diversity is an imponderable no architect can foresee— only the inhabitants and time can create it."

Another example of the fruits of Katan's public-spirited labors was a projected multi-service center planned with local residents—a kind of shopping center for social services such as legal advice, daycare, healthcare, and education, which took care of these and a host of other needs expressed by the residents of this teeming neighborhood.

After having spent ten years in East Harlem, Katan went on to work for the United Nations and other international organizations in West Africa and Latin America. He helped create in Burkina Faso one of the first micro-credit organizations. He also spent close to twenty years in South America working directly with communities on the design and construction of housing and other vernacular structures that utilized indigenous building techniques. He was a strong proponent of traditional building methods, pointing out how these practical alternatives offer superior affordability, ecology, and cultural appropriateness to industrialized systems. Katan also pioneered ways to improve traditional architecture and demonstrated to both local communities and international development agencies how valuable such building technologies can be.

Readers of this volume will further appreciate that Katan has invited his long-time colleague in advocacy architecture and planning, Ronald Shiffman, to add his own exemplary experiences in citizen engagement from the last few decades in New York.

After a lifetime as a professor and critic of modern and contemporary art and as the author of more than thirty books on art and architecture, I can attest to the timeless worth of Katan and Shiffman's case studies. *Building Together* with all its diversity, depth, and experience-from-the-field perspective is destined to become a classic for architects, planners, citizen planners, and planning students.

Foreword

Kenneth Reardon

I n 1990 I was invited to work with other planning and design faculty from University of Illinois at Urbana-Champaign (UIUC) in establishing a new community development assistance project in East St. Louis, Illinois. Eager to support local activists, religious leaders, and elected officials involved in a variety of community development projects, I was distressed when one of the city's most respected grassroots leaders said, "The last damn thing we need in East St. Louis is another university researcher telling us what any sixth grader in town already knows."

Ms. Ceola Davis, a long-time community worker, went on to explain how waves of faculty from UIUC and other institutions had routinely collected disturbing health, education, employment, income, housing, and public safety data from East St. Louis and used it to secure research grants to advance their academic careers and campus balance sheets, while doing little to address the serious problems confronting this once-vibrant riverfront community. By continually highlighting the city's deficits and barely mentioning its many strengths, these scholars had contributed to the East St. Louis's negative public image as a hopeless case of urban decline.

In spite of these concerns, Ms. Davis and her neighbors agreed to enter into a new partnership with UIUC with the proviso that local leaders select the issues to be investigated, collaborate with faculty at every step of the process, share in all externally generated funding, receive a minimum five-year commitment from UIUC, and secure help in creating a new nonprofit to sustain this work after the University's departure from the community. While many architecture, landscape architecture, and urban planning professionals and faculty were involved in research, planning, and design projects in low-income communities in the early 1990s, few appeared to be engaged in the kind of highly-reciprocal and mutually-beneficial partnership Ms. Davis sought to build in East St. Louis.

Roger Katan and Ron Shiffman's *Building Together: Case Studies in Participatory Planning and Community Building* addresses this gap in urban planning and design. Their book builds upon Katan's critically acclaimed *Bâtir Ensemble* to provide a rich set of domestic and international case studies that demonstrate the transformative power of resident-led revitalization and development. Katan and Shiffman's cases feature highly participatory planning and design projects undertaken by the authors and their colleagues over a fifty-year period in Europe, Africa, South America, and North America. In fact, I first encountered Ron Shiffman when working with Ms. Davis. My UIUC colleagues and I were searching for a compelling example of a non-exploitative community/university development and discovered how Shiffman and his Pratt Institute for Community and Environmental Design (PICCED) colleagues had established a thriving community development assistance center within Pratt. The center was brilliantly co-generating, with community partners, inspired solutions to many of the most critical issues confronting Brooklyn's poorest neighborhoods by using highly participatory methods to support resident-led revitalization.

In *Building Together*, Katan and Shiffman draw on the most salient participatory community transformation projects of their long and distinguished careers to assemble exactly the kinds of collaborative models that neighborhood leaders, design professionals, elected officials, and urban scholars can use for guidance. Their stories will be invaluable to those advocating more democratic and equitable forms of development because they illustrate how design professionals can work with community partners to overcome local skepticism and resistance to participatory planning. Besides its innovative solutions to common urban problems confronting low-income communities, one of the book's most compelling features is its authors' honest discussion of mistakes they made while seeking to transcend the racial, class, gender, religious, political and cultural barriers that so often complicate grassroots efforts to build the just city and region.

The release of *Building Together* could not be more timely! These cases highlight the capacity grassroots activists and equity-minded professionals have to work together to produce context-sensitive solutions to complex urban problems and enhance the capacity of community-based networks and groups. Furthermore they show ways to overcome the objections of powerful local institutions, and challenge development policies of elite dominated agencies and institutions in order to assist historically marginalized groups and communities in achieving meaningful voice in affecting the quality of life. As such, these case studies provide a strong counterpoint to the neo-conservative and libertarian arguments of groups, such as the Tea Party, that describe community planning efforts, especially those supported by government, as infringements on personal liberty and the free market. At a time when conservative organizations in the U.S. and abroad are attacking local planners and planning agencies for advancing U.N. Agenda 21 at the expense of local economies and democracy, Roger Katan and Ron Shiffman's projects demonstrate how local citizen planners and their design allies have and are working at every level of government policy-making to promote more vibrant, sustainable, and just communities and healthier and more robust civil societies.

Preface

T hanks to a grant from the Graham Foundation, we have had the opportunity to translate, update, and expand *Bâtir Ensemble*. Originally written in the 1980s in French by Roger Katan and published in France in 1988 by the International Council for French Language in partnership with the International Institute of Mediterranean Architecture, *Building Together* has now been translated for an English-language audience[1] and expanded to include recent South American and New York City case studies. In this updated publication, Ronald Shiffman, cofounder of the Pratt Center for Community Development[2] in New York, will be joining me, Roger Katan, with two New York City case studies. Together, we will look back at the different work that we have been engaged in over the past half-century and comment on the methodology and processes that emerged.[3]

---

1. The largest audience for *Building Together* is among English-language readers. In the United States, the birthplace of participatory planning and advocacy architecture, this book should prove to be a valuable reference text for students, professionals, and community organizations.

2. Originally known as the Pratt Institute Center for Community and Environmental Development.

3. Portions of the text that discuss how advocacy planning emerged in the United States as an outgrowth of the 1960s social movements and has since been internationally adopted have been added to the original text by Ronald Shiffman, a former colleague and friend of Roger Katan.

The purpose of this 2014 edition is to give a new generation of community activists, architects, planners, and decisionmakers insight into the importance and significance of integrating action and place. It is our intent in the following chapters to show how participatory processes and the engagement of people lead to the emergence of better places and seeds the civil society structures upon which communities are sustained and democratic institutions can be built. Our intent is to share with the reader a range of firsthand experiences and explain what they were and how they were done, as well as demonstrate how grassroots people, primarily elderly and new immigrants, had a distinct influence on group decisions, informed the way we worked, and, more importantly, animated the communities in which we and others engaged in participatory practice. *Building Together* has the connotation of rebuilding people and community through engagement in the design and building of one's immediate environment. It outlines a methodology of participatory practice learned from forty-five years in the field.

Acknowledgments

We want, firstly, to acknowledge the people of East Harlem and Brooklyn for their ongoing struggle to sustain and revitalize their communities and for the time they spent with us striving to create a new paradigm of professional and community interaction. Their willingness and skills for collaboration—an effort in which client and professional learn from each other ways to enhance the community and empower its people—also enables the architect, urban designer, and planner to better understand and serve the community without compromising creativity or accountability. We appreciate the patience and contributions of these community members to social, economic, and environmental equity. They helped prove to us and society that citizens can work hand-in-hand with professionals to become agents of progressive, positive change, be it in New York, Paris, West Africa, or South America.

We are deeply grateful to our French translators of *Bâtir Ensemble*, Lisa Walsh and Maggie Calt—their work was foundational to the creation of *Building Together*, as was funding from the Graham Foundation for translation, updating, and expansion of the original *Bâtir Ensemble*. Special thanks goes to Isabel Aguirre for her patience and invaluable assistance in helping make this book possible by organizing the photographs and illustrations and other tasks too numerous to mention. In kind, we thank the Pratt Institute's Programs for Sustainable Planning and Development for their invaluable support of this work. Warm thanks, too, to the generosity of photographer Ian Lunn, who helped make old photographs usable.

We are indebted to Ben Gibberd for helping us get started on the revisions, to Yvette Shiffman for her consistent encouragement, support, and editing assistance, and to Julie Katan for her patience, support, and understanding. Without the support of Julie and Yvette the efforts that led to the collaboration with community that resulted in the stories and lessons contained herein would not have been possible.

Our gratitude goes also to dear friend Robert Crumb for not only designing the cover of our book that features his legendary hand-lettering of the title, but also for his early encouragement and enthusiasm for this work.

Finally, we would like to thank editor Laura Leone and New Village Press director Lynne Elizabeth, as well as the press's parent organization—Architects, Designers, Planners for Social Responsibility—for their leadership in directing our profession from one of egotistical self-absorption to one of designing and building a more humane and socially responsible world. *Building Together* is a testament to moving our profession from the "I" to the "We" in order to benefit us all.

The Emergence of Participatory Practices in Architecture, Planning, and Development

I. Setting the Stage

The objective in writing this book is to provide as wide a range of people as possible—elected officials, community groups, prospective urban planners, and concerned citizens in general—with the tools necessary to participate in the social, economic, environmental, and physical revitalization of their own communities, an arena previously and erroneously reserved for so-called experts. My belief, honed after decades of professional experience around the world, is that only when the public is involved in the process of planning, designing, and building their own neighborhoods, can truly successful and long-lasting communities be created.

I will be presenting a variety of case studies experienced firsthand by myself, as well as a number from the career of my friend and colleague, Ronald Shiffman, a New York City-based urban planner with whom I have worked in close collaboration in the past. Although these cases appear on the surface to be highly disparate, involving very different communities in very different parts of the world and at very different times, they were all inspired by the same overall goal: to help people, whatever their socioeconomic status, better understand the forces acting upon them and to organize themselves to have a true say in the construction

1

of their environments. This form of "participatory" or "advocacy" planning, as it is known, involves a great deal of personal commitment on behalf of all those involved and a mutual learning process between the community and the various experts—planners, architects, politicians, and so on—addressing that community's problems. Each side must learn to listen to, learn from, and, above all, respect what the other has to say.

My own experience as an architect, designer, and urban planner has taken me over the course of the past fifty years to three continents—Europe, Africa, and the Americas—with populations as diverse as those of East Harlem in New York City; communities in France and outside of Paris; areas around Colombia's Pacific coast, including Bogotá, the Chocó Department, and Tumaco; and the West African city of Ouagadougou in Burkina Faso. Ron's professional experience, which spans almost as many years as my own and has taken him to many corners of the world, is focused primarily in New York City. He was trained as an architect, but has spent the majority of his career focusing on the social, economic, and environmental aspects of urban planning and development. This book, which is based on an earlier French version written in 1980 and published in 1988, has been updated and enormously enriched by Ron's comments and two new case studies in New York, and it is my hope that the remarkable parallels between our seemingly very different work will help enlighten anyone attempting to understand the new methodology of participatory planning we have come to see.

While both our professional lives have been inspired by the rationality of the pure sciences, we have benefited immensely from the sharing and exchanging of ideas and the ingenuity and compassion of the different cultures and traditions we have worked with—values far beyond the price of anything money can buy. Traditionally, professionals and elected officials most often judge such participatory projects as impractical, claiming that people don't know what they want or that they'll never be able to come to an agreement. Above all, this sort of reaction exhibits impatience and the inability to truly understand the context in which they are working, and it is often a defense mechanism masking a fear of being excluded from the myth of an (already crumbling) ivory tower of professionalism.

In order to assist people and help them mobilize, we, as professionals, must start by dispensing information freely and committing ourselves to learning from others. In this way, the standard prejudice that participatory planning merely generates delays and stymies development is turned on its head since the definition of development shifts from being based purely on quantitative criteria, such as programing and completion dates, to one based on qualitative factors, such as human satisfaction.

Most importantly, in this process of planning and building, knowledge and information ceases to be the domain of a few, and the generation of ideas no longer the exclusive preserve of specialists, no matter how talented they may be. On account of their very diversity and their understanding of what the community's everyday problems and opportunities are, those who are part of the community have within them the ability to make the most valid and well-founded decisions once the complexity of the various options open to them are made clear. What could be more exciting than planting the seeds of an alternative society where, far from being an empty notion, development in a democracy translates into a true physical reality? What could be more fulfilling than building on the assets inherent in every community rather than dwell solely on the issues that have provoked unfortunate problems in the first place?

Origins of a Practice

Fresh out of the *École* des Beaux-Arts in Paris, I won the annual Grunsfeld Fellowship for Massachusetts Institute of Technology (MIT) studies and architectural travel, and arrived in the US in 1960. After completing the MIT master's degree program in two semesters and touring the country from east to west, visiting most of Frank Lloyd Wright's buildings, I joined the architectural practice of Louis Kahn in Philadelphia from 1962 to 1964.

As I indirectly experienced the social upheavals of the 1960s—race riots in the ghettos of every major US urban center and demonstrations demanding changes in the social structure at the universities—I began to question the ambiguous and often contradictory roles of architecture in a society in the midst of such change. The tension within me between the pure aesthetic vision of architectural practice—as exemplified in Kahn's prestigious company—and the diverse movements driven by the ideals of justice, freedom, and ethnic expression flaring up all around was becoming untenable. Wasn't the practice of architecture, as I knew it, simply contributing to this unrest whether consciously or not? And how could one remain professionally passive in the midst of a major social crisis?

In search of a new form of practice, I left Kahn's office in the spring of 1964 and began commuting to New York City to teach architecture to graduate and undergraduate students at the Pratt Institute in Brooklyn. At the same time, I was offered what seemed an exceptional opportunity in East Harlem, in Upper Manhattan, and I moved there to live and work with the numerous community-based organizations and individuals that were springing up. The board of a nonprofit organization in East Harlem needed to develop a feasibility study for the construction of a new settlement house, along with one hundred housing units for the elderly, to replace the old, rundown La Guardia Settlement House on the east side of 116th Street. They had bought three empty row houses adjacent to the existing settlement house, which they planned to demolish for the new project. For their initial presentation to the state authorities, they didn't have enough money to pay professional fees for the preliminary architectural studies that would help them determine the amount of construction funds needed. In exchange for carrying out the feasibility study, I was offered one of these houses to use as my own office on the ground floor and as a residence for my wife and young family on the second. The neighborhood, called Italian Harlem since the 1930s, was then becoming known as Spanish Harlem, home to the new waves of Puerto Ricans, Dominicans, and other Latin American immigrants seeking work and a better life for their families in New York City. The community, which was once approximately 90 percent Italian and 10 percent Puerto Rican, was gradually reversing these figures.

It was at this time that I met Ron Shiffman, who had been hired by Pratt in the winter of 1963 to work on a special project started within the graduate urban planning program to assist communities suffering from urban decline in the Bedford-Stuyvesant neighborhood of Brooklyn and elsewhere. Ron was introduced to me by Mannie Lionni, another architect teaching in the undergraduate program, and by a group of students associated with them who were engaged in protests to improve the quality of their education at Pratt. The three of us quickly became the only Pratt faculty or staff members to support the students in their struggle. I began my work in East Harlem by engaging a number of these students to help me first with the settlement house design and later with a number of other local community projects in order to give them some firsthand experience. (Though, unfortunately, Pratt declined to credit their work.) We met constantly at Pratt, in their apartments, or at my new office in my row house, sharing with each other late into the night our ideas as to what the ideal architectural education should be and what the role of architects and planners must become in this newly emerging society.

Ron, Mannie, and I all encountered the official ire of our Pratt colleagues for our work and beliefs. They questioned both the pedagogy and the content of what we were doing with the students. But the desire of the students to work directly with struggling communities on real issues rather than abstract and irrelevant design problems was overwhelming and helped forge a powerful alliance between us all. Ultimately, the intense and numerous conversations with each other and with our students led to the adoption of a new philosophy of participatory and experimental education; a philosophy that, in time, became the model for a new form of professional practice.

Sometimes during our meetings, faculty and students from Columbia, Yale, and other universities joined us. Over the following weeks, our ideas about architecture and urbanism began to change, and the discussion moved beyond the improvement of architectural and urban planning pedagogy to issues of aesthetics and the process of civic engagement, empowerment, professional responsibility, ethics, and accountability. These discussions were often quite heated, yet always intensely creative, and, ultimately, of vital importance. We concentrated, above all, on the idea of community: How could we, as professionals or soon-to-be professionals, learn from those struggling to empower themselves, and how could we forge valid working relationships with them? What did we, as professionals, have to offer them in their fight against the poverty and decay that pervaded their communities and that was the legacy of decades of exclusion and exploitation? As a result of this intense interaction, many of us became truly radicalized for the first time.

The 1966 Pratt student strike took place at the same time as similar actions were underway at Columbia and the University of California, Berkeley, and these soon were to impact places like Yale and other academic institutions in the US, as well as in France and Italy. Interestingly, enough of the sparks that were ignited in the political climate of that time seemed to originate within the schools of architecture.

A few months after the student strike at Pratt, the Association of Collegiate Schools of Architecture (ACSA) and its chairman, Sydney Katz, invited me to address the 1967 National Institute for Architectural Education (NIAE) in New York in a seminar-forum entitled, "The Student and His Future Development." The subject was on architectural education and the period of practical experience that a student needed in order to acquire a license to practice. The French system was structured in such a way that it not only allowed but also encouraged the student to work flexible periods of time in an architect's office so that their final degree was the license to practice. In the US, the system did not allow the same flexibility: between graduation and licensing, a period of three years had been designated during which the student was supposed to receive practical experience, which was until then absent from their education. I believed that rather than restructure the internship, as was generally proposed, it was the educational process that most needed to be restructured. It was easy to underline the increasing awareness of our social ills and the movement at all levels of society and among restless youth in particular to help cure one of the most pressing of human problems: life in the metropolis. How could the university be a dispenser of knowledge without firsthand contact with reality, a contact that only internships could offer the students? An urban architectural peace corps could accomplish a great deal while involving the students in real-life problems, which were becoming more serious each day we ignored them. In my address, I spoke about the concept of architectural students' involvement in neighborhoods. As part of their curriculum, students would be immersed in the problems of urban America and learn firsthand of the ills and of the possible solutions by participating in the work of newly created community design centers.

While the most famous and publicized student protest was Berkeley's Free Speech Movement, followed by the sit-in and the much-publicized

Roger Katan addressing the NIAE National Board on architectural education, New York Hilton, May 15, 1967.
PHOTO BY JON NAAR

police action at Columbia University, Pratt was the first school to experience a walk out by its architecture students. While the events at Pratt did not garner the same notoriety or press coverage as its more elite cousins, they were to have a significant impact on architectural education and on the practice of architecture and urban planning both in the US and abroad.

One can only speculate as to why the student unrest of the 1960s started in architectural schools. In Pratt's case, the spark was unquestionably the desire of a number of its students and research staffers to engage in participatory processes with community-based organizations and to work with the emerging leadership in those communities. Other students initially joined for more prosaic reasons—they may have decided to walk out because of their frustration over the lack of desk space, poor facility maintenance, or overcrowded classrooms. But, whatever the reasons for their initial involvement, through their participation, they all developed a political perspective that fueled and sustained the strike. I remember particularly one Pratt student handing Ron, Mannie, and me a copy of a treatise written by a group called The Architects' Resistance (TAR), which proclaimed:

> We live in a country where power lies in the hands of a few, and we serve those few—as the Master Builders of history served their kings. The people do not power over the formation of their environment, but must accept whatever is forced on them. We, as

architects, are not taught, or even permitted, to go out to the user and apply our skills to put physical form to *his* vision. We serve only to put "aesthetic" form to the avarice and power of rulers—even those who have openly enslaved millions under Apartheid.

TAR, which was started in the summer of 1968 after a walk out at a meeting of the New England chapters of the American Institute of Architects (AIA), included students who went on to make important contributions to the profession and to society in general, such as Anthony Schuman, now the ACSA's Distinguished Professor at the New Jersey Institute of Technology, and Bruce Dale, a banker at the Community Preservation Corporation, who has dedicated his life's work to community building and neighborhood revitalization.

One of TAR's specific targets was the famous architectural practice of Skidmore, Owings & Merrill LLP (SOM), which the group accused of putting its "skills, resources and name behind the brutal racism of South Africa." "Somewhere," TAR proclaimed, "a SOM architect is drawing three sets of bathrooms—'White,' 'Colored' and 'Black'—in a project that they were designing for the Anglo-American Corporation of South Africa." The treatise went on to state that it wanted to:

> Move towards a society where the power lies with the people, and where architecture is a tool of that power. . . . [And] find a means to assist the re-humanization of society by restructuring the architectural profession to deal with living people on human terms. Architecture is a tool for mobilizing people, for making them more aware of themselves and their human dignity. . . . It is an integral part of the totality of forces molding our society: political, economic, social. It cannot continue to function in a moral void.

These declarations, and others like it, animated much of the student discussions that followed and captured the rebellious spirit that was in the air at the time.

The location of institutions such as Columbia and Pratt, adjoining the primarily African American neighborhoods of Harlem and Bedford-Stuyvesant, respectively, also left a powerful impression on the students.

At either university, it was impossible, unless you simply closed your eyes, to ignore the issues of poverty and racial discrimination made manifest in human form all around. In 1968, the issue of race was specifically drawn to the architectural and urban planning community on a national level when National Urban League Executive Director Whitney Young, Jr., speaking at the AIA convention, challenged the profession for its exclusion of African Americans in its role in rebuilding American cities, something that only further heightened the political and social consciousness of the students and the profession.

A general shift in the overall political and economic context of the late 1960s also played a key role in stimulating the discourse that took place. For some time, the intellectual community had been shaking off the legacy of years of lethargy and blind acceptance of a post-war conservatism borne of the materialism of the time and spurred by a booming economy. It was a conservatism that, combined with the explosive growth of the suburbs and the manufactured ideal of the nuclear family (the single-family home with its white picket fence in a whites-only neighborhood), had drastically and often adversely affected the structure of our cities and metropolitan areas. But the paranoia of the 1950s, with its hunt for a Communist in every nook and cranny of our society, began to yield slowly to a more nuanced acceptance of a country born with the best of democratic intentions yet seriously flawed and defective—a country that had crafted both a democratic constitution and a bill of rights, yet had not extended those rights to all of its citizens. It was a country that had within it another country; it was a country of contradictions, a country with places of intense poverty where people of color were segregated either by the force of law or the force of their economic circumstances.

In the early 1960s, the United States experienced a serious social crisis, which, in the long term, threatened to call into question its entire political and economic system. The disparities between the beneficiaries of a wealthy society who were the majority of the population, on the one hand, and blacks and ethnic minorities, on the other, had become too vast to sustain. Moreover, these disparities were exacerbated by the forced geographical segregation of large urban metropolises—blacks in the inner cities and whites in the suburbs. All of these issues weighed on us and seeped into the consciousness of the students. And yet, the official education they continued to receive—assignments to design a suburban school or a two-bedroom beach house in the Hamptons, for example—failed utterly to address these issues. The world these students saw in simply walking from the subway to the classroom, looking out of the windows of those classrooms, or turning on the television was substantively different.

Fortunately, we found we were not alone in our protest; a chorus of diverse and sympathetic voices was beginning to make itself heard. On the political level, President Lyndon Baines Johnson had taken over the reins of his predecessor's antipoverty initiatives following Kennedy's traumatic assassination in November 1963. In his 1964 State of the Union message to Congress, Johnson declared:

> Let us carry forward the plans and programs of John F. Kennedy, not because of our sorrow or sympathy, but because they are right. . . . This administration today, here and now, declares an unconditional War on Poverty in America . . . wherever it exists. In city slums, in small towns, in sharecroppers' shacks, or in migrant worker camps, on Indian reservations, among whites as well as negroes, among the young as well as the aged, in the boom towns and in the depressed areas.

Both Kennedy and Johnson had been widely influenced by the writings of the American democratic socialist thinker Michael Harrington, whose 1962 book *The Other America: Poverty in the United States* was a catalyst for much of their domestic policy. In the following decade, the chorus grew louder as sociologists, planners, and urban policy critics followed Harrington's insights about what was going on in America's cities and rural communities and what was needed for those communities to advance themselves. Figures like the urban planner Sherry Arnstein, author of the classic article "A Ladder of Citizen Participation," Paul Davidoff, urban planner and author of the influential paper "Advocacy and Pluralism in Planning," Herbert Gans, sociologist and author of *Urban Villagers*, Robert Goodman and Chester Hartman, urban planners and authors of numerous important books and papers, Lewis Mumford, writer and critic of American cities and author of *The Myth of the Machine*, and, perhaps most importantly, Jane Jacobs, author of the enormously influential *The Death and Life of Great American Cities*, all used their own unique perspectives to call for greater professional accountability to communities and the need to engage people in the planning and development processes that affected their lives. Each built upon and reinforced the concept of empowerment, and all had a profound effect on public policy and on how planners and policy makers should function. Collectively, they firmly established the need for substantive citizen participatory processes and the need to redefine how policy makers, urban and regional planners, architects, and others engaged the public and practiced their respective disciplines.

All of this directly influenced how Ron, Mannie, and I came to feel about our profession, and, more importantly, how we began to put into action our newfound beliefs. At this time, I renewed my friendship with Troy West, an architect I had known in my days working for Louis Kahn, who, to my delight, I found through our respective writings for various architectural magazines to be now working full time in the Hill District, the poorest African American community in Pittsburgh. Interestingly enough, the difference between practitioners and theoreticians of this new participatory discipline became increasingly and happily blurred since much of what the latter wrote about was the result of their direct engagement and practice with the former and much of what the former practiced—ourselves included—was the result of our reflection on what we were engaged in and our ongoing conversation with the communities we were working for.

There were, however, two major problems with working with the politically disenfranchised: first, our clients did not have the resources to pay for our architectural, planning, and development services, and, second, they also didn't have the influence, money, or power to implement any plans we might develop with them. We quickly learned that architecture, planning, and development in a diverse, pluralistic, and democratic environment requires a broader set of skills than practicing in a homogenous and more autocratic environment. The planner and design professional must move beyond physical planning, design, and structure to understand a range of issues such as finance, government policies, decision-making processes, the environment (including environmental justice issues), and community economic development. The planner must, in addition, be an organizer, tactician, educator, student, and communicator. Experience taught us—the hard way—that community meetings are often contentious, comprised of people who move in and out of the picture, operate at different speeds and levels of information and disinformation, and have differing needs and values, but, in the end and despite all this, provide the vital spark for creative planning and design. Just as importantly, once you have gained the confidence of the community, the people of the community not only provide your inspiration but also become your powerful ally in the inevitable battles to come against entrenched bureaucracies and the attitude of business as usual.

The practice of community-based planning and design has a modern history of over four decades, but its contribution to the practice of architecture and its role in the building of place, communities, neighborhoods, and cities are still often misunderstood and misinterpreted. Community participatory processes and designs—when practiced genuinely—go far beyond the planning, design, and development professions contributing their know-how and talent to low- and moderate-income communities. It is a fundamental recasting of planning and architecture from that of the signature architects and top-down urban planners with their product-oriented, know-what's-best-for-you approach to a more transdisciplinary approach to design and community development. It is an approach that moves from a superficial development of functional— and, too often, dysfunctional—forms to a substantive understanding of the way people live, work, and grow.

True decision making and real empowerment can arise only from choosing among informed alternatives. Without a substantive and honest dialogue, neither the architect/planner/designer nor the community/ citizen/advocate can make an informed decision, for neither can possibly know all of the alternatives. Any outcome is doomed to mediocrity at best and will, in all probability, result in an embarrassing and aesthetically and functionally irrelevant undertaking.

In the chapters that follow, I, with input from Ron Shiffman, who has agreed to help edit and add some commentary to this book, hope to show how people from enormously varied communities around the world have discovered how to build, preserve, and rehabilitate hundreds of thousands of housing units. We will show how they have maintained the historic character of many of their cities, generating greater attention to sustainable planning practices and green building approaches, and helped give birth to the environmental justice and industrial retention movements that have recently emerged.

It is our hope to show that participatory planning, far from being a fashionable or politically correct form of practice, is probably the only approach that can achieve a community's goal for security, shelter, stability, and human happiness.

II. Influence of the Advocacy Planning Movement

The following section will focus on another form of advocacy planning in France and in Europe, which was inspired by the US advocacy movement. Whereas our US experience had started at the grassroots level, the one in Europe started less than a decade later and was generated and led by government organizations in parallel with grassroots organizations.

The Public Workshops in France and Europe

France's creation of public workshops in 1969 was based on a public service concept inspired by the American tradition of the town meeting (or community meeting), in which any action seeking to transform all or part of a city was subject to public discourse (a similar tradition is still at work in Dutch and British cities). Initial experiences modified the structure of the public workshop, paring it down, making it more flexible, and decentralizing it. The best known workshops were in La Rochelle and Juvisy-sur-Orge in France in the 1970s. The municipality of Grenoble was considered a model of everyday democratic management. These experiences had in common the support of a local territorial base (often the neighborhood) with a particular emphasis on the built environment: architecture of the everyday (habitat, social services, social equipment, etc.). This resulted in the establishment and, at times, the institutionalization of more flexible relationships between elected officials, technicians, and residents.

When they appeared on the political scene in 1968, the Groups for Municipal Action (GAM) seemed particularly sensitive to the architecture of the everyday. These groups had been created by residents determined to protect their role as citizens, a role not limited to voting, but one inscribed in the heart of the everyday urban struggle. Their objective was to disseminate unrestricted information, provide support for struggles, and demonstrate that another way of fostering democratic engagement was possible. As for knowing whether GAM would be able to transform institutions and install new power relations, or if power would transform those who acquired it, it turned out that GAM remained as sites of activism and vigorous debate. It had to assure that the majority of the group's most militant members, in particular its leaders, remained separate from the municipal team while continuing to encourage a counterpower to the city's normal democratic organizations. In this context, the circulation of information was primary, and conflict and contradiction were never negative—unless they were stifled.

GAM's ideology took shape within a hierarchical, highly bureaucratic society, and this seriously constrained the experiments attempted by several of the municipality's elected teams. Despite a desire for more open politics, participation functioned in a middle-class vacuum (represented by the municipal team, study groups, and the intellectuals who gathered for the experiment).

Every country in Europe, in particular, Belgium, the Netherlands, and the Nordic countries, had experienced examples of similar forms of popular participation to GAM. The most striking examples took place in Bologna, Italy beginning in the 1960s and in Portugal after 1974 with the institution of the new democratic regime. The experiment in Bologna was innovative in its goal of allowing the population to plan and approve development projects. The progressive municipality delegated all management of its own interests to the residents via neighborhood and municipal councils. Henceforth, projects were not to be formulated in abstract terms or isolated rules, but were rather integrated into collective urban politics grounded in place. They were simple solutions directly grasped and understood by the population. In all these areas, experiments were conducted in constant communication with residents, along with ongoing refinement based on feedback. With its deliberately social agenda, this experiment sought collective ownership of their part of the city and, in some cases, of the entire city. In Portugal, after the 1974 revolution, the Mobile Local Aid Service (MLAS) was created to help poorly housed populations across the entire country. In 1978, the MLAS was renamed Technical Action Groups (TAG)—public workshops run by the previous leadership.

While European governments were well structured, the governments of South America were less centralized, allowing for a form of grassroots action to take place there. In South America, one could describe many examples of participatory actions and community self-help groups. Some of these groups had to disappear with dictatorial governments, as was the case in Uruguay, El Salvador, and Chile, where military power felt menaced by their existence. However, Colombia is one of the few Latin American countries that developed self-help practices and encouraged community participatory actions. In Case Studies 6 and 7, we will see how these organizations influenced other South American countries once they became democratic. Case Study 6, the example of the "Homeless" group in Pereira, Colombia, demonstrates the impact that that group had both locally and nationwide, while Case Study 7, with examples from the Pacific coast of Colombia, will show how their impact spread all over South America.

In the United States, where grassroots organizing, advocacy, and participatory planning processes emerged, there was little or virtually no governmental planning or development initiatives like those that existed in Europe or Latin America. Planning and development were ceded primarily to the private sector, which had little interest in and often abandoned low- and moderate-income communities. The US had bottom-up planning without the ability to bring their plans to fruition, and Europe had top-down planning and development efforts with little engagement with the people who would be directly affected. In order to address the disengagement of the government, a number of US communities decided that if the government would not aid in the development of their plans, they, in turn, would develop the institutions and the mechanisms to develop their plans and visions themselves. The community development idea was born: communities fearing the continued decline of their neighborhoods and worrying about government inaction led area residents to organize a planning and development effort that resulted in a new model of development in the United States.

In 1965, residents of the Bedford-Stuyvesant neighborhood acknowledged their innate ability to revitalize their own community. The residents undertook a revitalization initiative together with the Central Brooklyn Coordinating Council and aided by the Pratt Center and launched the first community development corporation (CDC) in the country. The foundation for the CDC model was built upon a three stage involvement strategy originally applied for an initiative to turn vacant lots and underutilized buildings into productive spaces. The three levels of community involvement were (1) involvement in the development goals and the evolution of the plan itself, (2) involvement in the process and the beneficiary of change, and (3) involvement in the end product and its use. The model of the first CDC provided the framework for local revitalization undertaken by communities on their own or in partnership with governments, other organizations, and the private sector.

The formation of the CDC was a result of a participatory process in planning and of the desire to continue that process in the development or product of that participation by engaging in and controlling, owning, and managing the developments or products that emerged from their efforts. In essence, community members initiated the action after organizing and engaging in a participatory process.

III. Case Study Summaries

CASE STUDY 1: *Choices for '76: A Participative Regional*
Planning on the Scale of the New York Region

In 1971–1972, New York's Regional Plan Association (RPA) launched a massive information operation called Choices for '76 to encourage the diverse population of the state to define the parameters of a new regional plan. This covered five areas: housing, transportation, environment, poverty, and the development of satellite cities and suburbs. From television to newspapers, books to radio, a variety of means were employed to expose the problems. This information campaign lasted almost two years.

The consultation itself took place over a three-month period, during which various groups and associations remained in permanent contact in order to develop, debate, and encourage responses from the concerned populations. (Five hour-long documentaries were produced and aired on television that examined the challenges facing America's cities and asked citizens to provide their views on how to address these mounting issues.) The larger campaign included mailing five thousand surveys to residents and asking them to complete and return them, providing a compelling experiment in the emerging field of advocacy planning. This project reached more than three million people, and more than one million participated actively.

In the wake of the devastating attack on September 11, 2001 that destroyed the World Trade Center and a good portion of Lower Manhattan's financial district, the RPA led a civic alliance to plan for the area's rebuilding—the Civic Alliance to Rebuild Downtown New York. In a similar effort to Choices for '76, the RPA, working with the Pratt Center and other organizations, launched a major effort to engage New York City's and the region's diverse population in the plans to rebuild Lower Manhattan. Using new and innovative communication and information technologies not available twenty-five years earlier, the civic alliance engaged thousands of people directly into planning for the rebuilding effort. This case highlights the similarities and the differences between the two RPA efforts and draws a number of lessons from the two experiences for citizens, planners, and decision makers.

CASE STUDY 2: *The Williamsburg Community*

The Williamsburg case study is an in-depth description of how a dedicated set of community leaders working with professionals committed to participatory planning principles enabled a community to emerge from a tragic event and develop a strategy and a mechanism to facilitate the resurgence of their community. The case documents the emergence, growth, and success of a community-based development organization and how it worked to stabilize and revitalize one of New York City's neighborhoods that was on the edge of decline.

CASE STUDY 3: *Three East Harlem Projects in New York City
and the Vassar College Experience*

1. Settlement House and Housing for the Elderly

What sort of rights can residents have with respect to the design of buildings destined for or granted to them? In response to this question, an experiment conducted from 1968 to 1971 puts forward tools of reflection and action in order to allow residents to appreciate and decide on the forms and uses of architectural spaces. It is important to be able to decide not only on the form of one's habitat but also on the forms of institutional spaces designed to serve members of the community such as neighborhood services (educational, health, recreational, etc.).

2. Wards Island Hospital and Mental Hygiene Services

The second East Harlem case study describes how the community stopped a four-thousand bed mental hygiene hospital from implementing a plan for institutional expansion on Wards Island and convinced the authorities to scale down new types of smaller mental health facilities run by and integrated into the fabric of the Harlem-East Harlem community.

3. East Harlem Multiservice Center

Designed to house multiple social services, the East Harlem Multiservice Center was initiated and launched by neighborhood residents. The plans were developed collectively over the course of a reciprocal training experience. Technicians worked and learned directly from area residents, discovering and helping others discover new forms of practice. The project's goal was to encourage groups of residents to make decisions likely to affect the ways in which community buildings were used.

4. Vassar College Experience

The Vassar College case study describes how motivated Vassar students defended the rights of the community that surrounds their institution and actively worked in helping to improve it.

CASE STUDY 4: *Creation of the First Microcredit Organization in Ouagadougou, Burkina Faso*

Case Study 4 tells the story of how, in 1976, in a country that the United Nations classified as one of the world's twenty-five "least developed countries"[1] and the World Bank deemed a place where "progress is bound to be slow,"[2] a population proved the contrary and provided the economic means—though modest at the start—to manage the development of their neighborhoods. Step by step, this case study describes the creation of a microcredit union as a tool for neighborhood self-management. It also describes the motivation and organization of the inhabitants necessary to set up and collectively bring about neighborhood improvement projects. This effort could not have succeeded without a respect for the indigenous social structures inherited from a still recent rural way of life. Success was possible because of the absence of hypercentralized, paralyzing techno-bureaucratic structures common in developing countries. It is the story of a neighborhood organization that evolved into a national savings federation by 2012.

CASE STUDY 5: *Production of a Self-Managed Habitat: The Jardies in Meudon, France*

The Jardies in the Meudon housing cluster attempted to create and symbolize a new way of life. This is the only case study included that was led by a relatively affluent and particularly influential group of professionals—made up of ten families—that found the same engagement and solidarity in organizing and collective action as those found in more disenfranchised areas. At the start, these ten families refused to live in standardized housing because they wanted their lives to be richer and to create an urban social life together. The realization of their project inspired many similar sorts of developments. Trying to set up a new way

---

1. World Bank, *Current Economic Position and Development Prospects of Upper Volta*, report no. 564a–UV (Washington, DC: World Bank, 1975), *i*.

2. World Bank, *Main Report*, vol. 1 of *The Economic Development of Upper Volta*, Western Africa series, no. AW–19 (Washington, DC: World Bank, 1970), *i*.

of life, this pioneer group has influenced many projects that gave birth in the last forty years to the cohousing movement, first in Denmark in the 1980s and extending to most of Europe, the US, New Zealand, Canada, and Australia.

CASE STUDY 6: *Self-Managed and Self-Built Project in Pereira, Colombia*

Case Study 6 describes how a motivated and organized marginal group spontaneously and independently set about to create and build their community in an innovative and integrated way. They provided an environment for their own needs, and later had a large influence on national institutions, as well as on many self-help groups. The self-managed organization, the Destechados (Homeless) from Pereira, was a group experience that allowed individuals to participate in the construction of a collective housing project. They attempted to attain several objectives: create small production enterprises to reduce the cost of construction materials, reinforce solidarity among association members, keep participants informed about their social rights, establish a working framework in the technical and sociocultural domains, and demonstrate to participants the importance of engagement in collective projects. This experience had a great impact on the Colombian national scene.

CASE STUDY 7: *Several Projects in Colombia*

1. Chocó New School in Rural Areas

This project describes how, in 1984, black and indigenous communities, living in total isolation in their jungle in African Colombia, helped create a "New School" adapted to their needs, culture, and environment. The experiment has influenced the building of the same type of learning centers in rural areas throughout many South and Central American countries in the last three decades.

2. Tumaco Self-Help Assisted Project

At the southern tip of Colombia, Tumaco is an island linked to the mainland by a small bridge. It has been plagued by countless tidal waves, many illegal settlements, and uncontrolled urban growth. My first intervention with the French Technical Assistance in Tumaco in 1984 involved the construction of two hundred houses according to local typology and the creation of a self-managed savings and loan cooperative.

3. Bocana and Brick Making along the Pacific Coast

Addressing the problem of intense humidity in Colombia's Pacific region led to a search for alternative construction materials to wood. What resulted was an effort to make and teach brick making and brick building, which was then mandated by the European Union (EU), all along the Colombian Pacific coast.

4. European Union Project in Tumaco

The fear that tidal waves and the resulting surge would erase a good part of Tumaco prompted the Colombian government in 1995 to ask the EU for help in moving two thousand families living in shacks on stilts away from the highly vulnerable Tumaco beaches to the mainland. The project ended four years later with problems of corruption and with the construction of only 1,060 housing units. Also discussed are the various proposals for the development and growth of Tumaco projected through 2015 made in conjunction with the former mayor and the present municipality. The chapter concludes with an analysis of the EU and other international organizations' attitude when facing corruption problems.

IV. Methodology Utilized and Lessons Learned

While this book is not meant to be a how-to book, we will attempt to tell the reader how we did things. And while this is not meant to be a textbook, we hope that what we have written will instruct a new generation of citizens, activists, architects, planners, developers, and decision makers on the processes and methodology of place making and community building. As we engage with you on this journey, we hope that neither the issue of aesthetics—the art that makes our world a more beautiful and more livable place—nor the intangibles—the elements that make our homes, work areas, and play places safe and enjoyable—will be forgotten or seem unimportant—we believe that both are enhanced by the participatory processes and the methodology discussed.

1. Identification of Problems and Assets

This is the first and most crucial step. Often problems are unclear to both the planners and the residents involved, and the assets of the community are ignored. As a result, an important tool in overcoming an area's problems is often ignored. The process usually begins by reacting to vague and often unfocused discontent. At other times, the problem is defined in terms of presupposed solutions to a perceived problem (e.g., the problem may seem to be the need for a new hospital when the problem may really be a lack of accessible and affordable health care). Many times, communities react to the proposals of others that ignore or trample upon their needs. Advocacy planners, architects, local political leaders, and others working in the field of participatory planning must help the local community become aware of their asset base as well as the basic issues—architectural, political, economic, environmental, and otherwise—that surround a particular crisis or situation. Recognizing the area's asset base provides a foundation upon which to build.

2. Organization of People to Help Them Act on Their Own Behalf

Organizing, animating, and engaging people in the process of problem and asset determination, and continuing to broaden the base once these have been identified, is an important and ongoing task. Once the key assets and issues have been determined, leaders within the community and steeped in the issues involved must spread the word and engage the rest of the community, persuading them to get involved. Outside professionals can assist in this process, but it must essentially be by the people and for the people not only to avoid the appearance—and reality—of an external technocratic authority taking charge once again, but, more importantly, because it is a fundamental aspect of the development process. How this is done is more of an art than a science—one has to not only know the community, its traditions, its practices, its fears, and its memories but also, most importantly, gain the trust of the people or the group that one would be working with and representing. In homogenous communities, the process is fairly straightforward, but in heterogeneous and multiclass communities, it becomes more complex, and the concept and use of pluralistic strategies may be applicable. Controversy and conflict are healthy as long as there are conflict-resolution and decision-making mechanisms in place.

3. Organization of a Work Group or Groups

The more complex a project, the more groups or subgroups will be required. This includes technical, legal, economic, and other committees, and all will work to create a plan that can modify—or, if necessary, entirely counter—the official one. Information discovered, strategies and goals articulated, and ideas generated by these subgroups must be regularly explained to the general population generally in meetings run by an overall residential steering group. For maximum efficiency and transparency, the size of these groups should never be less than seven or more than fifteen. A major goal of the steering committee should be to achieve integration of ideas, avoiding the silo effect that leads to the segmentation of the issues. In essence, they should evolve into an entity that facilitates communication, establishes feedback loops, enhances mutual education of all those involved, and fosters synergy.

4. Establishment of a Relationship between Technical Experts and Residents

This is a reciprocal and symbiotic process: both technical experts and residents must learn how to talk the language of the other and each has to educate and learn from one another if the project is to be a success. Such experts (architects, engineers, planners, etc.) have to be evaluated, reviewed, and chosen by the residents themselves in public meetings. Most important is the recognition that the technician works for the residents and does not speak for them. The technicians' role is to transfer ideas, information, and options to the clients—the community, village, residents, etc.—in such a manner that will allow them to make informed decisions based on the best available information.

5. Analysis and Exposition of the Program

Once the team of technicians has been determined, they should, jointly with the community leadership, outline the specific problems faced and assets available so the community can be fully conscient and confident in their ability to make decisions based upon informed choices. It is of vital importance that, at any given moment, those residents who have not as yet participated may be allowed—and, indeed, should be encouraged—to do so. In this way, the traditional trap of simply falling back on the expert's knowledge can be avoided. If at all possible, the community should be organized into an ongoing entity that can carry out the results of the initial effort, monitor and evaluate its progress, and launch additional efforts in the future.

6. Process of Engagement

How the community interacts with their technical consultants will vary from place to place and from time to time and is dependent on a variety of factors, including, but not limited to, the issues, problem or project being addressed, experience, history, and culture of the community, as well as the technician involved. Techniques can vary, but should include participatory processes such as visioning, community-based design charrettes, etc. These should utilize surveys, experiential data, and popular education techniques, among others. The process of engagement builds trust, maximizes the exchange of information between all of the actors, and allows for ideas to percolate, be discussed, and, eventually, visualized, decided upon, and integrated into what, hopefully, will be a comprehensive and synergistic approach to the issue or objective being addressed.

7. Conceptions and Written and Visual Representation

This is the stage at which the architects, urban planners, engineers, and other technicians, working closely with the community, offer up to the community at large the proposals that have emerged from their collective efforts. If any residents are unhappy with any aspect, they must be made to feel free to say so—this project will affect their lives, not the technician's, and alternative proposals, in part or whole, can always be explored and proposed. For this to work, the community must have participated in some capacity-building effort that gave them a minimum of technical, economic, and visual understanding so that they can make valid, informed responses to the experts' often mysterious preserve. Conversely, it is the obligation of the technician to demystify and clearly present the ideas and proposals in a form understood by all. This can be done effectively only after the technician/consultants engage in their own capacity-building endeavor of learning from those experts in the community about the community's memories, assets, concerns, visions, and aspirations.

8. Establishment of a Preliminary Outline

Once the community concurs on the general approach, the technicians can then proceed to offer up a highly concrete proposal. At this point, the residents should have come to understand the essential vocabulary of the experts, and the technicians, in turn, should be deeply familiar with the local vocabulary and the needs and wishes of the residents. If satisfied, the residents and technicians can begin the next phase of the effort—obtaining the resources and developing the strategies for implementation.

9. Project Execution

At this stage, resident intervention should be encouraged even if it gives the perception of delay. The social costs emanating from the old model of imperious and irresponsible execution, and the resultant social dissatisfaction, are a powerful reminder of the alternative's dangers. In a community development context, it is constantly necessary to give priority to the human concerns and needs. Community development differs from traditional development because of its focus on the human scale and the need for people to achieve food, shelter, love, participation, and freedom, including freedom from hunger, poverty, and exclusion.

10. Project Evolution

It is relatively easy to foresee the implementation of a plan or a building's development over the immediate five- or ten-year future, but it is far harder to envision plans for a mid- to long-term future. In this light, after the launching of a building or project, the community needs to develop and maintain an organizational structure that can ensure its proper functioning and go on to design, finance, and execute any future changes that the community may need or deem necessary. The process of developing a project must always be tied to the constantly changing social, political, economic, and environmental requirements of the individuals and communities that it serves.

Participatory Planning on a Regional Scale, New York

Introduction

P articipatory planning and design is essentially a process that engages people. How that engagement occurs varies from place to place, from issue to issue, and from time to time, but the principles, practices, and techniques that lead to that engagement are important to understand. Throughout this book, we will be examining those issues. Since it was originally published in 1988, much has been learned about participatory planning processes, and yet much remains the same. There continues to be a need to inform and animate people to take action, and there is still a need to identify the means of transferring decision making from the few with power and resources to the many whom the decisions impact the most. It is this latter group that, at the outset of any planning or design effort, often lacks access to information and does not have the power to make decisions or the resources to implement those decisions. The lessons learned in observing and participating in Choices for '76 as practitioners working in New York City powerfully contributed to the way both of us approached our subsequent engagement with communities.

Choices for '76: A Strategy to Engage People in a Large-Scale Regional Planning Effort

To mark the 1976 bicentennial of the United States, the New York Regional Plan Association (RPA), set up an investigation in 1971 aiming to know the choices of the New York population concerning regional planning decisions. To develop a follow-up to their first regional plan (1929–1965), the RPA set up, beginning as far back as 1963, an effort to engage the twenty million citizens of the tristate region surrounding New York City (comprising New York, New Jersey, and Connecticut) in a regional participatory planning effort. It used the new technology of the time, which included television, newspapers, businesses, and community-based and community-led discussion groups, to solicit public reaction to the planning approaches for the region if the current trends continued. A committee of 125 diverse leaders evaluated the research and policy proposals for a second regional plan looking to the year 2000. This was the beginning of a regional planning participatory process that was eventually expanded and intensified to mark the bicentennial of the United States. It was called Choices for '76.

The RPA is the oldest regional planning association in the United States, and has its main office in New York City. It is a voluntary citizens' organization—a nongovernmental entity supported primarily by individual memberships, corporate subscriptions, foundations, and government grants. While the RPA is a highly professional planning organization representative of the region's diverse geographic areas and independent of any governing body, it is also, given its financial structure and board, one that tends to represent the more powerful regional interests, such as major corporations, utilities, larger and more powerful environmental organizations, and politicians that favor planning efforts, rather than neighborhood and community-based organizations or environmental justice organizations. Planning in a region as extensive as the New York metropolitan area is a minefield of complexity with an array of interests and a multiplicity of administrative structures and governmental decision-making bodies. This, coupled with regional versus local neighborhood needs and a plethora of other competing demands, contributes to the challenge of undertaking a regional plan—a challenge that many

A copy of original RPA flyer announcing Choices for '76.

PHOTO BY RONALD SHIFFMAN

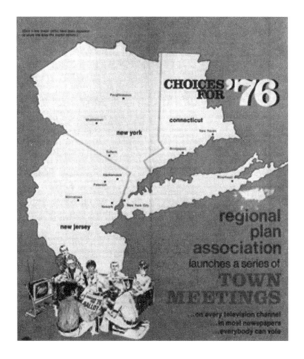

feel close to impossible. The complexity of regional problems, together with the unfettered growth of administrative and private sector interventions, often makes the responses to urban issues incoherent, scattered, and outdated. The RPA is the only entity willing to take on the challenge to deal comprehensively with the problems of the region and to respond to the needs and goals articulated by undertaking regional planning initiatives.

There are very few organizations like the RPA in the United States, although a couple of regional planning entities have emerged in recent years, and internationally, there is only a handful, most of which are government run. In the 1960s and 1970s, there were a few in noncommunist or unplanned economies. In France, the most notable was Les Oream et l'amenagement du territoire, which operated between 1966 and 1976 and was engaged in the development of ten regional plans, which mostly focused on the spatial needs of the regions they studied.[10][1] Oream was

1. The regions studied were Marseilles-Aix, Lille-Roubaix-Tourcoing, Nantes-Saint-Nazaire, Nancy-Metz-Thionville, Lyon-Saint-Étiennne, Grenoble, Vallée de L'Oise, Vallée de l'Aisne, Loire Moyenne, Bordeaux-Aquitaine, Alsace, and Midi-Pyrénées.

essentially a national effort to undertake the development of regional spatial plans, while the RPA, a nongovernmental entity, tried to develop a regional planning mode that, while it could be replicated, addressed the complex set of issues affecting one particular region's needs.

Apart from the municipal structures for planning that existed in the 1960s and 1970s in the US, there were at a local level over 1,400 different planning and decision-making agencies in the New York area planning for health, education, roads, water treatment, and other forms of infrastructure. If anything, that number has grown since then, making the problem today even more acute.

Choices for '76 was divided into three main steps:

1. **Inform** by enabling the public to gain information on a range of specific problems regarding the present and future needs of the New York metropolitan area.

2. **Stimulate discussion** by ensuring that the information and questions asked of the public would result in intensive discussions on the various options available.

3. **Generate the expression of views** by means of an informed vote by the public on projects that affected them.

Its goals were to:

1. **Engage in the planning process with as broad an audience as possible**, including social groups who might not have previously been engaged in such activities.

2. **Offer positive alternatives**—a goal based on the RPA's belief that neighborhood associations and local communities, due to their lack of information, often tend to oppose projects rather than find alternatives. (In part, this goal reflects the organizers' top-down view that they—the organizers—know the solutions and that participation in this case is merely consultative.)

3. **Encourage the greatest number of people to participate in the process**, thus stimulating a sense of community by encouraging discussions in a multitude of places and venues.

CHOICES FOR 76—PLANNING

Identification of problems	Sensibilization	Operational stage project organization	Operational stage

1971	1972	1973

A	M	J	J	A	S	O	N	D	J	F	M	A	M	J	J	A	S	O	N	D	J	F	M	A	M	J

Creation of the committee of citizens advisory.

Organization of 500 000 participants to the groups reunion.

Groups monitoring.

Newspaper articles.

Study and final report from the citizens' commission

Establishment—preliminary organization of the project.

Publication of the basic analysis.

Paperback publication.

Study of the scripts for TV films.

Shooting of 6 films in 1 hour.

Editing films.

Experts' reports.

Cooperation from:
• Government
• Civic organizations
• Survey institutions

Growth •
Habitat •
Transportation •
Environment •
Poverty •
Government •

Timeline for Choices for '76. Image recreated by Isabel Aguirre based on the original. Diagram taken from an RPA Choices for '76 publication

In many ways, Choices for '76 was highly successful in reaching its stated goals. It engaged nearly three million people, or about 15 percent of the population of the New York metropolitan area, and it helped launch a broad debate in committee discussions throughout the region on numerous critical issues and the various options on how to address them. Using ballots available in banks, libraries, large corporations, and newspapers, people were encouraged to express their choices after each of five documentary films were aired on television. In addition, information was broadcast on all major television channels and two radio stations, and a book entitled *How to Save Urban America* was prepared for the occasion and sold at newsstands and bookstores. The book was also distributed free of charge to teachers in many of the region's social and political science programs, as well as to large companies, which, in turn, distributed them to their employees. Through these various outlets, five topics were addressed: the environment, housing, transportation, poverty, and cities and suburbs.

Preliminary Project Organization

To start the effort, the RPA sought the support of organizations, civic leaders, and personalities to both launch the program and help raise the funds necessary to carry out its aims. For this, it was vital to identify allies who were respected and could reach out and engage both the general public and those institutions that would be of greatest help to them. The RPA chose to address the television industry first because, if it were accepted, it would serve as a catalyst and stimulate the imagination of other potential supporters by making the project more credible.

Participants

In essence, the RPA wanted to motivate people who had never previously participated in civic- and planning-related activities and prepare them to participate effectively in a sustained way in regional policy discussions. In addition to reading material prepared for them, watching specially developed television documentaries, and soliciting written responses, the participants were asked to organize and participate in small discussion groups that were held throughout the region. It was at this level that difficulties arose. For many, this step seemed too complicated, and they did not relate to the regional context of the discussion. Unaware of even belonging to a region, they had first to be convinced that the regional problems were directly related to the local issues that affected them. The RPA was also unknown to many in the region, and a major challenge was introducing it and explaining its objectives and methods. The frequency of meetings and the commitment of time (a few hours a week for five to eight weeks) often frightened off potential participants as well.

Strategy

In order to organize and motivate people, Choices for '76 was able to get the commitment of eighteen of the area's television channels to participate in the project. Their involvement helped to legitimize it, and made it a very important event. Major stories in almost every newspaper and advertisements in local libraries, banks, train stations, restaurants, and businesses, as well as on television and radio programs, all helped further bolster the enterprise. Among other organizations, several women's groups, including the League of Women Voters and the American Association of University Women, actively participated in this outreach effort, as did both of us, participating alongside the neighborhood organizations in Bedford-Stuyvesant and East Harlem that we were working with at the time.

Content Identification and Discussion of Area Problems

The identification of issues and the various alternative approaches to them required a constant effort. The pros and cons of each potential solution had to be very carefully and painstakingly laid out. This involved creating an awareness of the complicated interrelated nature of many of these issues—the way a solution was arrived at for one particular problem might impact a whole host of other issues in unimagined ways. Above all, it meant presenting the various alternative solutions clearly enough to make them understandable to the general public without oversimplifying the issue or talking down to them. The principle issues looked at were as follows.

1. The Environment

Environmental issues in the mid-1970s were framed in a completely different context than they are today. Climate change and the need to reduce the consumption of carbon had not yet been recognized although the media reported sporadically on environmental concerns such as smog alerts and other air pollution-related events. Rachel Carson, in her 1962 book *Silent Spring*, had raised concerns about our reliance on synthetic pesticides, and her book is credited with launching the growth of the modern environmental movement, which, in turn, increased media focus on environmental issues. But air pollution was commonly accepted as the price one paid for progress. Environmentalists and conservationists were often considered elitist and concerned more about protecting nature than people or the economy, and were often considered prophets of doom. The end of the 1960s and the early 1970s saw the emergence of media and public attention to the state of the environment. Books, newspapers, and television—which, at the time, was emerging as a powerful new medium—helped to propel what previously was a nascent environmental movement into the national consciousness. News stories about oil spills, polluted rivers, floods, and smog alerts all helped to make the environment an important new political, social, and economic issue. In April 1970, an estimated twenty million Americans gathered for the first Earth Day celebration, including tens of thousands in Lower Manhattan. Many of the organizers of that event were from New York City's community-based development organizations. As a result of the organizing and political action that took place, Congress quickly passed federal legislation, including the establishment of the Environmental Protection Agency (EPA). In 1972, the Clean Water Act was passed, lending further legitimacy to environmental issues and spawning increased media attention.

Legislative efforts to address environmental concerns continued in a bipartisan fashion until the mid-to-late 1990s, when some on the right abandoned or politicized environmental issues. The issue that led to the environmental backlash more than any other was the near unanimous international scientific recognition that climate change was the result of human activity and that we had to find ways to reduce our consumption of carbon, which meant oil. Fueled by funds from those in the oil industry, some groups were heavily financed to question the scientific basis for the claim or to argue that any attempt to limit carbon consumption would lead to economic calamity.

Choices for '76, therefore, looked at the issues of the environment at a time when the environmental movement was just beginning to emerge and when issues of climate change, environmental justice, carbon use, and peak oil—in other words, the realization that petroleum is not a renewable source of energy and will, in the not too-distant future, become unavailable and expensive—were all issues not fully recognized yet.

These issues, plus many others that planners and the public were unaware of in 1976, continue to be the focus of our attention today. The struggle between individual actions and desires and the collective needs of society, the debate between suburban sprawl and urban concentration, and the controversy over who benefits and who pays for the costs of our actions in both dollars and quality of life are all enduring questions. Today, the challenge of building resilient sustainable communities and livelihoods, be they in Tumaco, Colombia or in New York City, is one we can no longer avoid. While the discussion during Choices for '76 did not focus on the same environmental issues that we need to address today and in the future, it did help deeply inform those of us who participated, kindling a desire to learn more and to expand on what we read, saw, and discussed. The environmental movement that emerged at that time provided a vehicle for accelerating change, continued learning, and ongoing engagement that no one event, no matter how well thought through, financed, and planned, could have brought about. It led us to the awareness that planning and development is a process and not just an event or product and that engaging in participatory planning requires more than consultation, but also the building of capacity, including the organizational capacity to engage in the process over time. This was the great lesson of the experience that we have been privileged to have engaged in.

2. Housing

Housing was selected as one of the key topics to be discussed since it encompasses far more than the shelter one occupies. It allowed the sponsors of Choices for '76 to introduce an array of interrelated issues such as race, segregation, and residential choices, transportation, income and housing needs, neighborhood decline and housing abandonment, affordability and accessibility, and many others. As the original authors of Choices for '76 put it, "everyone has a housing problem":

> We start with housing because enclosed within it are most of the other dominant concerns of the Region. Until we have made up our mind about where and how we live, about the relationship between that and the way we work and play and get from place to place, about the relationships between ourselves and people of a different race or ethnic heritage or income or age—until we've made some decisions about housing and home, we can't have a clear idea of what we want to do or have done. . . . We start with housing because this series looks at the whole New York Urban Region and housing is a truly region-wide issue . . . housing is fundamental because it occupies most of the built-up urban

land. . . . What housing is like and where it is located gives the Region its basic appearance. Housing location and the number of households per acre determine whether people drive their cars a great deal or walk and use transit, whether they feel part of a community or not, whether they stay close to nature or not.[13][2]

Many of these questions still challenge us today. Some that have been addressed have, in turn, led to other problems, such as gentrification, displacement, and housing affordability. As was the case for Choices for '76, housing today continues to be a gateway issue to many of the other issues our regions face.

3. Transportation

In the early 1970s, as well as today, the issue of transportation focused on the conflict between individual choices and collective solutions—in other words, between the personal automobile and public transit. The debate took place even though the issues of climate change and the imperative to reduce carbon emissions were not yet in our vocabulary. Also discussed was the interrelationship between housing and the workplace and the spatial implications that such interrelationships warranted. Evidence of sprawl and the decentralization of the city were beginning to become an issue of concern to our principal cities. Highways facilitated the growth of the non-trolley or transit-oriented suburbs and accelerated the migration of upper-income and predominantly white families to the suburbs. The racial segregation of our metropolitan areas was becoming increasingly evident and problematic. This pattern of residential segregation had been spawned a few years earlier due to the confluence of the new post-war housing and financing opportunities that had become available to white working families, many of whom were veterans eligible for low-cost housing mortgages. Such opportunities were closed to people of color and female heads of households because of discriminatory lending and real estate practices. Closely linked to the issue of race was that of poverty.

2. William B. Shore, "The Town Meeting on Housing," in *How to Save Urban America: Choices for '76, Key Issues Confronting Cities and Suburbs*, ed. William A. Caldwell (New York: A Signet Special/New American Library, 1973), 14.

4. Poverty

The issue of poverty and the strategies to address or eliminate it were far more front and center in the 1970s than it is today. In particular, the relationship between poverty and race, more than any other individual issue, was perceived to have had the most profound influence on the development of the region. The discussions on this issue attempted to address several questions, including the social and racial integration in schools that was exacerbated by the growing residential segregation in the region; job creation, especially that which focused on those who were most often the victims of cyclical as well as chronic unemployment, and the means by which how best to engage the poor in the process of addressing this issue; the establishment of a minimum wage, and in some circles, including conservative groups, the establishment of a guaranteed minimum income; and the redistribution of wealth through a progressive system of taxation.

Ironically, one of the key questions asked at that time was: do you favor making people with higher incomes pay more federal income tax? The top marginal income tax rate at the time was 70 percent in the US and 60 percent in France—as compared to the post-Bush era when it dropped to 35 percent in the US and 46 percent in France.[14][3] Yet, in the material developed by the RPA for the discussion on poverty, the organization wrote:

> The experience of West European countries indicates that the United States is still far from the point where higher taxes on the upper income portion of the population would hurt the economy as a whole. Of course, if far reaching income redistribution schemes are to be considered for implementation, detailed studies of the changed flow of money and the changed allocation of resources would have to be carried out to estimate their impact on all of society.[15][4]

---

3. Kevin L. Kliesen and Daniel L. Thornton, "Tax Rates and Revenues since the 1970s," *Economic Synopses* 2011, no. 24 (2011).

4. Boris S. Pushkarev, "The Town Meeting on Poverty," in Caldwell, *How to Save Urban America*, 183.

The political pendulum has swung so far to the right since Choices for '76 that any discussion of income redistribution and higher taxes on the wealthiest of us is practically a nonstarter unless, of course, it leads to the greater distribution of wealth to those already wealthy since, as the argument goes, such people are the job creators. However, the key point here is that the RPA, despite its somewhat corporate and elite status, raised critical issues about equity and poverty. The organization demonstrated the need for planners and civic leaders to frame the debate and to propose solutions to genuine problems affecting society. Choices for '76 did that and, in doing so, taught us that urban planners and decision makers have a responsibility to address hard and often unpopular issues.

5. Cities and Suburbs

The town meeting session on cities and suburbs raised the question of relations between the town and the periphery of urban areas, balancing sprawl and density and tackling the issues of population dispersal. Issues that were discussed at these meetings included the safeguarding of the countryside during periods of rapid urbanization, attaining a better system of public transportation, and diversifying housing opportunities for disadvantaged groups such as women, the poor, and minority populations, many of whom were now confined to cities.

As well as such specific elements, there was also a close examination of what the overall allocation of resources between the city and the region should be. As the RPA put it:

"Do we re-channel some of the energy of prospective urban growth from the fringes of the Region back into its central cities? Or do we continue the long-term trend toward dispersal and decentralization?"[16][5]

In many ways, the discussion of the cities and our suburbs was the most contentious and, at the same time, most farsighted topic Choices for '76 examined. It forced us to address the issue of centralization versus decentralization of the city, which, in turn, was a factor in determining the physical armature for our region's development. It raised issues of race

---

5. Boris S. Pushkarev, "The Town Meeting on Cities and Suburbs," in Caldwell, *How to Save Urban America*, 186.

and class. It forced the participants to tease out how they wanted to allocate resources over time. It forced those assembled to address whether or not we should abandon our center cities, erode our agricultural and rural communities, and reframe how and where we lived, worked, and played. It questioned the very need for a center and opened up discussions of alternative systems of urbanization.

All of these factors had an impact on how and where we lived—our housing. It set the framework for how we circulated through and serviced our region—our transit and transportation. It addressed how we were going to consume or preserve our natural capital, our land, air, and water—our environment. And it forced us to address our human capital needs or whether we were going to ignore them—the issue of poverty and social and economic equity. In doing this, it addressed how and where different segments of our society will live and the opportunities and choices available to them and to us. These are questions planners and politicians like to sidestep, but are critical to the process. Most of all, these are the threads by which all of the elements of this intricate regional web can be woven together.

Observations

Reflecting on this process in the January 1975 *National Civic Review*, William B. Shore, who had been the vice president for public affairs at the RPA, commented on the lessons learned from running a media-based mass public participation project as follows:

> Three components are necessary, and a promise of all is needed before the project can go ahead: (1) mass media dissemination. (2) Competently selected and presented choices and background information. (3) A very large organized audience. So television time will be contingent on having a trusted, well-financed research agency and a civic network committed to recruiting participants.[17][6]

---

6. William B. Shore, "Choices for '76: The Results and the Lessons," *National Civic Review* 64, no. 1 (2007): 7.

Based on some of the evaluations reviewed and some of our personal observations of Choices for '76, the following principles emerged that might help guide any future, large-scale participatory planning effort:

1. To achieve maximum participation, use of the mass media—television, newspapers, and radio—does not suffice alone: one needs to engage in personal relationships in order to recruit, organize, and sustain the involvement of people.

2. It is also not enough to simply get the answers to questionnaires; it takes work and constant contact and engagement with people and organizations at all levels.

3. It is important to show that regional issues are not separate from local issues; they are simply at a different scale and put a different perspective on the issue. Often, they can lead to new approaches and solutions that would not have emerged if one looked at the issue from a purely local perspective.

4. The use of audio-visual technologies was essential in raising awareness of the issues and helping to pose alternative approaches to addressing those issues. If done well, it can help people to begin to envision alternatives and to generate their own informed approaches to those issues.

5. The question of how to tailor the issues and information so that they engage different audiences needs to be a major consideration. This must be done without compromising the common theme and integrity of the effort.

Today, we are confronted by many of these same questions. However, the context in which we address these questions and the many factors we were unaware of in the 1970s, such as the relationship between urban sprawl and carbon consumption, will condition how we respond. Revisiting Choices for '76 is a strong reminder of the need to discuss such interrelated questions, and the RPA and other planners today are struggling with a means to do this while largely lacking the resources and political support that was available almost half a century ago.

Participatory Planning at the New York City Scale:
Listening to the City

Twenty-five years after Choices for '76, shortly after the attack on the World Trade Center on September 11, 2001, a similar effort was launched by the RPA in concert with the Pratt Center for Community Development called Listening to the City.[7] Ironically, that effort was, on the whole, oblivious of what had taken place a quarter of a century earlier.

The year 2001 was very important for the Pratt Center. In the spring, it had released a report about the role that manufacturing played in New York City's economy and the need to preserve industrial space. At the same time, thirty-five business, labor, and academic experts, known as the Group of 35, worked with the RPA and issued a very different report that called for rezoning and other actions to insure that New York City had enough land to accommodate growth in the office sector, in essence, calling for additional square feet of office space to be built over the next years. The RPA and the Pratt Center studies were essentially staking out two alternative economic visions of the city: one that sought to reinforce the trend of New York as a world financial capital and another that argued that we needed to diversify the economy, maintain our manufacturing capability, and provide economic opportunities to a population with a broad range of educational and technical skills. To a degree, the different approaches reflected the different constituencies that these organizations worked with. But on September 11, 2001, the entire framework for this debate was abruptly shattered.

The attack on New York City's World Trade Center took place on a beautiful late summer day. Not a cloud in the sky and low humidity: the kind of day one ranks among New York City's best. It wasn't. News of the two planes hitting the World Trade Center alerted New Yorkers and the world alike to changes that still reverberate. However, on that day when our attention was riveted by the news and concern for our family, friends, and neighbors, people began assembling in public places. The

---

7. In addition, in late 2001, the Municipal Art Society, working with a broad coalition of community-based organizations and an advisory group that included the Pratt Center and Ron Shiffman, also launched a regional visioning process entitled Imagine New York.

parks and streets were filled. People lined up in long, almost unending, lines to give blood. In Brooklyn, residents and small shop owners set up chairs for people to rest and served water to those walking over the bridges to their homes in Brooklyn, Queens, and Long Island. Everyone was helping someone—race, class, age differences, and tensions evaporated. The city was united in ways that surprised even the most jaded observers, and some of that unity was to last for months and even years after the terrible events of that day.

The trauma of the September 11 attacks to New York City, the US, and the world was deep. The attack rendered sixteen acres of dense commercial space in the heart of the city's downtown central business area useless. It threatened to weaken its financial sector and even undermine its economy entirely. The immediate task was to find places for those displaced businesses to relocate to and be able to once again function effectively. The second task was to make sure that the lost functions and jobs returned to New York City and, at the same time, allowed for redundancy and resiliency to be achieved so that essential economic functions would not be lost in the event of another disaster. There was still a need to rebuild and to engage New Yorkers in a dialogue concerning rebuilding. The reasons for this were multifaceted. First, it was important to make sure New York City retained its vital financial sector and that it was not weakened through a process of decentralization. Second, Lower Manhattan was a major part of the city, home to many businesses and surrounded by a vibrant and creative set of residential communities. It was also home to tens of thousands of jobs filled by people from all walks of life that resided in neighborhoods throughout the city and region. And third, but not least, it was vital to simply engage in some attempt to help others for the sake of one's own mental health.

In concert with other organizations, the Pratt Center embarked on a number of interrelated planning, rebuilding, and memorialization endeavors. Underlying them all was a belief that many of New York's low-, moderate-, and middle-income communities should be engaged in the process. These communities had suffered dramatically, but because the attack had been on the financial district, many assumed the victims to be limited to the businesses there and their higher-income employees. This was, of course, true to an extent, but many of those left unemployed or killed were first responders, restaurant employees, service personnel, cleaners, elevator operators, street vendors, taxi and limousine drivers, and so on who were from low- or middle-income backgrounds. When they lost their jobs, their neighborhoods suffered, their rents and mortgages went unpaid, and the impact quietly reverberated throughout the city. Yet, many of those who were advocating for aid from Washington ignored the needs of these New Yorkers and focused their attention almost entirely on the needs of the financial and real estate sectors.

The Pratt Center's Principles and Work Tasks

In the weeks following September 11, the Pratt Center had been invited to participate in discussions convened by representatives of the many sectors who were assessing the issues raised by the attack and the recovery process. It was contacted by some elected officials, civic organizations, and researchers, but above all by community-based organizations engaged in struggles for social, economic, and environmental justice that were concerned about the short- and long-term impacts of the events on low-income neighborhoods and communities of color.

Setting the Stage: The Actors

A number of civic groups organized to engage in the planning and rebuilding process. To some degree, these were duplicative and often made up of the same set of actors, but they were focused on different aspects of the overall rebuilding effort. These endeavors included Rebuild Downtown Our Town (RDOT), a community-based effort organized by residents of the Lower Manhattan community; Imagine New York, an effort organized by the Municipal Art Society (MAS) Planning Center, which initially organized to focus on memorializing those lost and engaged in exploring the response to the bombing of the Alfred P. Murrah Federal Building in Oklahoma City in 1995; the Labor Community Advocacy Network (LCAN), a collective of progressive organizations that emerged to advocate for the needs of labor, new immigrant groups, the poor, and environmental justice organizations; New York New Visions, a coalition of architecture, planning, and design organizations under the auspices of the AIA New York City Chapter, which aimed to address some of the physical planning and architectural issues involved in the rebuilding; and the RPA, which took the lead in convening an umbrella organization called the Civic Alliance to Rebuild Downtown New York.[18][8] These efforts and others that emerged all overlapped, but each was essential to keep the needs and issues that it considered important on the agenda. The Pratt Center was a key player in all of these efforts, and to a great extent, it helped facilitate cooperation between all of the groups—a task that was made easier by the level of cooperation after September 11. The Pratt Center and the RPA each received funding to support their endeavors and organize their respective constituencies in the rebuilding effort.

Setting the Stage: The Issues

A handful of the leaders of the groups involved in the planning and re-building process were asked to attend a retreat in November 2001 organized by the Rockefeller Brothers Fund and held at the Pocantico Center, New York. Also present were representatives from the Rockefeller Foundation, Ford Foundation, Surdna Foundation, and a number of other foundations. At the meeting, the Pratt Center presented the case as to why the rebuilding effort was of such importance to New York City's low- and moderate-income population. Others discussed the impact on the city's cultural and business communities, and Robert Yaro, RPA president, presented the need for an umbrella group and to get the states of New York and New Jersey to cooperate on the rebuilding effort.

The Pocantico meeting was called at a critical time. The Partnership for New York City, the city's leading business group, had just issued *Working Together to Accelerate New York's Recovery*, an economic impact analysis report outlying priorities and initiating discussion with the federal government on the rebuilding process. The Partnership's report was timely and excellently crafted. It articulated the needs of its audience and its constituency—the business community of Lower Manhattan and, in particular, the financial sector. The report documented the unquestion-

---

8. The Pratt Center, New York University, and The New School all assisted in this effort, and the Pratt Center emerged as co-convener of the group with the RPA through the spring of 2004.

able and critical role that Lower Manhattan played in the economy of the city and the interrelationship that existed between the health and vitality of the financial heart of the city and the other communities of the region.

For all its competence, however, the Partnership Report fell short. While it enumerated the numbers of people that had lost their jobs because of the attack, it did not focus on the fact that of the estimated 105,200 jobs lost to the city, 79,700 had been held by low- and moderate-income people who had been employed in the restaurant, retail, hotel, air transport, and building services. It failed to acknowledge that 60 percent of the men and women working in these sectors earned an average of 11 dollars per hour and had an annual salary of less than 23,000 dollars, a figure well below half the median income of the city as a whole.[9]

The report also failed to mention the additional 76,000 workers who had avoided layoffs, but who still had to accept reduced work hours, resulting in dramatically lower earnings.[10] While the attack had a major impact on the financial sector, its impact was somewhat lessened by the relocation within days of most of the financial sector jobs outside of Manhattan and, in some cases, outside the city altogether. That was not the case with the other sectors that were badly impacted. For instance, the apparel industry, which was the second most impacted sector, suffered outright layoffs. Unlike financial sector jobs, apparel industry jobs were not relocated in the region, and while some employees had to wait for months following the attack to be rehired, others found that their jobs were lost permanently.[11] As the Labor Community Advocacy Network to Rebuild New York noted in April of 2002, "in many ways, low-income New Yorkers, immigrants, and people of color have borne the brunt of the resulting economic hardship. Some of the hardest-hit sectors have been those such as airports and hotels that were key sources of family-supporting jobs for New Yorkers without college degrees. And other devastated sectors—for example, the apparel, taxi and car service

---

9. Fiscal Policy Institute, *World Trade Center Job Impacts Take a Heavy Toll on Low-Wage Workers: Occupational and Wage Implications of Job Losses Related to the September 11 World Trade Center Attack* (New York: Fiscal Policy Institute, 2001), 2.

10. Ibid.

11. New York State Assembly, *The Lower Manhattan Economy after September 11th* (New York: New York State, 2005), 16–18.

industries—were ones where even in the best of times, workers struggled to get by."[12]

The cumulative effect of all this made it apparent that while the physical damage and destruction had taken place in Lower Manhattan, the economic toll was devastatingly high in New York's low- and moderate-income neighborhoods. In mid-October, just before the foundation-led meeting was called and a few weeks before the Pocantico session, the Pratt Center, working with LCAN with the support of the Federal Reserve Bank of New York, brought together some of the community-based development organizations working in these communities to help identify what the impacts were. At this session, anecdotal evidence regarding the impact of the attack on New York's low- and moderate-income neighborhoods began to emerge—increased demand on food pantries and a spike in housing court actions (particularly in the Bronx) were observed. Local community-based organizations reported that they were experiencing higher than usual walk-in inquiries for jobs, housing, small business loans, and protection against evictions.

It was clear to those in close communication with working-class communities that the impact of the September 11 attacks went well beyond Lower Manhattan. It influenced, for instance, the welfare of communities throughout the city where those dependent on Lower Manhattan lived— e.g., the so-called outer boroughs; the public services and the agencies providing them; the immigrant enclaves now put under suspicion; the residents, parents, and children living in or using the city's public services, including its transportation and school systems; and the tourist-dependent services throughout the city. All these points were presented to those assembled in Pocantico, and, as a result, support for a broader response began to emerge.

The Partnership's report, which was the basis for many of the comments made at the Pocantico retreat, also proposed a five-borough strategy to decentralize the financial industry. Everyone agreed that this was important and that it needed to be planned and undertaken carefully.

---

12. Labor Community Advocacy Network, *Labor Community Advocacy Network to Rebuild New York Policy Statement* (New York: Labor Community Advocacy Network, 2002), 13–14.

From the perspective of the progressive groups and community-based organizations present, this had the potential to both improve the economy in many of our neighborhoods and generate needed jobs. At the same time, there was concern that there was a need to minimize any adverse effects of decentralization, including the direct and indirect displacement of residents and of manufacturing and industrial jobs.

In essence, we were calling for a program that both maximized economic benefits on a macro (city-wide and by sector) level and maximized economic and social benefits on a micro (neighborhood and community) level. The progressive groups also saw the need to not only decentralize the city's economic base but also diversify it. They advocated for a more diverse economy that would generate more moderate- and middle-income jobs rather than concentrating growth at the top and bottom ends of the economic scale. In order to achieve this, it was argued that a local community economic development plan was needed that mirrored the one being undertaken for Lower Manhattan.

The foundations that assembled at Pocantico and at some of the meetings that took place before and after realized the key role that the RPA, MAS, some of the city's cultural advocates, and the Pratt Center could play in the rebuilding effort. The Rockefeller and Ford foundations, both of which shared the progressive perspective put forth by the Pratt Center and its allies, supported these efforts because they realized that unless New York City's low- and moderate-income population were engaged, their needs would be ignored. The Pratt Center was aware that it could not speak for this constituency, but at the behest of a number of neighborhood and community-based development organizations, it was encouraged to take on the role because these organizations lacked the resources to participate themselves. In addition, some of the funds received by the Pratt Center were, with concurrence of the donors of the funds, funneled to a number of grassroots and immigrant organizations. The work of all of these organizations continued and intensified over the next years, and the outcome of these efforts, and those of countless other groups, could easily be the subject of a book in and of itself. However, for the purposes of this book and this chapter, we want to focus on an initiative of the Civic Alliance called Listening to the City.

A Second Listening to the City

Listening to the City, like the RPA's Choices for '76, attempted to engage in a broad-based regional participatory planning approach. Interestingly enough, discussion of the earlier RPA effort was rarely, if ever, raised. Yet, the effort was strikingly similar even though the impetus was different. Both attempted to engage the larger public in the process of planning, and both used the technologies of the day to facilitate that participation. Both efforts engaged others to advise them in framing the participatory planning efforts that they were launching, and both attempted to develop techniques to inform those that were to be engaged in the process. Both also took place over an extended period of time.

The Civic Alliance to Rebuild Downtown New York sponsored hundreds of planning and coordinating meetings, planning sessions, and mini-charrettes. Among these were two major town hall meetings entitled Listening to the City. The first of these, sponsored by the Civic Alliance in cooperation with America*Speaks*, a nonprofit organization that specializes in bringing citizens together in large forums, and the Robert F. Wagner Graduate School of Public Service at New York University, was held on February 7, 2002 at the South Street Seaport. A second meeting followed on July 20 at the Jacob K. Javits Convention Center in Manhattan.

The first town hall discussion was an important one. It addressed many issues of concern, and what was learned helped in the redesign of the second meeting. One of the principal things discovered was that many of those directly and indirectly affected by the attack were not in attendance. This was an error of omission rather than any attempt at exclusion, but such errors tend to occur when a particular constituency is not of concern to those in leadership at the time. While the Pratt Center was an active member of the Civic Alliance and the Civic Alliance was a sponsor of the February 7 event, the event was mostly planned and organized by New York University, the RPA, and America*Speaks*. At the first meeting, there had not been an effort to ensure that the lower-income communities that adjoined the World Trade Center site, namely, Chinatown and the Lower East Side, were in attendance. Nor had there been any attempt to reach out to labor, new immigrant, or the multitude of low- and

*Cover from
Listening to the
City, Report of
Proceedings.*

PHOTO COLLAGE
ORIGINALLY PRO-
DUCED AT THE
PRATT CENTER USING
PHOTOS BY RON
SHIFFMAN

moderate-income communities that had been severely impacted. This
was a serious drawback and one that was recognized by MAS, LCAN, the
Pratt Center, and some in the progressive donor community. In addition,
the America*Speaks* process described later in this chapter was only as
good as the questions it framed and the diversity of its theme teams, the
groups of men and women summarizing the feedback from the thousands of participants.

The progressive donor community stepped up by funding more progressive players to be able to take a more aggressive role in the planning
process, and the Pratt Center became a conduit for that funding. Thus,
the organizers of the second town hall meeting included, in addition
to the original sponsors, the Milano School of International Affairs, Management, and Urban Policy at The New School, LCAN, a new immigrant
coalition, and the Pratt Center as integral parts of its planning team.

To the RPA's credit, they welcomed the progressive community's more in-depth engagement, and a healthy and supportive partnership was forged. The issues of broadening the base of participation, of how to reach out and make sure that those previously excluded felt comfortable to participate, were openly and honestly discussed. In addition, the agenda and how the questions for the second Listening to the City meeting were to be framed, and in what order they would be discussed, were intensely debated. Such a partnership required the RPA to balance the needs and demands of those representing big business and the real estate and finance industries, as well as the Port Authority of New York and the Lower Manhattan Development Corporation (LMDC), which shared jurisdiction over the World Trade Center site, with those of New York City's progressive community.

Between the two events, the Civic Alliance continued to meet regularly and issued a series of background briefing and policy papers. Some were the result of special technical forums while others came from its various committees. These focused on issues such as the memorial, economic development, transportation and circulation, urban design, civic amenities, social, economic, and environmental justice, green buildings and sustainable systems, and regulatory review processes.

A compendium of recommendations entitled *A Planning Framework to Rebuild Downtown New York* was prepared, presented, and discussed at the RPA's twelfth annual regional assembly held on April 26, 2002. LCAN had just released a policy statement two days earlier that touched on the same issues, but stressed the need for rebuilding the economy, good jobs, infrastructure, and revenues. LCAN strongly advocated for a rebuilding process that would be "broad-based, transparent and inclusive."[13] All of these reports were widely distributed, discussed at smaller meetings, and the subject of a score of newsletters, newspaper articles, and briefing sessions. As a result of all this, it was decided that the following issues had to be addressed at the forthcoming event:

- Employment and economic development concerns that retained the FIRE (finance, insurance, and real estate) sectors but diversified the city's economy.

---

13. Labor Community Advocacy Network, *Labor Community Advocacy Network to Rebuild New York Policy Statement* (New York: Labor Community Advocacy Network, 2002), 2.

- Environmental and ecological concerns and a focus on the environmental justice issues that arose from the demolition of the World Trade Center site and the removal of the debris, such as where would it be removed to and how, as well as how environmental justice issues would relate to the rebuilding effort itself.

- The need for housing that was truly affordable to New York City's low- and moderate-income population, many of whom were directly impacted by the events, such as EMS personnel, elevator operators, maintenance personnel, street vendors, and other emergency workers.

- Ensuring transportation, security, infrastructure, and quality of life concerns were dealt with in a way that benefited all New Yorkers equally, and that the burden of development did not fall disproportionately on the poor.

- Developing a strategy for substantive and ongoing public input.

Understandably, the discussions leading up to this second and far larger event were not free of conflict, with the LMDC (a subsidiary of the Empire State Development Corporation formed to expedite the planning and rebuilding of the area) and the Port Authority, in particular, which were seeking to narrow the discussion to that of their plans for rebuilding on the site. However, the way the event was designed ensured that any particular interest group could not hijack it. Every aspect of it was planned and scripted—not in terms of the outcomes, but in the issues to be discussed, their order of presentation, who would be in the theme teams, and even the specific questions to be asked and voted upon. In the end, a consensus was achieved. The LMDC's key issues were to take place in the morning, while the broader and so-called softer issues, such as employment, were put on the agenda in the afternoon session. Commitments and program adjustments to make sure that people did not leave before everything was discussed were agreed upon. As a result, issues such as job creation, environmental justice, design, and memorialization were all given space alongside major economic, construction, and financial matters.

A participant guide for everyone involved in the July 20 event was distributed, which covered all the issues, the history of the area, and some of the major policy alternatives. Posters reflecting and illustrating some of the same material were hung throughout the Javits Center. The space held over five hundred tables, with an average of ten seats per table, and a computer at each one. Every participant was given a hand-held device that could respond to questions from the podium. A theme team and an area for receiving, distilling, and feeding back the information was set up. Miles and miles of cable were laid on the floor for the event. As the process continued and the participatory plans became increasingly more intensive and costly, the Port Authority and the LMDC were both approached for funding and both entities agreed to help defray some of the costs.

Conclusion of Listening to the City

Altogether, the partnership between the Civic Alliance and America-*Speaks* yielded a degree of civic participation that far exceeded any previous discussion focused on development issues. Planning, urban design, and excellence in architecture were all publicly discussed and supported by a broad array of people from all walks of life and groups representative of all of the city's diverse constituencies. As the steering committee noted in the cover letter to the proceedings of the event:

> More than 5,000 people came together to make a difference in the city that they love. Total strangers sat with each other at diversely assembled tables and over the course of a day shared their stories and emotions, puzzled over plans and the challenges facing this city and our region, and pondered how to create a suitable and moving memorial for those who lost their lives on September 11. Unlike public hearings or traditional town hall meetings, at these forums everyone had a chance to speak and everyone had a chance to listen.[14]

---

14. Civic Alliance to Rebuild Downtown New York, *Listening to the City: Report of Proceedings* (New York: Civic Alliance to Rebuild Downtown New York, 2002), 1. The cover letter was signed by the sponsors of Listening to the City: Ed Blakely, Milano Graduate School, New School University; Arthur J. Fried, Center for Excellence in NYC Governance, NYU/Wagner; Carolyn J. Lukensmeyer, America*Speaks*; Ron Shiffman, Pratt Institute Center for Community and Environmental Development; and Robert D. Yaro, Regional Plan Association.

Javits Center before the July 20, 2002 event.

Javits Center during the event. PHOTOS BY RON SHIFFMAN

The cover letter to the report, which was released on the first anniversary of the attack, concluded:

> At the one year anniversary of September 11, the pain, sadness, and disruption caused to so many lives is still fresh in our minds and our hearts. The rebuilding process that served as the focus of Listening to the City is an opportunity born out of tragedy—an opportunity we wish we had never been given. Therefore we dedicate this report to every victim of the terrorist attacks of September 11 and every person whose life was irrevocably changed.[15]

The event led to short-term and substantive changes in the Port Authority's and LMDC's initial plans for the rebuilding of the area. It led to a greater public appreciation of planning, urban design, and good design than had existed in the New York area for decades. It brought community-based development organizations, developers, and the government to the same table for the first time in years. Mutual respect for differing opinions began to emerge. A template for planning was slowly taking place. New York's architectural and design community came to life, contributed time and effort, and engaged in ongoing discussions concerning the form and quality of the city. Design competitions for the rebuilding effort were launched and were eventually undertaken for other affordable housing efforts in the city. At a community level, planning was no longer considered a dirty word, and qualitative development was not only acceptable but also being courted. Longer-term fledgling efforts like New York 2050 emerged to be quickly replaced by the mayor's sustainability initiative, PlanNYC2030, a few years later and the RPA's major initiative, America 2050.

The quality of the discussion that took place among those assembled at the two Listening to the City town meetings and the feeling of those that participated far exceeded anyone's expectations. The diverse nature of those who planned and participated in the events enormously broadened the debate. It made the rebuilding of Lower Manhattan more than just a construction initiative. It avoided addressing memorialization in

---

15. Ibid.

Listening to the City, July 20, 2002.
PHOTOS BY RON SHIFFMAN

....

Listening to the City, 2002:
An Excerpt from the Civic Alliance to Rebuild Downtown
New York's Listening to the City: Report of Proceedings

"Listening to the City" combined technology with face-to-face dialogue, using a format developed by America*Speaks*, a non-profit organization that has pioneered techniques for bringing citizens together in large forums while preserving the benefits of face-to-face discussion. The America*Speaks* 21st Century Town Meeting model captures the full range of participants' ideas and allows these ideas to be heard and discussed not only by people at the same table, but by the entire assembly.

Participants in "Listening to the City" held 10-to-12-person round-table discussions, each led by a trained facilitator skilled in small-group dynamics. A network of laptop computers recorded ideas generated during the discussions. Each table's input was instantly transmitted to a "theme team" composed of volunteers and America*Speaks* staff that identified the strongest concepts from the discussions and reported them back to all the participants.

Based on the roundtable discussions, the "theme team" quickly developed a set of priorities and questions that were posed on large screens throughout the meeting hall, allowing people to get quick feedback about

....

a narrow sense, and it made rebuilding more than the mere task of replacing what was there. The broadened engagement made it a discussion about what kind of city we wanted and, ultimately, what kind of lives we wanted to lead. It addressed the lessons of September 11, but sought to engage in a larger discussion that would lead to a rebuilding effort that sent an important message to the rest of the world, reflecting our diversity, our pluralism, and our democratic way of life. The end result would be a community that would honor those whose lives were lost by addressing our vision of a better world rather than retreating and developing a plan based on our fears and a desire for retribution. Nikki Stern, whose husband was killed on September 11, presented to those five thousand men and women assembled during the second event a mission statement that how their perspectives compared to the thinking of the larger group. Each participant used a wireless polling keypad to vote on these questions and the results were immediately displayed. This process also allowed the agenda to be modified to correspond more closely to the tenor of the discussions.

The facilitators were volunteers from all 50 states and from countries as far away as Afghanistan, Australia and South Africa who paid their way to New York because they wanted to help the city heal and recover. Services available to participants also included sign language and simultaneous spoken translation; facilitators who spoke Spanish and Chinese; foreign-language, Braille and large-print copies of important discussion materials and constituent services and grief counselors.

Another key component of "Listening to the City" was a two-week online dialogue. Between July 29 and August 12, a total of 818 people exchanged ideas and expressed their priorities through this dialogue. The format and technology were developed in conjunction with Web Lab, a non-profit organization dedicated to creating innovative, Web-based projects that bring fresh perspectives and new voices to the discussion of public issues.[17]

17. Ibid., 5.

was written and adopted that day concerning the proposed memorial. It concluded with the following words:

> For all who come to learn and understand, we dedicate this memorial to the unfulfilled dreams of those lost, to our country and the strength of our democracy, to our resolve to preserve an open, diverse and free society, to our determination to remain ever vigilant in order to safeguard our nation and to those peoples around the world who unite with us in a joint quest to end hatred, ignorance, intolerance and strife and promote peace.[16]

16. Ibid., 14.

Choices for '76 and Listening to the City:
Lessons Learned

Serious concerns about such participatory events remain, however. Listening to the City, like its predecessor, Choices for '76, was very costly. The sponsors, in addition to their own resources and time, rose close to two million dollars to cover the cost of planning and holding the event—a figure that worked out to be approximately four hundred dollars per attendee. And, inevitably, its extraordinary momentum, though not entirely diminishing, began to fade with time, and as the economy recovered, an attitude of business as usual once more emerged. The rebuilding process was also subsequently politicized in an unfortunate way. In 2004, New York State Governor George Pataki, President George W. Bush, and the Republican Party decided to hold their nominating convention in New York City following the US attack on Iraq, military engagement in Afghanistan, and start of the War on Terror. While this did not entirely erode support for the effort, it unquestionably dampened the participatory engagement of many in the process. Coupled with New York State's allocation of September 11 funds to primarily benefit the business sector and the construction of housing for higher-income families, others were further alienated. The process also simply burned out some of those who participated; yet, others inevitably ended up refocusing their efforts on their original missions. Slowly, the various civil organizations—the Partnership for New York City, the Real Estate Board, the RPA, MAS, and local community boards—fell back into serving the interests of only their principle constituents.

All of this underlines the issue that unless there are mechanisms for sustaining public interest, support will slowly fade. The fact that RPA did not even reference its previous regional participatory effort while planning was underway for Listening to the City is, in and of itself, a lesson. Somehow, we need to find ways to learn from our past efforts, sustain the efforts that are worthwhile, and overcome the tendency to burn out or disengage. This means finding ways to assure that such broad-based participation will be supported in the long term. The inevitable tendency of foundations to lose interest and of organizations to be forced, often by sheer financial restraints, to refrain from engagement has to be addressed. In the end, the need to sustain engagement in the process and to find ways to support that engagement must be developed, and civic groups like the RPA and MAS must find ways to sustain the engagement of all sectors and not just the powerful and the moneyed.

Williamsburg-Greenpoint Case, New York

Introduction

R oger's work in East Harlem, South America, and Africa was predicated on building trust with those with whom he worked (see Case Studies 1, 3, 4, 6, and 7). It required collaboration not only with his clients but also with other interveners and professionals. Social, economic, and political change is predicated on the cooperative effort of a number of committed actors transcending what any individual person or group can accomplish. My work in New York City and elsewhere was similar. This often involved working with people over long periods of time and being available and responsive to needs as they arose. It involved learning to work with a variety of different groups with differing perceptions and skills that will ultimately decide to unite to benefit their communities and use their knowledge and skills toward that end. It often meant abandoning one's self interest, acknowledging biases, and sublimating personal and institutional egos. The lessons that we learned decades ago turned out to be more applicable today than they were when we first had to confront them.

In this chapter, I will describe the role that my Pratt Center colleagues and I played in the Williamsburg-Greenpoint communities of Brooklyn over the past forty-five years, from the late 1960s to the current day.

An article in the New York Times *discussing the City's agreeing to create new housing for displaced residents in their former neighborhood.*

Ousted Brooklyn Tenants Promised Co-Ops by City: Plan Called Acceptable Company
By MURRAY SCHUMACH
New York Times (1923-Current file): Sep 18, 1973;
ProQuest Historical Newspapers: The New York Times (1851-2007) with Index (1851-1993)
pg. 47

Ousted Brooklyn Tenants Promised Co-Ops by City

By MURRAY SCHUMACH

Tenants from the Northside community in the Williamsburg section of Brooklyn, who are being relocated to permit expansion of a factory, will be in new, permanent homes by next summer, city officials said yesterday.

Construction of 10 three-story brick buildings will begin before the end of next month, according to Robert M. Heller, assistant to Mayor Lindsay. Mr. Heller was assigned to the area when it became a scene of turmoil last week as residents were forcibly ejected by the police on orders from the city.

The new buildings, between Bedford Avenue and Berry Street and from North Fourth to Norh Fifth Street, will contain 30 apartments. The rent will be $29.19 a room and the down-payment on the Mitchell-Lama cooperatives will be $2,000, according to William A. Smith, director of Brooklyn development for the Housing and Development Administration.

Plan Called Acceptable

Ron Schiffman, who has been a frequent spokesman for the community in its numerous disputes with the city, said this plan was basically the one presented to the city last January by the community.

"If the city had accepted it right away," he said, "there wouldn't have been any forced evictions. We've been talking to families. This is what they have been fighting for, and they will accept it."

Mr. Heller conceded that the city had learned "a lesson" from this dispute and would not make the same mistakes again in planning industrial expansion.

The city officials said the new apartments would be made up of 18 one-bedroom units, six two-bedroom and six three-bedroom.

Though the land for these buildings has not yet been acquired, they said any dispute about getting it would be over price and would not hold up construction.

Mr. Heller said that acquisition proceedings would be initiated in Supreme Court in Brooklyn on Oct. 3.

The assistant to Mayor Lind-

The New York Times/Sept. 18, 1973

say predicted that the City Planning Commission would approve the proposal and that the Board of Estimate would hold hearings no later than Oct. 25 and would also vote in favor of the plan.

He said that the city hoped to put up additional housing of the same sort in this area.

"We're looking to expand beyond this," he said. "We're putting new housing into Northside for the first time in a generation."

The new housing will be, for the most part, almost directly across the street from the buildings demolished last week in the forced evictions.

Company to Expand

The houses were demolished to permit expansion of the S & S Corrugated Paper Machinery Company, which has 500 employes and plans to hire 200 more if it can expand. Officials of the company had told the city that unless they could expand soon, they would move to New Jersey.

The Board of Estimate last week passed an item to permit rezoning of the area from manufacturing to residential to permit construction of the new houses. The builder, Aaron and Sol Arker, was chosen by the community.

Mr. Heller said the $2.000 down-payment for the new apartments would be covered by payments by the city to the tenants being relocated.

Williamsburg-Greenpoint is a community in the northern section of Brooklyn and is separated from the Borough of Queens on the north by a highly polluted waterway known as Newtown Creek. The western boundary is the East River that separates the Williamsburg-Greenpoint from Manhattan. Manhattan's high-rise buildings and iconic skyscrapers create a dynamic and breathtaking sight when viewed from the Williamsburg-Greenpoint waterfront.

Williamsburg-Greenpoint Community

When I first began working in the Williamsburg-Greenpoint community in northern Brooklyn in the late 1960s, its population was a microcosm of New York City's polyglot ethnic neighborhoods. The southernmost section, known as the Southside, primarily comprised ultra-Orthodox Jews with a significant and growing Puerto Rican population. As you moved north to the belt that straddled the Williamsburg Bridge and its access roads, the percentage of Puerto Rican families increased with a commensurate drop in the number of Jewish families—however, you were still in the Southside if the street numbers began with an "S," as in South 3rd Street, South 2nd Street, etc. Once you crossed Metropolitan Avenue, you arrived in the Northside. The two neighborhoods—the Southside and the Northside—made up a significant portion of the Williamsburg community.

The remainder of the community was east of the Brooklyn-Queens Expressway, which, just a few years before, had ruthlessly slashed through the community, displacing thousands of people and jobs and leaving a deep divide between the two sides. The area to the south remained primarily Orthodox Jewish. The strong religious ties of the Orthodox Jews were able to bridge the divide created by the highway because of the strong allegiance to Hasidic traditions and its growing political clout born out of its solidarity. The area separated by the highway further north was known as Italian Williamsburg or East Williamsburg and was under pressure, having been brutally separated from one of the major Catholic churches, and remained isolated to the west of the great divide.

The Northside itself, however, was principally a low- and moderate-income blue-collar Polish and Slavic community made up of immigrants from Poland, Ukraine, and Lithuania. East Williamsburg was primarily Italian with a sprinkling of Latino families and some black families located in the area's one public housing community, Cooper Park. The areas to the south and east were primarily African American and West Indian. As one moved north to Greenpoint, the area became primarily Polish and Slavic. All of the communities were mixed-use, walk-to-work neighborhoods. However, in 1961, many parts of the area were zoned for manufacturing uses, a category that allowed the residential uses to be grandfathered in, but that limited their expansion and favored the eventual shift in use from a mixed-use community to an entirely manufacturing one. It was a designation motivated by the desire to preserve manufacturing, which was a good thing, but that did not reflect the reality on the ground and, in many ways, proved to be shortsighted, as we shall see.

Every one of the Williamsburg-Greenpoint neighborhoods had its own "ballet of the street" accompanied by its own "symphony of sounds" reflective of the languages and noises that emanated from its homes, factories, and commercial enterprises.[1] Each had its own distinctive smells, sounds, and often disorganized aesthetic.

The genesis of my involvement in Williamsburg-Greenpoint began with a series of meetings a group of New Yorkers had in the late 1960s. We were concerned that many of those in the white ethnic communities of New York were reacting to the civil rights and antipoverty movements in a negative way and that many politicians desirous of holding on to their power were trying to divide communities based on race and ethnicity. At the same time, we realized that the conditions that were undermining stability in communities of color were also at play in many of the new immigrant communities and in the older low- and moderate-income white ethnic communities. Much of our understanding of these issues had come from the Pratt Center's continuing involvement in the Bedford-Stuyvesant community working on a series of programs to better the neighborhood and address some of the systemic issues afflicting that community. We

1. Jane Jacobs, *The Life and Death of Great American Cities* (New York: Random House, 1961).

Brooklyn Residents Pray to Keep Their Homes
New York Times (1923-Current file); Sep 4, 1973;
ProQuest Historical Newspapers: The New York Times (1851-2007) with Index (1851-1993)
pg. 17

Brooklyn Residents Pray to Keep Their Homes

About 150 residents of the Williamsburg section of Brooklyn took part in a street mass on North Fourth Street between Bedford and Berry Avenues yesterday to pray for 10 families living on the block who are scheduled to lose their homes Saturday when a city eviction notice takes effect.

They are being put out to make room for the expansion of a paperbox factory a block away.

"We assembled the community to pray for strength of the families who are about to be evicted," said the Rev. James Hunt of St. Vincent de Paul Parish on North Sixth Street, one of the concelebrants of the mass.

Mrs. Adele Proetta of 122 North Fourth Street has lived on the block for 38 years, has two children and now must get out. "It helps when you are desperate and you see a lot of peoople get together to pray," she said. "It gives you the reassurance you need to face up to things."

North Fourth Street was festooned with pennants and flags left over from a block party that was held last week to celebrate a temporary stay of eviction granted by the courts while certain legal technicalities were debated, but it was only a brief reprieve.

Twenty-six blocks of the area, which is called the North-side section of Williamsburg, are about to be rezoned to residential status by the City Planning Commission to prevent similar evictions.

Brooklyn residents pray to keep their homes. THE NEW YORK TIMES, SEPTEMBER 4, 1973

realized that the political reaction to the changes the community was seeking would inhibit progress not only for the African American community but also for many of those same communities that were reacting to the changes proposed. Many in the white ethnic community had the misperception that people of color were getting everything and that they, the white ethnic communities, would pay the price, and they did not realize that the changes would, in essence, lead to a better life for them as well. At the same time, many of us in the progressive movement were too quick to dismiss the fears, needs, and aspirations of those residing in these communities and to brand them as reactionary or even worse.

Some of the technical assistance providers, community organizers, and other progressives met and decided that our focus only on communities of color had contributed to this reaction and that it was incumbent on us to try to assist these white ethnic communities to address similar issues when they arose in their areas. One of those participating in these discussions was a community organizer by the name of Jan Peterson, who, at that time, was director of the Conselyea Street Block Association, which had received a grant to organize in the ethnic neighborhoods of Williamsburg. Jan was an expert community organizer and one that recognized it was important that the needs of white ethnics not be ignored or left to those with questionable motivations to prey upon them for their own reactionary purposes. She was committed to furthering the rights of low- and moderate-income people irrespective of their color, religion, or country of origin. She was also a feminist. She believed, acted, and organized in concert with her beliefs. She was also not averse to using a certain degree of manipulation to achieve her objectives. She and her organization forged an alliance with the Pratt Center, and together, we established a unified effort to organize and develop the area based on principles of inclusion and equity, rejecting calls for the exclusionary and short-term "me only" policies being promoted by some at the time.

Threat to Northside Tenants

In the late 1960s, Jan was working with a group in the Northside and East Williamsburg on establishing a senior citizen center to serve the area. While working toward this goal, she was made aware by a group of residents attending one of her planning meetings that the city intended to use eminent domain to take two blocks of the Northside adjacent to the S&S Corrugated Paper Machinery Company so that the company could expand, thereby preserving and possibly expanding job opportunities. One of the residents, Rudy Stobierski, the owner of a funeral parlor on Metropolitan Avenue, had read in the *Daily News* that these two blocks would be designated as an urban renewal area. This meant that ninety-two homes would be lost. Rudy's funeral parlor was on one of the blocks to be acquired. In addition, Rudy was a member of the local community board and was aware that they had already rejected the proposal to designate this area of decent worker housing as an urban renewal area. The residents asked Jan the simple question: why should we plan a senior citizen center if so many families will be forced out of the neighborhood?

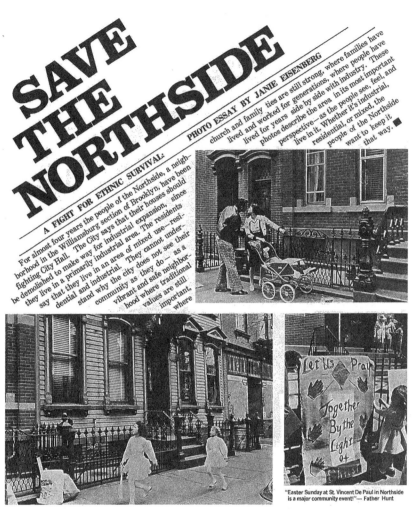

SAVE THE NORTHSIDE

PHOTO ESSAY BY JANIE EISENBERG

church and family ties are still strong, where families have lived and worked for generations, where people have lived for years side by side with industry. These photos describe the area in its most important perspective—as the people see, feel, and live in it. Whether it's industrial, residential, or mixed, the people of the Northside want to keep it that way. ■

A FIGHT FOR ETHNIC SURVIVAL:

For almost four years the people of the Northside, a neighborhood in the Williamsburg section of Brooklyn, have been fighting City Hall. The City says that their houses should be demolished to make way for industrial expansion, since they live in a primarily industrial area. The residents say that they live in an area of mixed use—residential and industrial. They cannot see their stand why the city does not see their community as they do — as a vibrant and safe neighborhood where traditional values are still important, where

"Easter Sunday at St. Vincent De Paul in Northside is a major community event!"— Father Hunt

Pages from publication of the Pratt Center called Street: Magazine of the Urban Environment, *Winter 1973–74.* PHOTO ESSAY BY JANIE EISENBERG

Jan's response was to offer help in fighting the proposed urban renewal plan. She organized a group to go to the various agencies to get more information. She arranged for a meeting with the mayor's liaison to ethnic communities, who suggested she meet with the city's economic development agency, who, in turn, suggested they meet with the housing agency, who, in turn, told them to go to the mayor's liaison! When they appeared at city hall for the second time angry, frustrated, and de-

"This is my community. I don't want to live anywhere else." — John Ehresmann, North 4th Street.

"I take good care of my bushes. And now the city wants to take them away."

"Being bored in Northside is like being bored anywhere else."

"I don't want to live in one of those new tall buildings. I feel at home here."— local resident

Janie Eisenberg has been very involved in trying to save the homes in the Northside.

Pages from publication of the Pratt Center called Street: Magazine of the Urban Environment, *Winter 1973–74.* PHOTO ESSAY BY JANIE EISENBERG

jected, a policeman told them that they would continue to get this kind of bureaucratic runaround until they began acting the way that those uptown acted—referring to the black and Latino groups in Harlem who were engaged in acts of civil disobedience. When a policeman suggested that perhaps they should organize a sit-in, or something similar, they listened. This was particularly important to a group that historically had enormous respect for authority. Once someone with a uniform said this

Northside Housing.
PHOTO COURTESY OF THE
PRATT CENTER

to them, they felt that they had a license to act. And so Jan, Rudy, and their followers took this piece of advice from an officer of the law quite literally. A few days later, Rudy and Jan led a funeral procession onto the Brooklyn-Queens Expressway and stopped the procession just short of the Kosciuszko Bridge, blocking traffic for tens of miles in both directions and bringing New York City traffic to a halt. As the *Village Voice* recorded:

> Three years of quiet anger on the part of the community that believed blindly in democracy and freedom and in the right to own your own home had changed the people of the Northside. "They're not even allowed to do this in Russia," they said to each other. The residents were becoming radicalized. . . . Three days after Christmas in 1972 a group of Northsiders began walking up to the entrance ramp of the Brooklyn-Queens Expressway [BQE] during rush hour. A roving patrol car spotted the string of people and forced them back from this suicide mission. An hour later, Rudy Stobierski's black hearse gently angled up the ramp, onto the expressway and stopped. To the screech of brakes and the amazement of passing motorists, out of the hearse emerged not one, not two, but seemingly endless numbers of live bodies who proceeded to lock arms across the highway. They blocked the rush hour traffic . . . waving signs which said, "Mayor Lindsay has a home, what about us?" Forty people in all demonstrated

NEW HOMES FOR NORTHSIDERS

By Brian Sullivan

Just suppose for a minute that you are 65 years old, on Social Security and paying $45 a month to live in the same four-room apartment that you've lived in for the past 50 years. Not bad, right? Now suppose that the city bureaucracy decides that they have to tear down your house to make way for a factory expansion project. Where do you go? What can you do?

Well, if you're anything like the residents of the largely Polish Northside area of Brooklyn, you stay right where you are and fight. The odds on winning are very, very slim. But this is a story about a long shot that paid off; about a group of "little people" who fought City Hall and won.

Northside, if you haven't heard, is in the Williamsburg section of Brooklyn just above Grand Avenue, west of the Brooklyn-Queens Expressway. It's the type of place where your neighbor might be a sheet metal warehouse or a garage. But everybody there likes it and tries to keep it clean and comfortable. Perhaps it's because they work so

and comfortable. Perhaps it's because they work so hard to keep it up that the people of Northside refused to believe it when the city took away their homes a few years ago.

Their refusal set the stage for a battle that lasted over four years. On Saturday, November 3, 1973, the community held a victory celebration on North 4th Street where less than two months before the city had, at last, physically routed them out of their homes.

Pages from publication of the Pratt Center called *Street: Magazine of the Urban Environment*, Winter 1973–74. PHOTO ESSAY BY JANIE EISENBERG

and eighteen were arrested for disorderly conduct. The protest weary news media had seen thousands of demonstrations since Jane Jacobs took on the West Village [urban renewal] project, but a group of blue collar workers tying up the BQE in a hearse was news. Television crews rushed to the scene and the term ethnocide was coined.[2]

The protest took the issue out of the closet and put it on the front page of every newspaper and radio newscast. While being interviewed by one of these radio stations, Jan stated as a fact that Pratt Center planners and architects had agreed to assist the residents in fighting the renewal plan and were preparing an alternative plan. She lied. We had not yet agreed to do that, but once she made that statement, it was impossible to then deny it—she had hooked us into working with them. Had she asked, our answer would have been "yes," but she asked only after our

2. Nancy Seifer, "Northside: Another Corona: The New Ethnocide," *Village Voice*, February 15, 1973.

participation had been publicized. It was the sign of a truly effective community organizer.

The Pratt Center's engagement was part of a team effort that began to give the community some assistance in balancing the array of support that had been marshaled by the city to assist S&S. The company claimed that they needed room to expand and that the expansion would enable them to add 100 to 150 new jobs—jobs that the city desperately needed and that the community, many of whom worked for S&S, wanted to see created, but not at the expense of their homes. Residents were also concerned about the future of their church, which was the focal point of their tightly knit community. The construction of the Brooklyn-Queens Expressway had already begun to weaken the fabric of the community, and with the loss of some of its members, many feared that if the urban renewal plan was allowed to proceed unabated, many more parishioners would be forced to leave.

S&S had originally looked at other locations in New Jersey to transfer their production operations to, but despite a number of meetings, their efforts to get their skilled employees to consider relocating failed. Once S&S realized the difficulty in relocating, they asked the city, state, and federal officials for assistance. Immediately, each level of government lined up to assist. Congressman Rooney, a powerful Democrat who represented the waterfront communities of Brooklyn, got the US Economic Development Administration to designate the area and helped to obtain federal commitments to finance the expansion. In addition, the New York City Public Development Corporation (PDC)[3] began to aggressively assist the company, and the New York City Planning Department began processing the urban renewal application while the city's housing agency, the Housing and Development Administration, began to identify relocation housing for the residents. Not one of these agencies reached out to the

---

3. The Public Development Corporation (PDC), created by Mayor Lindsay as a quasi-governmental nonprofit corporate entity, was empowered to manage and develop land for industrial and economic development purposes. PDC had the power to buy, sell, and lease land at below market prices without competitive bidding to companies desiring to expand. This, when coupled with the city's ability to exercise the power of eminent domain for urban renewal purposes, made it an important development entity.

residents, who were left to fend for themselves. The balance of assistance was dramatically tipped in favor of the company.

The result of all this collusion was that a deal was arrived at between New York City and S&S where the city agreed to, as the PDC put it,

> Create an urban renewal project in the area, condemn the houses on 3rd and 4th Streets and in turn lease the land to the Public Development Corporation [PDC]. The PDC, in turn would lease [the property] to S&S at very good terms, 60 cents a foot for 63 years, after which time S&S would have the option to buy. Even without the option to buy S&S was getting a very reasonable rental and 63 years of depreciation. Moreover, the City's Economic Development Administration and Congressman Rooney got the company a $2,225,000 million dollar Federal EDA [Economic Development Administration] loan at extremely reasonable interest rates to finance the proposed expansion. It was, as they say in the trade, a sweet deal.[4]

In order to accelerate approval of the plan, the city calendared both its acquisition of the land in the area and the disposal of that land to S&S at the same Board of Estimate[5] public hearing in 1969. As Joyce Haney pointed out in an unpublished history of the Pratt Center, "The nature of the deal between the Company and the City, however, was not presented. All of these legal technicalities only became important three years later when the community began to protest the action."[6]

In all, the proposed condemnations would raze forty houses and two businesses, requiring the relocation of ninety-two families. In terms of the larger picture, of the jobs retained, the numbers were small, but to those directly involved, this type of reckoning was irrelevant.

---

4. Joyce Haney, from an unpublished and untitled manuscript commissioned by the Pratt Center in the mid-1970s based on interviews with the Pratt Center staff, primarily with the then director, Ron Shiffman.

5. The Board of Estimate, which was eliminated by a New York City Charter change in 1990 after the city was found in violation of the one-person-one-vote rule, comprised three citywide representatives, who each had two votes, and borough presidents, who each had one vote.

6. Haney, unpublished and untitled manuscript.

Not surprisingly, the community became very upset. They went, as they had done before, to their political representatives. Congressman Rooney, who had arranged the loan, was not in a position to reverse the agreement. The other politicians all told them the same thing: the Board of Estimate had acted, and it was too late.

After the stoppage of traffic on the Brooklyn-Queens Expressway by Rudy, Jan, and their followers, the picture began to change. The higher media profile this act achieved led to the support of some of the more progressive political leadership in the city, and, through them, a legal team was organized to assist the residents. The Pratt Center team of urban planners, architects, and financial packagers that I directed became a central part. We worked closely with the lawyers, community organizers, and members of the press that followed the issue closely, and Jan and I worked jointly with the residents to build their capacity to negotiate and make informed decisions based on alternative planning and housing proposals that we proposed and developed. Most importantly, we worked collectively on political issues and built the community's and the technical team's capacity to strategize. We met before every meeting with the community leadership, developed a clear agenda, clarified objectives, and identified who would present what. We brought in leaders from other communities who had been through similar struggles to help the residents think through their options. Many of these folks were picked not just because of their skills, but because of their racial and ethnic diversity. Jan and I were intent on dispelling some of the racial and ethnic biases held by some of the residents, which had prevented them from seeing that they were being oppressed by precisely the same forces that other, very different ethnic communities were facing.

At these meetings, the group decided who would play the good cop, or the agreeable community resident, and who would play the bad cop, or the community agitator who refused to accept any compromise. Also, and most importantly, we decided who would play the role of the cool, calm mediator who would bring the parties to some agreement. We strategized about every aspect of our pending meetings with the city, including such details as the shape of the table, who would sit where, and even who would wear what. Eventually, after much discussion, the community came up with not just a plan it wanted to implement, but the delicate strategies that would be required to get it both approved and implemented.

This alternative plan was hammered out only after collecting information concerning S&S's real needs, the number of people that had already sold their homes, the buildings that were already in the hands of S&S, and the condition of the buildings that remained. It was agreed to allow the company to expand, but it would need to keep the residents in the same social community rather than being dispersed to all parts of Brooklyn. The new housing was to be woven into the community in vacant parcels within a five- to ten-minute walk of the church. The community wanted the displaced families to have to move only once to their new homes—something that proved, eventually, not to be the case although the community never yielded to the city's two-move proposals. To get the new housing built, the community needed to get the area's zoning designation changed, and a totally new zoning classification needed to be established—one that allowed manufacturing and residential uses to exist side by side. To guarantee affordability, we worked out a financing plan tailored to each of the displaced families. Affordability was predicated on obtaining low-cost financing, a significant increase in the relocation benefits that the city agreed to pay those being relocated, and a guarantee that the new housing was qualitatively equivalent or better than the housing the families presently lived in and was to come in at a fixed cost. The city agreed to all of the demands, including the rezoning, changes in relocation reimbursement policies, and the financing plan that was developed, as well as acquiring and turning over the sites that were preselected to a community-established housing entity. The only point that separated the community and the city after months of meetings, refining of the plan, and scores of negotiating sessions was whether the families would have to move once or twice to their final new residences. We knew that we needed ironclad guarantees witnessed by the public at large or the city would never fulfill their commitment.

The New York City Planning Commission passed the rezoning application creating the first mixed-use zones in the city—a manufacturing, residential (MR) zone that favored manufacturing over residential, but which allowed new residential, and a residential, manufacturing (RM) zone that favored residential over manufacturing.[7] This set the frame-work for the new housing to be built. However, S&S, which worked hand-in-hand with some of the city agencies and very closely with some of the city staffers to the point it was often impossible to tell who worked for whom, pushed for the immediate acquisition of the property held by the residents.

The community was keenly aware that the city might move to forc-ibly evict them from their homes. They met and reaffirmed their desire to move only once and directly into their newly built homes. They did this fully realizing that if they refused the two-move solution, they could be forcibly removed from their homes and still have to move twice. They decided on going with this option because they felt that the forced move, if it were to occur, would create such a public outcry that the city could not then renege on the commitment for the new homes. They rejected the city's two-move offer and stood their ground, but they planned for the possibility of police action and their forced eviction.

In Poland, whenever a village was attacked, the church bells would ring, summoning everyone to the village square to resist the enemy. A number of community leaders, working with Our Lady of Consolation Parish and its various committees, began preparations for the worst while praying for the city and S&S to come to some accommodation to the community's needs. Their prayers were not answered.

Northside Tenant Eviction

Late in the evening of September 11, 1973, while listening to a news report about the coup in Chile and the assassination of Salvador Allende, I re-ceived a call from a former student working for the city, alerting me to the fact that early next morning there would be an attempt by the city to evict the remaining eight families that had decided not to voluntarily move. Immediately after receiving the call, Jan and I talked, and, within minutes,

---

7. These existed and maintained the balance between home and work for close to two decades, but were eventually and unfortunately weakened by the city in the late 1980s, which eventually tipped the balance to residential.

Tenants Evicted in Brooklyn as Demolition Begins

Police officers remove demonstrators as Mrs. Anastasia McGuinness, one of last to be evicted, shouts defiance.

Photographs for The New York Times by MEYER LIEBOWITZ
Sophie Rzasa, a Northside resident, at eviction scene

By MARY BREASTED

Angry holdouts in a long fight against eviction in the Williamsburg section of Brooklyn were dragged from the stoop of a condemned building by sheriff's deputies yesterday, and bulldozers immediately moved in to begin demolition making way for an expanded industrial plant.

But even as the struggle of the families in the Northside area of Williamsburg to retain their homes appeared to be over, their supporters obtained a court order late last night temporarily restraining further demolition.

State Supreme Court Justice Irwin Brownstein signed the order after hearing charges that the city had acted with undue haste to tear down the homes and was endangering nearby residents. He set a hearing for 9:30 A.M. tomorrow for argument on whether the restraining order should be extended.

The evicted families made their last stand at 144 North Fourth Street, on a block that the city plans to lease to the S & S Corrugated Paper Machinery Company for an addition to its plant that, the company says, will create 200 new jobs.

Residents have been protesting the expansion plan for months, but by yesterday only eight of the 94 families who had been living on the site still remained, refusing to move un-

Continued on Page 93, Column 5

Tenants evicted in Brooklyn as demolition begins, September 12, 1973.

THE *NEW YORK TIMES*, SEPTEMBER 13, 1973

word went out to folks throughout the Northside that the eviction would happen the next morning. Calls also went out to community-based organizations in Bedford-Stuyvesant and Fort Greene in Brooklyn and to allies in Manhattan and the Bronx, and, within hours, city hall and the mayor's office received calls and letters in support of the residents of the Northside.

Jan arrived on North 4th Street early the next morning. Cathy Herman, a Pratt Center colleague, was there as were other Pratt staffers and hundreds of residents from the Northside. Catholic schoolchildren led by their teachers joined the nuns who came to support the residents, and neighbors young and old came out to show their support and to join the residents in blocking the bulldozers and moving trucks that seemed to have appeared from nowhere overnight. Even some of the local politicians who had at first refused to help were there. The street was filled with people as if it were Times Square on New Year's Eve. The idea of mobile phones at that time was still a fantasy left to characters in comic strips and science fiction movies, so the only means of communication we had were landline phones and the telephone booths that were sprinkled sparingly throughout the neighborhood. This meant that only the police with their walkie-talkies could efficiently communicate, and while the community had numbers on their side, their opposition had equipment and was well trained.

The police, many of whom were not pleased with the assignment, moved efficiently, wedging barricades between Jan and myself, who were in the middle of the street. They proceeded to slowly push the crowd back to the corners, all the while emptying the street to allow the moving trucks and bulldozers to enter. The plan was to vacate the buildings of people and their possessions and to immediately begin to demolish the houses so that they could not be reoccupied. Frank Kulikowski, a disabled war veteran, stood tall atop the stoop to his and his wife Carol's home. He proudly unfurled an American flag and held it in front of his large body, believing it would provide him and his home sanctuary from eviction. A group of police officers, trembling with remorse, scaled the few steps to Frank and tore the flag from his hands and carried him away from the door, and with it any hope Frank had that he could save his home. The New York Police Department had faced many demonstrations in the city, but they were usually antiwar, black, Latino, or college student protestors. The protes-

NORTHSIDE ZONING TO ALLOW HOUSING: Homes for Families Evicted for Factory Gains in Estimate Board...
By MURRAY SCHUMACH
New York Times (1923-Current file); Sep 14, 1973;
ProQuest Historical Newspapers: The New York Times (1851-2007) with Index (1851-1993)
pg. 43

Northside zoning to allow housing. THE NEW YORK TIMES, SEPTEMBER 14, 1973

tors had always been an "other." But now Frank was one of them, and the despair the police officers felt in carrying out their orders was palpable, and some even expressed their frustration. I believe that the residents there that day all began to understand that if you stand in the path of the powerful, you would have to yield to their demands regardless of who you are. I know that many in the crowd that day began to understand the struggle of blacks, Latinos, and others who are similarly disenfranchised.

Eviction Aftermath

Attorneys who volunteered to assist the families of the Northside immediately went to court and obtained an injunction forcing the city to stop its demolition, which actually violated city codes for such actions.

The bulldozers came to a halt, but not until after enough was destroyed and the families removed. The city had achieved its objective; yet, the community had also achieved a moral victory and a public commitment to build the new housing. The next morning, September 13, 1973, on the front page of the *New York Times,* below an article about the coup in Chile and assertions that Allende had committed suicide, was the headline: "Tenants Evicted in Brooklyn Demolition Battle." The article, written by Mary Breasted, included photos of Mrs. McGuiness, one of the last residents along with the Kulikowski's to be evicted, and a photo of Sophie Raza, an elderly resident who weeks after being relocated was found wandering through the neighborhood and who a few weeks after that died.

That November, ground was broken for the forty-two housing units that the community had fought so hard to have in place in order to allow families to move only once. The Pratt Center staff worked with the families to enable each of them to afford a share in the new cooperative that was organized. The cooperative was comprised as a group of three family houses. Every apartment had its own entrance, thereby avoiding any interior space that was not in an apartment so that all the built-up space was used and maintained by the residents. Each building maintained the sidewalk and backyard space. We located the Kulikowski's in an apartment on the top floor, where Frank could continue to raise his pigeons on the roof the way he had done in his own house for years. He planned to do just that until he read the warranty covering the roof of the newly built building, and, despite our assertions to the contrary, believed that if he ever walked on the roof, it would void the warranty. He never raised the pigeons there, and I often wonder what happened to them.

Conclusion and Lessons Learned

The Northside had some very pointed lessons and some important victories that influenced planning and public policy for years. We had needed to rethink zoning policy and when that was done, it resulted in a new fixed mixed-use zoning category that worked well for years until it was eventually watered down. There were important relocation assistance victories that changed city policy for over two decades until redevelopment was essentially turned into a private sector effort rather than a publicly led effort. Our engagement with the community led to the development of stable affordable housing that to this day, some forty years later, continues to serve that purpose. The level of community awareness and engagement that was developed at that time has also sustained itself. Despite demographic changes, the Northside continues to be a place where engagement in planning, development, and environmental issues that date to the S&S struggle continue unabated. From a personal perspective, we at the Pratt Center and our partners learned the importance of a team effort, where community residents and organizers work hand-in-hand with lawyers, journalists, and socially committed builders and developers. Most importantly, people learned that if they banded together, they could challenge city hall and win, and they recognized the wealth of community assets that for too long were ignored could be built upon and exploited for a better future.

While working on this Northside project, a few buildings in the adjoining community of East Williamsburg were consumed by a fire, which took the lives of a number of people. Residents, while still grieving, reached out to Jan to see if she could assist in the rehabilitation of the damaged buildings. Jan, in turn, reached out to me, and we set up a meeting at the home of Marion Wallin, a resident of Powers Street, who lived right across from where the fire had destroyed a family and the building they occupied.

Marion and her neighbors were concerned about finding a way to rehouse those who had survived the fire and to find ways to rebuild the block. After inspecting the site, we were convinced that the houses were beyond repair and that the best course of action was to see if we could build new housing on the block and work with the nucleus of folks who had come together to see what they could do to stabilize the area in general, which, like many neighborhoods in New York, was on the verge of dramatically declining. The area to the north was already experiencing abandonment, and fears of that spreading to this area were real. A large former convent, which anchored the block on one end and had been used as a detention home for troubled young men, added to the fears and tensions on the block. The community had fought to close the detention facility, which they felt did not serve its occupants or their neighbors well, and the facility had recently been closed. The empty building remained, however, as a public reminder of the area's insipient decline.

The meeting at Marion's house was historic in that it was decided then and there that merely replacing the housing would not be a viable option in the absence of a larger concerted effort to revitalize and stabilize the area. The decision was made to form a community-based development group focused on housing preservation and development. The area had excellent access by mass transit to Manhattan and other parts of the city and was a low- and moderate-income, working-class neighborhood that had what I would call "good bones." Despite all of this, it still faced onerous social policies, such as redlining and municipal disinvestment—policies that were pursued because of the extensive economic problems of the city and the high rate of unemployment in the country. However, unlike the response to the near depression in the wake of the George W. Bush presidency in 2008, Congress in 1973 enacted a law entitled the Comprehensive Employment and Training Act (CETA) to train workers and provide them with jobs in the public service. The program also offered work to those with low incomes and long-term unemployment, as well as summer jobs to low-income high school students. The legislation provided funding for full-time jobs for a period of up to two years in public agencies or private nonprofit organizations. The intent was to impart marketable skills that would allow participants to eventually move to an unsubsidized job, and was predicated on the success of President Franklin Delano Roosevelt's Works Progress Administration from the 1930s. Luckily for the residents of Williamsburg, the area's settlement house was allocated a few hundred slots to hire unemployed or underemployed area residents. Jan learned about this opportunity and immediately reached out to me, and together we were able to secure twenty-five slots for this emerging community development corporation (CDC), which soon became known as the St. Nicholas Neighborhood Preservation and Rehabilitation Corporation, and today goes by the name of the St. Nicks Alliance. The vast majority of the slots were filled by area residents although a five were set aside for two CETA-eligible architects who had experience working with me at the Pratt Center and for three other people with planning- and community development-related experience to supervise those recruited from the community. In addition, I assigned one of my senior staff, Cathy Herman, to function as the acting director of the emerging CDC.

A board was formed based primarily of community leaders, including Father Vietro of St. Nicholas Church, who today is a monsignor serving the community, and Sal Abramo, a respected community leader and owner of a local funeral home. Sal died many years ago, but did live long enough to see the area and the organization that he had helped build become a true success. Ironically enough, the leadership team of a priest and an undertaker was the same here as had been in Williamsburg's Northside. However, the core of the board and its worker bees were the women of the neighborhood who rarely took on the mantle of leadership, but who nevertheless enabled the organization to function. The role that these women and others played in the revitalization of the Northside, East Williamsburg, and countless other neighborhoods was something that Jan immediately recognized and was the impetus for her organizing the National Congress of Neighborhood Women—the story of which should be a book in and of itself.

The board of St. Nicholas took on the responsibility of raising money for the day-to-day operation of the CDC. The church lent the CDC space and for the first few months, supported the operation by running bingo games and "a day at the races"—raffles that helped pay for everything from phones to paper clips. The architects, former students of mine, were hired as CETA workers and were assigned to work with my staff and me at the Pratt Center. They developed and refined proposals for the new housing on the site the fire had destroyed, and they linked the new housing to the substantial rehabilitation of Jennings Hall—the vacated building that had functioned as a juvenile detention center. Once we knew that there was a strong possibility the project would become a reality, we joint ventured with a private architectural firm whose principal had volunteered to supervise the younger, less experienced CETA architects. We were also eager to build on the fact that the two CETA architects were women— Cathy Hutman and Ginny Yang—and that one of the principals at the architectural firm of Edelman and Salzman was a woman, which was a rarity at the time.

At the same time, Cathy Herman was working with my colleague Brian Sullivan to put together an application to the US Department of

Housing and Urban Development (HUD) for a new and evolving senior citizen housing program, which was referred to as Section 202 Senior Citizens Housing. The Section 202 program was designed to expand the supply of affordable housing with supportive services for the elderly. It provided low-income elderly with options that allowed them to live not only independently but also in an environment that provided common facilities and support for activities such as cleaning, cooking, and getting around. The program, if successful, would allow many of the area's elderly who were living in older walk-up buildings the opportunity to relocate to this new elevator building. At the same time, their moderately priced apartments would become available to younger individuals and families to move into, enabling them to remain in the community rather than having to move out, which was usually their only option. Without asking me, Cathy and Brian fronted the money for the application, which was submitted to HUD. Since the community was desperately in need of jobs and the emerging CDC was committed to the idea of community economic development, we decided to ask HUD for approval to build and allow community members to manage and operate the housing if and when it was built. HUD approved the application and the unique request for a community-based management operation—one of the first in the nation.

In 1980, Jennings Hall was dedicated, and soon after, 150 units of housing were built. A community management program was also initiated together with a range of other social, economic, and educational efforts launched by the St. Nicholas Neighborhood Preservation and Rehabilitation Corporation. Unlike its predecessor, the Bedford-Stuyvesant Restoration Corporation, which I had also been involved in at its inception, the St. Nicholas CDC at the time it was launched was almost penniless. However, like Bedford-Stuyvesant, its design was holistic and comprehensive, and it proved highly durable. Marion Wallin became the first manager of the revitalized Jennings Hall Senior Citizen complex, and her friend and another founding member of the group, Marie Leanza, who still works for St. Nicks, helped found a credit union that participated in the antiredlining movement that enabled mortgage money to finally flow to a neighborhood where banks had once discriminated by refusing to lend. In addition, many elderly individuals, some isolated and trapped in their walk-up homes because of disabilities, were re-

Ron Shiffman speaking at the dedication of Northside Housing.
PHOTO COURTESY OF
THE PRATT CENTER

located, and the availability of their now vacated apartments began to stabilize and revitalize the entire area. The result of all these activities was that many younger families remained in the area, and the community became a destination and did not, as many feared, fall prey to the forces of decline that engulfed many neighborhoods in New York in the 1970s and 1980s. Indeed, St. Nicks became a model for other such organizations and, I would venture to add, a leader in the renaissance that took place in the city overall. St. Nicks still exists today, and now employs over 1,100 employees, has assets in excess of 80 million dollars, and has an annual operating budget of 58 million dollars. It is a story of success built on local ingenuity, committed leadership, quality community organizing, and technical assistance. It is a story that needs to be told because it is a story of community self-sufficiency sparked by government assistance and investment—a policy that worked and a policy that needs to be re-enacted today to once again enable growth to occur and to economically enfranchise the next generation.

The story continues today, four decades after the partnerships that launched the revitalization efforts in Williamsburg and Greenpoint. I continue to work with an array of community-based organizations in the area dealing with new challenges, some of which have been borne out of the successes of the past and others of things left undone. My role today as an elder in the community development movement is a combination of technician, strategist, and storyteller, but the role of the scores of community-based organizations continues unabated and is as important to addressing the challenges of today as they were when this story began.

East Harlem Cases, New York

Introduction

n the French edition of *Bâtir Ensemble*, written in the late 1980s and published in 1988, several detailed case studies were devoted to East Harlem. In this 2014 expanded and updated English version, these studies have been shortened and compressed into one chapter. Over the past thirty years, the lessons from that experience inspired my practice as a consultant to international organizations in Africa (see Case Study 4) and Latin America (see Case Studies 6 and 7) in helping people help themselves.

The Settlement House and Housing for the Elderly

After working for two years in the office of Louis Kahn in Philadelphia, I moved to East Harlem in 1964 and spent close to twelve years working there. By mid-1963, I began commuting to New York to teach architecture at the Pratt Institute. At that time, I was offered the opportunity of some professional work: the board of an old rundown settlement house in East Harlem needed to develop architectural feasibility studies for the construction of new facilities. This nonprofit organization was unable to cover the cost of professional fees for the preliminary studies. The new building could be financed through a New York State loan on the condition that the new social and recreation facilities also included the construction of around one hundred housing units for the elderly, which was in great demand in the community and surrounding area. Preliminary architectural studies were necessary to determine construction costs for a presentation to the New York State Housing Authority. Over the years, the board had bought a couple of empty row houses adjacent to the existing settlement house. These buildings were to be demolished to make way for the future larger proposed development. In exchange for the architectural feasibility studies, I was offered one of these three-story row houses on the east side of 116th Street, rent free, to use both as my own office on the ground floor and as my residence above. It was the traditional practice for all settlement houses to give free room and board to their workers.

I moved with my wife and two small children (aged two and four) from Philadelphia to New York in the spring of 1964. In those years, the political climate was such that young professionals from all fields were offering their knowledge and time spontaneously to help people in communities in need. (With some friends from Kahn's office, I had given some work on weekends to help build vest-pocket parks in Philadelphia's poor black neighborhoods.) I took over the third floor for my family and furnished the ground floor with some drafting tables and second-hand office desks so as to start working on the project. The second floor was reserved for both office space and temporary lodging for students helping with the architectural studies.

Although in poor physical shape, 116th Street was a bustling center of commercial, civic, and recreational activities. Despite their diverse origin and economic background, the Latin American, Italian, and African American residents shared a common concern for the revitalization of their neighborhood. They were all battling against the problems of deteriorated housing, lack of jobs, deficient education, and substandard municipal services. I began to sense the explosive mixture of my new neighborhood toward the end of the summer of 1964 when I witnessed and participated in my first protest march against racism, poverty, and marginalization. I then realized that this neighborhood, known as Italian Harlem for the past thirty years, was becoming known as Spanish Harlem for the new waves of Puerto Rican, Dominican, and other Latin

American immigrants seeking work and a better life for their families in the area. While the community was once approximately 90 percent Italian and 10 percent Puerto Rican, these figures were being reversed.

During the protest march, I met some Puerto Rican leaders and discovered their opposition to our project. When I informed the settlement house board (essentially composed of Italians) of the fact that the Puerto Rican leadership was turning against the project because they felt excluded, the board convinced some of these leaders to join in and attend our project meetings. Only then did the new leaders realize that the future center's services would not be reserved exclusively for the Italian community and would benefit them and their families.

The first months in East Harlem were devoted to the establishment of a dialogue with the members of the board, settlement house workers, local youth associations, and elderly groups so as to develop an understanding of the overall activities of the building before commencing work on the first concept sketches. Since the overall site was so small, it became almost mandatory to propose locating the housing for the elderly right above the community facilities, leaving a small, planted outdoor space. The facilities included a spacious lobby and reception area, gymnasium, auditorium, day care center, community service offices, arts and crafts rooms, and music rooms. A kitchen was planned next to the elderly game room that could be transformed into a dining space. The recreational facilities were to be shared by both organizations serving the elderly and different youth groups. The two-story high gym and auditorium were on the ground floor below the apartment tower.

After taking a few months to analyze our preliminary project, the New York City Housing Authority finally agreed to finance the settlement house with 150 residential units for the elderly. Their public housing construction standards were very strict and quite forbidding: a real challenge for us to try and humanize. The problem was how to design apartments for the elderly in a high-rise building when all the elderly groups and individuals I consulted with were yearning to live together in a village atmosphere with a small garden where they could play cards and other quiet games. How do you interpret this village spirit in a ten- or fifteen-story building? With the board committee, we imagined a square tower where the service core is at the center and surrounded by an inter-

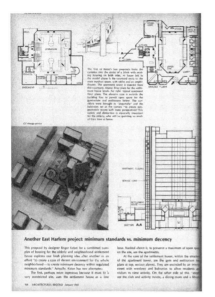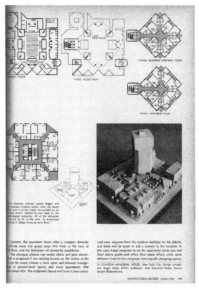

Architectural Record, *January 1966, "Another East Harlem Project: Minimum Standards vs. Minimum Decency", pp 168–169.* SCANS COURTESY OF *ARCHITECTURAL RECORD*

nal "street" naturally lit by and open to funnel-shaped, generous balconies at its four corners. On each floor, eight to ten housing units would share these balconies to encourage a village feeling among the friends choosing to live together. This immediate possibility of communication and entertainment through these common spaces was especially important for the elderly who spend so much of their time at home. At our first meeting presentation, the state authorities simply declared the building too beautiful and costly for low-cost housing. Getting rid of the balconies was their first and very insistent suggestion to lower construction costs. They underlined that the housing authority was not used to having balconies for low-income residents. Aside, they argued that the elderly didn't even want balconies! We immediately contacted several organizations for the aged, and in less than two weeks, the authorities were besieged with more than six hundred signatures on pro-balcony petitions.

That was the beginning of a long and difficult fight, an audacious and perhaps a hopeless one on our part. Who were we to dare confront and question a powerful long-established housing authority, which for years

Proposed La Guardia House for East Harlem housing for the elderly to the New York Housing Authority, 1964–1972.

La Guardia House as built by the New York City Housing Authority on 116th Street in East Harlem. (Photo taken in 2010.)

Middle-income housing project built in 1975 (around 110th Street). PHOTOS BY ROGER KATAN

had applied strictly tailored and regulated minimum standards in the construction of its low-income housing? Their standards had already created drab and rapidly deteriorating housing projects, making them instant slums, which lowered and were disrespectful of human dignity.

The New York Housing Authority found it insulting when we asked the housing standards guardians if they could live a week, a month, or even a single day in one of those instant high-rise slums they were helping to promote. Opposing the destructive and demeaning federal minimum standards, we dared the representative members of the board to fight at every one of our many meetings for a concept of minimum decency for the elderly. For the housing authority, the question of inhabitant participation and integration into the planning process remained unanswered. While being a distinct member of a community, each individual remained a statistic, a tightly planned-for entity, and not someone the housing authority would ask or expect to express any opinion. The authorities felt that their duty in life was to erect federal projects as gifts to the poor, and we made them feel that their gift was a poisoned one.

Our fight lasted around three years, during which time we presented several alternatives in an attempt to satisfy the bureaucracy's guardians.

We never gave up on some form of balconies, which changed shape and size, but persistently remained. We hoped that the publication of several versions of our presentations in the local press and national architectural magazines would influence the housing authority. Apparently, it became a point of honor for the housing authority to defend the usual low-income housing project look even though it was drab and devoid of any sign of humanity: what would the middle class say if this low-income group gets as good or a better design treatment in their housing?

Housing authorities all over the US had been so insistent in the 1950s and the 1960s with their poor design standards in their projects that they were obliged, starting in the 1970s and the 1980s, to acknowledge the acute social problems they generated and began destroying them to rebuild new ones. Finally faced with the pressing needs of the East Harlem community client to build according to the housing authority standards, and because there was no alternate financing possibility, I refused to associate myself with the final housing authority design that was built by another architect who had previously built a few of these types of projects. However, it is interesting to note that less than three years after I retired from this project, our tower design with balconies was built barely ten blocks south. Our *Architectural Magazine* publications had at least attracted some admirers! A well-known New York architect's office had built a middle-income building with enough slight variations in the design so that the designer could not be legally pursued.

In the streets of Harlem, I gradually began to unlearn most of what I had been taught in professional schools, and began groping toward a new way to practice that was more participatory and closer to people's needs. I began questioning my profession's social responsibility and the role of the professional school.

Wards Island Hospital and Mental Hygiene Services

In 1967, I was invited to participate in a seminar sponsored by the New York State Department of Mental Hygiene. There, I discovered that in addition to the 4,000 existing beds on Wards Island Mental State Hospital, the State was planning to build 850 new units for the mentally disabled.

The greatest part of the island was under the Department of Mental Hygiene's jurisdiction and the other part was used as a city park.

The island's planning had been random with buildings constructed in the 1940s and 1950s with little sense of the economy of the land. Any addition to the existing mental state hospital's four thousand-bed units would have only intensified and perpetuated the isolated and institutional quality of the island. The contrast was striking between its suburban planning and the densely populated urban areas of New York, Harlem, and the South Bronx nearby. After the seminar, I brought this project to the attention of the Harlem–East Harlem leadership. They then invited the commissioner of the Department of Mental Hygiene and top members of his staff to come to East Harlem to discuss their plans in front of twenty-five representatives of the Harlem–East Harlem community. After the Department of Mental Hygiene insisted that the island facilities were correct and appropriate, a medical student who was part of our East Harlem community development corporation (CDC) volunteered to be admitted to the hospital as mentally ill. After a month's stay in the hospital, his extensive findings forced the State to review its Wards Island policies. The unanimous opposition to the State plans prompted the commissioner to reevaluate all the Wards Island planning that had been done and reconsider it in terms of community needs and wishes.

The first consequence of our action was guided by a specific proposal jointly written by a community leader, a behavioral scientist, a psychiatrist, and myself. The proposal was addressed to the Department of Mental Hygiene, and further expanded on the development of mental health facilities in the Harlem–East Harlem community, how the present institutional methods had failed, and why it was of high priority to decentralize the mental health system.

The proposal argued that:

- The location of mental health facilities within the community minimizes family disruption when some form of hospitalization is required.

- The location of mental health facilitates led to early treatment and a broader range of clinical services with an increased relevance of services to community needs.

- The advantages of the proposal would result in shortened periods of hospitalization and could serve as foci for important educational functions.

- The physical improvement of the neighborhood and the availability of a large number of useful and well-paid jobs, which were a key component of the proposal, were expected to produce major beneficial psychological impacts on the Harlem–East Harlem community.

After an elaborate list of the specific advantages to patients and to the community, the proposal ended by stating that: "Play and recreational facilities, and sheltered business such as shops and coffee houses, could serve as specific examples of ways in which facilities could be shared between the mental health facility and the community. The project could then be transformed into a more informal, integrated community structure."[1]

As negotiations developed, the State of New York and the community reached an agreement. Out of the 750 units for the projected State-run school for mentally disabled and handicapped children, only 500 units would be built on the island and 250 of them would be built in Harlem in clusters of 25 to 50 units to be dispersed throughout the community. Although the architects for the State school were ordered to redesign the 750 units into a 500-unit facility, the State stopped this project because of budget cuts. For the community, the chance of achieving the desired decentralization increased after our CDC was contracted as a consultant to the State to help recommend policies. Our study included two phases: a code conformity evaluation of all physical structures with a proposal to update them and a long-range plan projecting the future of the institution with regard to its existing patients and to the population of Manhattan that it served.

However, the transition from hospital to community should have been made over a period of ten to twenty years. The hospital had to become more humane and provide for decreases mandated under the code of the bed capacities. It was also to permit future building uses to allow for the expected rates of attrition. We could not eliminate the need for the

---

1. Roger Katan, *Manhattan State Hospital Evaluation Report*, vol. 2 (New York: published by author, 1968–1971), 43.

hospital as we did not yet have a community delivery system to replace it with.

Our goal was to develop an equitable comprehensive mental health service system in Manhattan that would help the community meet its own needs by developing an open, flexible system of mental health care between hospital and community. Building housing facilities and some amenities had been, at times, in the planning stage by the Department of Mental Hygiene. We suggested that, ideally, a housing mix for hospital staff and neighborhood people could be planned on the island. This would have created a new community that would have integrated the hospital facilities that heretofore stood in isolation. On one hand, decentralization of mental hygiene services could have generated increased integration of services in the community, and, on the other hand, it could have been more appropriate to create a small community on Wards Island that would have integrated the reduced services of the Manhattan State Hospital. In this way, we believed that a healthy balance could be achieved. Harlem and Bronx community groups joined together to create the Wards Island Community Corporation to plan a new community in its unused areas. Based on that concept, the following proposals were to be fleshed out and evaluated:

- Effective use of public transportation from the island to Manhattan and the Bronx, and within the island.

- Creation of an open, new community composed of both hospital staff and residents from the surrounding communities.

- Apartment houses of various types and layouts to accommodate families should be planned.

A diverse number of amenities on the island, such as recreation, day care, education, and public services, along with a distribution of small stores, particularly those selling food and other necessities, were proposed. The desirability of planning low-rise apartments with parks and rents geared toward mixed-income residents was also to be explored. In 1972, a Manhattan-wide conference on mental health, sponsored by Harlem–East Harlem Model Cities, took place. The objective was to communicate the results of the Manhattan State Hospital evaluation, the community mental health services study, and the distribution of services review and to establish a long-range plan and blueprint for action in the decentralization process, which all came together in the *Manhattan State Hospital Evaluation.*

Uniting Social Services:
The East Harlem Multiservice Center

For about two million inhabitants in New York in the 1960s and early 1970s, poverty was the unavoidable context in which they lived, and promises of a better life streamed nonstop from the mass media. In reality, these were empty promises for the poor. Average annual income levels in East Harlem in 1970 stood at five thousand dollars, but that was still only half the New York City average. In 1965, 1.8 in 10 children in New York City were supported by welfare, but by the 1980s, the average had risen to 3 in 10 children—more than a two-fold increase.[2] All that could be found in deprived neighborhoods like East Harlem was poverty, which, in turn, generated other social ills—unemployment, drug addiction, delinquency, criminality, and unhealthy environments. It was almost impossible for an individual to escape this cycle of degradation.

As for juvenile crime statistics, while there had been a substantial increase rate of 16 to 19 per 1,000 of the population in the US between 1965 and 1970, juvenile crime in the population of East Harlem had actually gone down. In addition, more than half of the residents in East Harlem had no high school diploma. Housing was overcrowded and substandard, with 15 percent of accommodations housing more than 1.5 people per room and 32.8 percent of the houses considered substandard. On the health front, infant mortality rates rose from 31 to 33.6 per 1,000 between 1965 and 1970. Venereal disease rates were 2.5 times that of New York City, and for young people under the age of twenty-one, levels had risen by 75 percent between 1965 and 1970.[3]

---

2. Statistics provided by Roberto Anazagasti, president of Nuevo el Barrio para la Rehabilitación de Vivienda y Economia in New York. The goal of his organization is to provide low- and moderate-income housing for our communities.

3. Ibid.

Many of the specialized services that were developed to address the symptoms of poverty remained centralized, but soon they became inaccessible due to the rapid increase in demand in densely populated areas and the poor public transportation methods available. Even when these services were easy to access, services were compartmentalized. Faced with the complexity of problems in the ghetto, which compound one another, one could only find highly specialized institutions that tended to isolate individuals from their family context. This situation was particularly striking in the case of health services. For example, a five-year-old in good health was supposed to visit a particular dispensary. If that same child were to become ill, he or she would have to go to a different dispensary; and a sick adult would be required to visit a third center. There was, essentially, no health center that addressed the needs of the whole person, and, indeed, none to meet the needs of the entire family. Incomprehensible technical language, interminable procedures, and complex rules ended up simply confusing the people they were intended to serve.

As Nathan Glazer and Daniel Moynihan put it in *Beyond the Melting Pot*:

> [In New York City,] the schoolteacher or principal can do nothing about what goes on at home; the welfare investigator's role must be simply one of testing whether the family is qualified; the probation officer is supposed to keep in touch with each case, not the case's family, and can do nothing if the home in which the probationer lives is located in a tenement that is a center for drug addiction or thievery; the housing project employee (if the family was lucky enough to be in one) is concerned with financial eligibility, the payment of rent, and the maintenance of the physical property; the hospital hands out drugs and treatment, and so on and so on. And social workers and others now and then set up a joint project to see if out of the welter of bureaucratic confusion there can be fashioned an instrument that responds to families and individuals as full human beings.[4]

---

4. Nathan Glazer and Daniel P. Moynihan, *Beyond the Melting Pot: The Negroes, Puerto Ricans, Jews, Italians, and Irish of New York City* (Cambridge, MA: MIT Press, 1963), 120–121.

Although public social services were supposed to help people learn how to set things up for themselves and thereby increase their autonomy, the kind of assistance they provided only served to perpetuate dependency and disempower people. The situation became so serious that certain individuals and neighborhood groups got together. They were trying to solve their problems one at a time and, in this way, improve their lives. They enjoyed participating in the activities that had been created to help them, but these services were set up for them and not by them. Working in their own neighborhoods, Petra Lopez, Tony Rodriguez, Roberto Anazagasti, and Lucy Sanchez got together to try to link up these separate services and combine them into an integrated whole. A new concept for a community-controlled multiservice center soon began to emerge in East Harlem and other similar areas of New York City as a result. These new centers were to have a centralized and fixed location within easy access for most of the local population. They were also intended to have mobile units so as to reach the whole population and encourage people to use the available services.

While the multiservice center was a symbol of the decentralization policies of both New York City and the federal government, in East Harlem, it took shape through real grassroots participation and was not programmed or designed by the City. The multiservice center was a facility that was to be conceived with the maximum potential for overcoming all the difficulties of poverty. Rather than merely housing a number of unrelated service programs under one roof, it aspired to be a locus for encountering each person as a complex human being with interrelated problems, formulating with each person a viable strategy for family improvement, and systematizing community-oriented public and private programs so that, in concert, they could help each family implement its individual plan. The multiservice center building was to be located in the center of a concentration of poverty and was to provide services for a defined geographical area. The area it serviced was to be within walking distances of most residents and close to several public facilities, which could be utilized for some program components. It was to contain a built-in system of evaluation requiring effective interaction at the local level with representatives of the served community.

In East Harlem, the multiservice center was to be located between Lexington Avenue, Sylvan Place, and 120th and 121st Streets. The site was unique in that this block was divided by a street, Sylvan Place, and a park adjacent to the Harlem Court House, one of the rare city landmarks in Harlem, that opened into it. We developed interface tools that allowed us to better communicate with the community. These tools were helpful in defining the type and quality of programs needed, what their functions should be, and their complex relationships. We created diagrams that would help participants help us design and translate the constantly shifting needs and programs into physical terms. This procedure is illustrated in adjoining diagrams.

At this point, I would like to stress the difference of approach in design between the settlement house when I first arrived in East Harlem and the multiservice center. They were somewhat similar structures. The first one was mainly a community recreational facility, and the second was more of a social service facility. They were both strongly youth oriented. In the case of the settlement house, it was an architectural style of concrete splendor, a building for the ages, but in the case of the multiservice center, design was to be more flexible in a lighter steel structure, capable of change, spontaneous, and coming out of a much deeper interaction with and understanding of human needs. Fundamentally, the multiservice center had, in its essence, change and communication.

Change in the multiservice center building was expressed by an open design in which the structural framework would allow for the utmost flexibility to accommodate the constant evolution of community needs, both indoors and outdoors. Communication was expressed in the way the building would attract the street residents to be served and guide them through the different services. To that effect, large luminous billboards in Spanish, Italian, and English would announce special events and list community or individual improvement programs that were currently available.

The heavily frequented Lexington Avenue would also have an inviting arcade opening up from the main entrance and into the three-story lobby. One would find private interview spaces along with welcoming exhibits of general information about health, social services, housing, culture, and art. This would reinforce the sense that the individual was no longer alone in his or her struggle. A particular dream of Puerto Rican identity was realized through beautiful tropical island vegetation. A three-story high patio, around which workshops, library meetings, and other services would gather, was proposed. It was designed to have an indoor flavor reminiscent of the famous rain forest in Puerto Rico. After close to four years of exhilarating work with different community groups and hard struggles with different administrations, we received the final approvals for funding (one-third City and two-third federal sources). Unfortunately, soon after approval, the City was on the verge of bankruptcy, and the project was summarily dropped despite months of appealing to different levels of City, State, and federal government.

Vassar College Experience

Among the various fourth- and fifth-year students that volunteered their skills to the multiple activities in our East Harlem Community Design Center happened to be a Vassar College student, Jenny Young, who worked very closely with a local resident group dedicated to the analysis of the needs and the design of appropriate community health related services. Jenny presented her final work as a summer report to her college for credit recognition. Her analysis aroused such interest among her professors and fellow students that I soon received a phone call from Vassar asking if it could send a small group of students desirous to help while learning in East Harlem. I answered that I could not take on the responsibility of having in Harlem a dozen or more upper-class young girls from a prestigious women's college. Since that was a period of time of enormous unrest and turmoil in major US cities, Vassar agreed instead to allow me to develop a lecture course in their Department of Political Science called "Issues of Urban America."

I started the first of two weekly lectures by describing my East Harlem experiences. Vassar was an exclusive institution that was completely divorced from the life of Poughkeepsie, where it was located. At that time, mainly white Anglo-Saxon Protestant girls were admitted with a trickle of rich Catholics and Jews. Very few minority students, neither blacks nor Latinos, were ever accepted. This small town, about one hour's drive north from New York City, not only had its share of slums, but through reading the local press, I discovered that it also had its own Model Cities Program, the famous and often unfairly discredited federal program to improve America's blighted cities. I was lucky to have an extremely efficient assistant working full-time at Vassar, Sally Luther, who was politically active and very helpful in building contact with the local community. My plan for the course, after consultation with the students, was to get them involved with Poughkeepsie's Model Cities Project. The idea was for our seminar to move from the hallowed halls of Vassar to different storefront headquarters in the inner city, changing each week according to the local inhabitant's needs. There was also a resource center, accessible to residents and to our students, which was supported by the Model Cities agency, which served as a base of operations.

As the students' investigation of Poughkeepsie's inner-city problems advanced, we discovered that the mayor, as chairman of the Model Cities Board of Directors, had earmarked a major portion of the Model Cities Program funds for building a new city hall and extending the city's golf course to eighteen holes and only left a small portion for some token community projects. The elected neighborhood representatives felt frustrated and excluded from the very federal program that was supposed to be dedicated to improving their lives. I adapted the course contents and requirements to deal with this situation and decided to hold class sessions in different neighborhood venues every week. I invited Harlem leaders to prod and boost the courage of the local leaders and to help them build a stronger front so as to have their rights respected. In fact, the dynamic Harlem organizers that I had invited to talk in my weekly seminars inspired the hesitant local community leaders to go ahead and boycott the city government's program until the most needed community projects and other urgent necessities were included into the final submission to Washington.

This action greatly disturbed the fragile peace that had existed before my arrival in Poughkeepsie. The local establishment had worked hard to avoid conflict and keep the area's low- and moderate-income communities powerless. But I felt that Vassar's president and, especially, his wife, who represented him when he couldn't come to our weekly seminars, were sympathetic to our activities because they had attended several community meetings during the tense and most interesting moments of our course. They probably had never been in any neighborhood storefront meeting before and even less likely to have visited the rundown slums of Poughkeepsie. I am not sure what motivated them, but they seemed to be really concerned.

During the course of the semester, we invited city officials, business leaders, and leaders of local resident groups, particularly those who would be directly affected by this project, to give presentations to our class. The students attended community assemblies and met with local leaders who not only described their needs but also explained why they felt excluded from the project. The students met with urban planners and organizers from other Model Cities Projects. They were encouraged to analyze issues affecting their project not only through research but also through direct fieldwork.

The mostly upper-class students left Vassar's ivory tower behind and got their hands dirty while volunteering at day care centers, tutoring programs, and planning agencies. They visited schools, clinics, courts, and jails. Three students drew up proposals to improve the education system. Several students wrote in-depth studies of Poughkeepsie's public health and housing problems. Other students reported on traffic patterns disturbing neighborhoods, childcare services, and training programs. They packaged these papers in a seventy-five-page book entitled *A Search for Solutions: Poughkeepsie and the Model Cities Program*. They sold and distributed nearly three hundred copies to neighborhood block groups as well as to city officials.[5] The Poughkeepsie Model Cities agency incorporated the Vassar students' proposals on social services and welfare into their final federal application.

My lecture course not only transformed traditional passive academic research and observation to active fieldwork, but it moved the campus into the community, exposing the students to direct involvement in the turmoil and power struggles within Poughkeepsie. It was a microcosm of what was happening throughout urban America. It also raised questions about the university's role in the community: Should the campus be separate from the surrounding city or should there be a partnership?

---

5. Christiane Citron, "Students Complete Seminar, Stress Community Awareness," *Vassar Miscellany News* 53, no. 22 (May 1969): 7.

Should college students merely observe the community or should they become actively involved?

After our semester's experience, the students decided that there was a need for a symbiotic relationship. "We believe that our kind of work fulfills the dual function of obtaining valuable insight for the student, while also providing much needed and valued assistance to the community in the form of intelligent and diligent research," said Christiane Citron, one of my brightest Vassar students, in a conference handout. She added: "Personally, I certainly found my experiences in downtown Poughkeepsie completely relevant. Existence within the relative homogeneity of a college community can be both stifling and misleading. Most people at Vassar are unaware of the slums which exist only a very few miles away in Poughkeepsie."

Throughout the semester, the students felt that the course was unusually significant and compelling, and they made inquiries about continuing our course into the second semester. In December 1968, four months into the semester, the dean informed the students that there was little likelihood that I would be rehired as there was a "lack of special funds" and other faculty had already been hired to teach the second semester section of a normal political science course.[6] The mayor's pressure on the president of Vassar and his board of directors must have been very strong. They just couldn't accept the continuation of the students' work in favor of justice for the inner-city poor. But my ousting came a bit too late, and nobody could stop the ball of progress from rolling.

After much discussion from which I stayed away, twenty-one coeds (fourteen of the course's nineteen enrollees, four auditors, and three other concerned students) staged a sit-in on December 5, 1968, occupying the dean's office and demanding an extension of my contract. The sit-in, Vassar's first student protest, was peaceful and lasted close to six hours. The college considered calling the police, but after the students left the dean's office, Vassar's president met with them. He explained that my contract would not be renewed because of problems with sponsorship from the Department of Political Science and other financial problems. He sug-

---

6. Christiane Citron, "Students Sit in Dean's Office to Demand Katan's Rehiring," *Vassar Miscellany News* 53, no. 11 (December 1968): 1.

gested they look for alternative avenues for hiring me. The students found a solution: a combination of funding from the Student Government Association, the college administration, and a modest collection among Vassar College students to pay for my train fare so that I could come once a week. It was very symbolic and very encouraging to see the students' insistence and their determination to pursue this work. They organized their own second semester seminar on urban issues and followed with their active involvement in the Poughkeepsie Model Cities Project. They continued their volunteer work, surveys, and research, as well as hiring me and other experts as their consultants, and provided for guest lectures. Pressures at the national level were such that most Ivy League and other universities at large were starting to open admissions to minority students. Changes were finally coming to Vassar, and during my second semester, black students were admitted for the first time ever. This new wave of students slowly took over the work we had started, and Vassar itself found the necessary funds to continue in a permanent manner the work we had begun.

East Harlem: An Updated Postscript

East Harlem today is somewhat reminiscent of the East Harlem of the 1960s and 1970s where I worked and lived. It is no longer facing the prospect of the abandonment of housing or loss of population, as was the case almost a half century ago, and is no longer called Italian Harlem. With a population of 120,000 and growing, East Harlem is now primarily Latino, with its share of the population hovering above 50 percent, African American, at just under 40 percent, and white, at around 10 percent.[7] The Puerto Rican population of the 1960s and 1970s over the years shifted to a Dominican population that today is once again shifting to one dominated by a newly arrived immigrant population primarily from Mexico. The intergroup internecine competitions of the past continue to divide the area although much of the tension is not apparent to the casual observer and bubbles just under the surface.

---

7. United States Census Bureau, *2008-2010 American Community Survey* (Washington, Government Printing Office, 2001).

The Harlem area continues to be plagued by poverty and extremely high rates of asthma and incidence of HIV/AIDS, and has the highest rate of diabetes and heart disease in the country. Drug trafficking also remains high, leading to frequent crime, which, at times, bursts into violence that has an impact that goes far beyond the drug gangs that keep the area on edge. The overall crime rate for the city as a whole and East Harlem itself, however, is far lower than it was at the time that *Bâtir Ensemble* was originally written.[8]

What has changed is the dramatic shift from a community that faced the ravages of disinvestment to a community that today is facing the threat of displacement because of over investment and significant changes in the city's development and zoning policies. With the advent of a major regional shopping mall at the East River and a slew of zoning changes in the areas surrounding East Harlem, including one slated for the heart of the community, the area will be facing some dramatic changes in the near future. Beginning in 2012, the community board serving the area, known as New York City's Community Board 11 of Manhattan, working with a private consultant and the civic organization, Civitas, engaged in a vigorous participatory planning process that led to the development of a set of proposals for the area.

According to Jeff Mays of *DNAinfo New York's* neighborhood news, "Under the plan, Park Avenue would be rezoned to encourage light industrial and residential uses. The zoning for East 116th Street would include medium density contextual development to allow for the creation of affordable housing. Upper Madison Avenue would be down-zoned to help preserve the existing low-rise structures and neighborhood character."[9]

Hopefully, this plan will be adopted by the city as the community board has developed it so that it does not lead to the gentrification of the area—the outcome, or devil, will be in the final details. The result of similar rezoning actions that have taken place in Central and West Harlem have led to significant changes in the cultural, racial, and ethnic composition of those areas. So much so that civic and religious leaders of those communities have joined forces with other areas facing city-sponsored

---

8. Statistics provided by Roberto Anazagasti.

9. Jeff Mays, "East Harlem Zoning Plan Envisions Commercial Corridor, Affordable Housing," *DNAinfo New York*, January 30, 2013.

rezoning actions to try to stem the displacement trends underway and to oppose policies that many fear will lead to the hypersegregation of the city.

Lessons Learned

Looking back at the years spent in East Harlem, I can recall enthusiasm and frustration. Through this period of community planning process, I learned that knowledge and information ceases to be the domain of a few, and the generation of ideas is no longer the exclusive preserve of specialists. I felt enthusiasm because of an everyday discovery of a new way to practice architecture and planning, helping people give shape to their community in accordance with their dreams and possibilities, dispensing information freely, and committing ourselves to learning from those we work with. I felt frustration in trying to find a new way to practice and constantly being blocked by repetitive federal budget cuts, which always fell upon the poorest communities and their services, such as East Harlem's multiservice center, or by the guardians of age-old institutions, such as the New York Housing Authority in the case of the settlement house and housing for the elderly.

These Harlem years taught me that work at the grassroots level is productive if and only when one has the backing of some form of power to help execute a project, as we will see in the following case studies (for example, the UN backing of the creation of a national microcredit system in Ouagadougou, Burkina Faso in Cast Study 4, and the UN backing of a new rural school system in the Colombian Chocó in Case Study 7). It was an important two-way learning experience that helped me in the work that followed in my career.

Creation of the First Microcredit Organization in Ouagadougou, Burkina Faso

Introduction

Engaging people in the process of planning and development is fundamentally an empowerment tool. It satisfies a basic need for people to be involved and participate in the decisions that affect their lives. The grassroots democratic movements spreading throughout the world that from time to time capture the imagination of the most jaded news commentators are evidence of this basic human need. Most importantly, engaging with people allows the outsider or professional architect, planner, or economic development specialist to be informed by the accumulated knowledge of the people. Such indigenous knowledge is often unique to that culture or society. It is the basis for decision making in agriculture, trade, resource management, education, and other functions necessary for that society to function. It is nurtured by oral traditions coupled with internal creativity and exposure to and experimentation with external contacts.

What follows are two such efforts that yielded appropriate innovative solutions adapted to the context in which they were applied. The first and major initiative is a project that I undertook in what is now called Burkina Faso in West Africa. The second case briefly describes an effort on which Ron was engaged in South Africa. Interestingly, there are strands that connect the two interventions despite the fact that they took place at different times and in different places and were done independently of each other. Yet, in each case, the process of engagement created the linkages, which were then adapted to the different socioeconomic and political contexts to achieve locally defined outcomes.

Self-Help through a Microcredit System

Burkina Faso, originally a French colony called Upper Volta, gained its independence from France in 1960. Landlocked, the country is plagued with recurrent droughts. The most important ethnic group—the Mossi—rules and, essentially, dominates the country. Two nomadic groups—the Fulani and the Tuareg—also inhabit Burkina Faso. Its first president banned all political parties. Unhappy with the government, the military took over in a coup in 1966, keeping the same president until 1980 when worker strikes led to another coup. In 1983, the government was taken over once again by a military coup, which was led by Thomas Sankara and Blaise Compaoré. In 1984, Sankara, considered by the population as the African Che Guevara, became president. He changed the name of the country from Upper Volta to Burkina Faso—roughly translated as "Land of Incorruptible People." Sankara's presidency would not last, however, and after a five-day war with Mali in December 1985 and criticisms from France that Sankara was too radical, there was another military coup in 1987. When the coup was over, President Sankara had been killed and Blaise Compaoré, who remains president to this day, had taken his place. In 2013, Burkina Faso's population had grown to an estimated eighteen million, and its main products are peanuts, cotton, and livestock.[1]

In the immediate aftermath of the West African drought of 1968–73, the United Nations Sahelian Office (UNSO) was created to address the problems growing out of the drought in the Sahel region of Upper Volta. During that five-year period, up to 250,000 drought-related fatalities occurred, including vegetation and animal deaths in addition to the human

---

[1]. *Encyclopaedia Britannica Online*, s. v. "Burkina Faso," accessed March 10, 2014, http://www.britannica.com/EBchecked/topic/85420/Burkina-Faso.

Burkina Faso and
Ouagadougou location.
MAP ADAPTED BY
ISABEL AGUIRRE

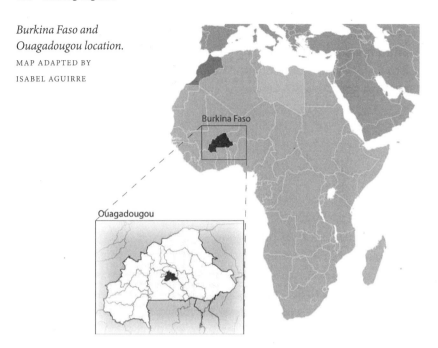

toll. The nomadic tribes that inhabited the area deserted their usual temporary settlements and moved to the outskirts of major towns in search
of food and water for them to survive. This dramatically changed their
lifestyle.[2]

Between 1973 and 1978, the United Nations Development Programme
(UNDP), at the request of the government of Upper Volta, began an
intervention called the Habitat Project. Two programs characterized it.
The first was the creation of a site and services project called the Planned
Area, which included 600 new lots that covered approximately 20 of the
495 acres of Ouagadougou's squatter community of Cissin.

The second program was the restructuring of each of Cissin's various
neighborhoods, which involved improving infrastructure such as roads,
sewage systems, and water. The site and services project had already
outlined six hundred lots in the Planned Area and had distributed them
by lottery to the people. However, after two years, only two hundred of

---

2. United Nations Development Programme, *Sahel Region Report* (New York: United Nations Development Programme, 1970).

the lots, owned primarily by privileged merchants and a few military and public employees, had been built on. The lucky but poor beneficiaries of the four hundred remaining lots had found it impossible to build because they couldn't obtain any government or alternative financing. They had no regular revenue or property, and, therefore, couldn't present any guarantees to secure the financing to build. The few goods they possessed had all been obtained through some form of barter. In other words, they were too poor to benefit from the land they had been given.

Clearly, the Habitat Project needed a program that could help these legal owners, and the many other illegal settlers, borrow the money they needed to either acquire or build houses in their own community. A housing bank or savings association seemed to be the obvious answer, and so the UNDP tried sending an economist and bank official to establish such a financing program. These so-called experts came back from their short-term mission concluding that the people were much too poor for a housing bank or any cooperative project. Most likely, these experts had just been driven through the peripheral neighborhoods in a minister's limousine, and had not been able to see any viable commerce or validity in establishing a lending bank in the areas that comprised the periphery of Upper Volta's capital. They felt that all the economic exchanges were through a system of barter and that any financing institution for this population would fail. Luckily, the United Nations (UN) officer who had sent these experts knew that something positive and more modest could be achieved with this population because he had worked closely with them for some time and knew that they were willing and capable of pulling themselves out of their poverty. He believed that the answer would have to come from the grassroots folks themselves and not from any conventional UN structure. William Easterly clearly defined this approach in his book, *The White Man's Burden*, by contrasting the different approaches between the well-intentioned, remote international organizations or "institutional planners," whose actions do not reach the poor, and the "searchers," who are advocates of an alternative approach, and finding the right or appropriate solution for curing the ills of a suffering community.[3]

---

3. William Easterly, *The White Man's Burden: Why the West's Efforts to Aid the Rest Have Done So Much Ill and So Little Good* (Oxford: Oxford University Press, 2006).

While I had no specific experience with banking or savings, through my East Harlem advocacy work, I had helped in the creation of community-controlled cooperatives and participated in many self-help projects. Senior UN administrators, who argued, logically enough, that my diplomas were in architecture and what they needed was a socioeconomist, blocked my candidacy at first. However, the officer who had worked in Ouagadougou insisted in finding the person who could help this population. He was apparently impressed by my grassroots participatory work in East Harlem and negotiated a three-month trial mission with the UN administration.

I flew to Ouagadougou on March 7, 1976 and immediately met three social workers who were also to be my translators from the local Moore language to French. My first action was to contact Cissin-area residents directly. For a good part of my first two weeks, the social workers and I walked the area, mainly in the afternoons and early evenings when people were back from their day's work, meeting people and engaging in what can best be described as warm and open discussions. Cissin's population was essentially agricultural. I soon discovered that Cissin was divided into specific sub-neighborhoods, each administered by a traditional chief, who, most of the time, had been the same chief they had had in their previous village prior to moving to the Ouagadougou outskirts. These sub-neighborhoods did not possess official institutional boundaries, and were more defined by physical forms like a tree, a road, or a feature of the land. Like in the village, these chiefs were tax collectors and ministered to the population living under their authority.

Problem Identification

The persistence of the Sahel drought reached a peak in 1973. Large-scale famine and dislocation on a massive scale had been recurrent, and the drought of 1968–1972 accelerated the problem, pushing rural populations seeking survival to move to areas around major cities such as Niamey, the capital of Niger, Ouagadougou, and Bamako, the capital of Mali. Without any legal status, these populations gathered on the periphery of these capitals, their settlements reflecting the social structure they had had in their previous villages.

Around 90 percent of the Cissin area's eighteen thousand people lived and were dependent on overexploited land parcels to the south of the community, which produced poorer harvests year after year in dry and exhausted soils. There were also some merchants, a few craftsmen, some workers, and a few others with undefined activities who could temporarily engage in farming in the rainy season. The remaining 8 percent were either civil servants or army recruits.[4] We visited primarily those identified as leaders in each area, meeting the traditional chiefs with their respective entourages, some schoolteachers, a few respected merchants, and some religious leaders, such as the local imam. From the very first day, I felt welcome. I was received with warmth and a climate of confidence, and a substantive desire for and receptiveness to community action emerged.

At first, the geographic area seemed endless. Walking away from the richer city center, with its cloud of dusty streets and colorful, immense marketplace, the winding irregular streets of Cissin looked like an endless conglomeration of poor and tiny adobe houses and small huts, an outgrowth of the same light red earth out of which they were built and from which they borrowed their material structures. There were also some rundown compounds enclosed by straw mats to keep the skinny chickens in and women out of view of the passersby. I slowly discovered that this immense informal settlement area that seemed unplanned and haphazard had a social structure congruent to the structured villages of origin, with each traditional chief allotting a piece of land to any newcomer from his own village in the age-old African tradition. Within the first two weeks, we identified six neighborhoods in Cissin's overall area. Each of the neighborhoods was named after the particular village its people had come from and remained under the authority of their traditional village chief.

Having met the people and identified the existing village structure, deciding what to do was not difficult. Several UN missions had previously studied the possibility of a savings and loan institution or a housing

---

4. United Nations Development Programme, *Report on the Sahel Drought* (New York: United Nations Development Programme, 1975).

bank at the national level, but these missions only helped the very few people with regular incomes and left out the majority who were poor. When people with low or irregular incomes were obliged to borrow, they were charged usurious interest rates of between 150 to 200 percent. Given the general poverty of the Cissin population, a national institution was clearly not the answer. On the other hand, I learned of the existence of micro savings and loan associations in many of the country's small villages that had been started by a Canadian organization called the Desjardins Group,[5] and it seemed obvious that, given the nature of the majority of Cissin's inhabitants, a micro savings and loan association was an ideal tool for community development. Given that each neighborhood had a traditional chief, or something equivalent that had been inherited from the village structure, it was clear that we could use these neighborhoods as a basis for organizing, and that the organization we created could also consolidate community cohesion. Indeed, the Canadians were building on an indigenous form of finance—the lending circle.[6]

Furthermore, with their rural origins, most of the people in the neighborhood had previously heard about the work done by the Canadians in many of the rural settlements of Upper Volta, where peasants had their own small village savings and loan associations of between twenty and fifty members depending on the village size. I visited a few of these associations and became convinced that the approach should be fundamentally the same when jumping from twenty to fifty members at the rural locations to two hundred to six hundred members at the urban site. We devised a questionnaire relating to the inhabitant's will to start a community savings and loan association. The reaction was immediate and

5. The Desjardins Group was and still is the largest association of credit unions in North America. Located in Canada, it is composed of some 536 local associations serving close to 6 million members regrouped in 11 regional federations. The Desjardins Group, through its subsidiary, Développement International Desjardins, has also been working in over 50 developing countries, including Burkina Faso.

6. Lending circles are when people get together to form a means by which to save and lend money to members of the group, negating the need to go to more formal lending institutions, such as banks. In a savings and loan scheme or lending circle, everyone contributes and everyone gets a chance to benefit. This practice has its origins around the world, and is known by different names in different places: SuSu's in Africa and in parts of the Americas inhabited by people of African descent, Paluwagan in the Philippines, Lun-Hui in China, and Tandas in Mexico. Its application is a result of understanding that emerges when exposed to indigenous knowledge.

FIRST INFORMATION FLYER ABOUT A COMMUNITY SAVINGS ASSOCIATION

A microcredit bank is not a charitable institution: it does not make a profit, but is set up to serve the population by providing folks a means of accessing credit. The purpose of such an organization is to enable people to work together for mutual benefit, with the general aim of serving their community.

How does it work?
A community micro-credit bank offers a combined savings and loan service. It serves people from the same neighborhood or the same region, who have come together to set up an association in order to serve their community and personal economic needs.

Remember that termites eat paper bills stored in clay pots and that huts can burn.

The community savings bank is a place where one can deposit or borrow cash and repay loans. The profits go exclusively to the membership.

Remember that thieves can also come and steal your savings

GUIDELINES FOR COMMUNITY MICRO-CREDIT BANKS

Free access to anyone of good reputation.
This gives every member the freedom to withdraw from the group if he or she wishes, once obligations to the institution have been satisfied. For example: the member can only withdraw once outstanding loans have been repaid.

One member one vote.
At annual general assembly meetings when a new board is elected, each member will have one vote.

Interest on deposits.
The interest on deposits will be disbursed at the end of each year.

THE COMMUNITY SAVINGS BANK ENCOURAGES ITS MEMBERSHIP IN THE FOLLOWING WAYS:

Solidarity is essential for a microcredit bank. For example a borrower has to understand that if he fails to repay a loan, it is the whole community that suffers.

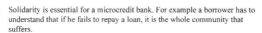

- One has to respect the rights of others;
- Respect the community elected board;
- Use borrowed money only to invest in projects that are useful to the community and families' well being.

Only through deposited savings is a member guaranteed secure placement for his cash and interest. The member is therefore able to:
- Invest in productive goods such as carts, machines and tools; -invest in consumer or professional activity;
- Set up a business;
- Renovate his or her home
- Invest in items such as bicycles, radios, etc…

First information flyer about community savings associations handed out to residents of Cissin. DRAWINGS AND COMMENTARIES BY ROGER KATAN positive given the fact that most of them had such an experience back in their villages. Those who were familiar with the process helped convince the ones who were hesitant, telling them of the many advantages of a community savings and loan organization. With the social workers, we devised a flyer to convince the most hesitant.

Most people were convinced that our sheer presence symbolized the official recognition of their new neighborhood. As squatters, they knew that they had no protection and that they could be ejected at any time by a government official coming with a bulldozer to take a big swath of land for a personal use. They understood that their membership in a community savings association could become the tool for the recognition of their neighborhood. In this way, their status could move from being squatters to being permanent settlers.

Structure for the Micro Savings and Loan Organization

Birth of Neighborhood Committees

Three of the neighborhoods in Cissin seemed highly responsive and ready to start saving immediately, and so, in my third week in Ouagadougou, we proceeded with the help of the social workers to organize the election of a local board of directors in each neighborhood. These local boards reflected the social structure of each quartier, or the neighborhood already identified with the existence of a respected traditional chief. It was natural and logical to keep and reinforce the traditional chief structure and make this traditional governance structure more democratic by electing five or six local distinguished members to work with the chief. These were folks who were beyond reproach, such as a teacher, religious leader, or respected business leader.

The next challenge was to spread the word about the organization in order to attract more members. During the first four weeks, we worked with the social workers each afternoon in a different neighborhood to train a few volunteers who could work closely with the social workers in their own areas. In turn, they reached out to future potential members by spreading the word about the advantages of a community-controlled savings and loan association and gathering memberships. We emphasized from the beginning that a savings tool would help them secure the land on which they were squatting. At the same time, this would help them create a microenterprise to build their houses and needed facilities in their respective neighborhoods and in the larger community.

We also set to work on education in order to foster the independence of both individual members and the organization as a whole. We subdivided each of the districts into cells of eight to ten members and taught simple arithmetic and functional literacy so that each member could read his or her own personal savings carnet and follow the progress of the community savings association. It was essential that each member could easily control his or her own account as this was the only way to ensure total confidence. They had to understand that when the time came to borrow, it was their own money that was involved. For those who wanted to borrow, but who possessed very limited savings, other members could offer their guarantee, and this also had to be clearly understood. Finally, although they were receiving assistance from the social workers and me, they had to understand that it was temporary and that they should learn to take charge of their own decision making because only they could best define their particular problems and plan their future. I offered a methodology and showed how to coordinate their initiatives and their wishes in relation to official programs. One month after the call for membership, the budding organization counted more than two hundred members.

Knowing the importance of women in the local African economy, I personally was disturbed by their total absence from our meetings in the first six weeks. When, at our second general assembly meeting, I said that I was puzzled by their absence, I was told by the chairman that if some of our social workers were women instead of men, there would not be any problem. A couple of days later, three women social workers were added to our team, and it was at this precise moment that the savings association started to soar.

Some two months after my arrival, we had enough members to proceed with the election of a local board of directors in the remaining three neighborhoods, which would then give us a board in each of the six Cissin neighborhoods. Following the election, we organized a general assembly that met every Saturday morning. These meetings were held in an open space with bare benches shaded by a canopy of straw mats in a central area where community facilities were planned. Remembering my success during the East Harlem summer festival in using video technology to stimulate participation, each meeting was videotaped, and, at the end of the meeting, we viewed the recording, as well as the videotapes of the individual neighborhoods' local assembly debates. Most of the attendants had never seen a movie, let alone seen themselves on a screen. To our great satisfaction, the general assembly grew larger and larger with every passing Saturday. Curious and puzzled about this increasing attendance, I inquired and was given the reason for their enthusiasm: they all wanted to see themselves on the screen at the end of each meeting and be part of the show! In addition to using these videotapes as a technique to stimulate participation, we decided to create a short documentary that we could use when we were ready to encourage other neighborhoods to start their own community-controlled savings and loan associations.

Relation between Inhabitants and Technician

Toward the end of my UN mission's third and last month, we began to receive protests from at least two surrounding neighborhoods that claimed to belong to the greater Cissin area and petitioned to become part of the association. After a few meetings with the elected representatives, the general assembly voted to include one of them, and the area grew from six to seven neighborhoods. The savings kept slowly but steadily growing. At the end of my first mission, the micro savings and loan association had close to six hundred members. There were seven neighborhoods that each had seven elected officials, making a total of forty-nine elected officials. The number of people attending the weekly meetings had grown from forty or fifty at the beginning to over two hundred.

The success of this first three-month UN task brought an immediate offer from the UNDP of a full-year renewable contract to continue our work for two or three years. While I was flattered by this offer, I could not accept it. If this were to be a community-controlled enterprise, when would the community take control of its self-help venture if I stayed full time with them? I believed that the members had enough experience, maturity, and will to control the growth of their nascent organization. It was normal that in the beginning, they relied heavily on my full-time presence for the conception and organization of the association. However, since they had been wholeheartedly involved in every step of its growth from its inception, I felt that it was time to leave them to manage it on their own for a while. Its success from the beginning was directly related to the respect that had been shown to their inherited village structures. The fact that they migrated within their own country left them with a continuing respect for traditional village culture, and I was fairly certain that they would act responsibly. I suggested to the UNDP that in this community's interest, as well as their own, the wisest policy would be to leave these groups to manage their newly created enterprise by themselves and empower them for a few months. I offered to replace the two or three year's full-time mission with two or three short missions to put the train back on the tracks if needed. This suggestion was well received by the UN, but not by the local elected boards or the community at large. At first, they seemed truly shocked by my decision. They relied on me to control and keep their collected savings safe. They had no confidence in banks and even less in the higher echelons of the national government, often accusing them of embezzlement and robbery. I explained that it was not normal for me to keep their savings and that someone could easily steal it from my house. I suggested that not only would their savings be more secure in a bank, but it would also bring them some interest. Addressing the board of director's anxiety about who would be responsible for accessing the account, I suggested that no money should be deposited or withdrawn from their savings account without at least three or four signatures of their most respected elected members. They accepted my suggestion reluctantly, and I left after they had deposited their money in a savings account with 5 percent interest.

Program Development Analysis: Consultation on Community Needs
Six months later, I returned for my second mission, and I found quite a surprise. I wish I had had a camera to record my arrival. The tiny Ouagadougou airport was jammed with smiling faces from the neighborhood and the open arms of the local board members, along with dozens of

representatives from the seven different communities. They were thrilled to announce that they had not only new memberships but also a lot more money saved. They were proud of the fact that they did it all by themselves. It was a happy moment for us all, which called for celebration. On the spot, I was introduced to some new people: a delegation from two very large surrounding communities that had come to ask for my help in starting the same activities in their respective areas. I had to tell them that my time for this mission was too short to help them, but that the social workers could offer guidelines and provide the same advice that had helped the Cissin neighborhoods to succeed.

Now that the community had gathered some money, the next step was to finance small local projects. We organized preliminary consultations in each of the seven neighborhoods to determine the community's needs and priorities. The reaction was practically unanimous: they all wanted the immediate restructuring of their entire neighborhood. At the core, their concern was to ensure the security of their respective parcels of land. Understanding their concern, I assured them that this was planned by a joint UN–World Bank action through the Habitat Project.

We needed more specific projects on which to focus, and I noticed once again that women had been absent from these first meetings. In the African context, I felt their presence was necessary to define community needs. While men's primary concern was land security, women were faced with a multitude of daily chores, such as lugging water for cooking and washing, grinding grains for meals, etc. We invited women to attend, and they quickly suggested close to twenty priorities, three of which were voted as the most important: water at low cost, a multifunctional grain mill, and the creation of a central market.

Parallel to these consultations, we decided to create a central board of directors that would be composed of an elected member from each neighborhood. I projected that such an overall direction would, in time, replace the social workers' coordination tasks in overseeing the problems that arise and supervising community activities. It would also coordinate the development of all the future community projects selected. At the Saturday general assembly, a central board was elected, and, less than three weeks later, it assumed total control of the overall organization. The social workers and I became temporary observers and advisers.

First Community Investments

1. Water Carts

While many members of the community were initially fearful about the transfer of power to the central board of directors, their fear was rapidly transformed into pride. The central board began with solving the water problem. Water in Cissin was only available through barrels transported by donkey-driven carts and sold at very high prices to each family. During the dry season, which was most of the year, water was even more expensive. Water was transported to each of the neighborhoods from the only public fountain, which was located about 1.2 miles away. The immediate solution was to buy one cart for each neighborhood, which could be pulled by one young man. After paying for all the expenses, including the salaries of the seven young cart runners, it was calculated that water would cost at least one-third of the existing price. While the carts initially worked well, three months after the start of the project, half of the carts ceased to function. Their runners claimed that they were much too heavy to pull. Only then did we discover that the former water salesmen had sent most of these cart runners to us, and it certainly was not in their interest to help our program. By that time, however, water was less of an issue since, in January 1977, they were two months away from the installation of a fountain in each neighborhood. The projected water tower, planned and built by the UN sites and services project,[7] was about to be completed. It had been designed with a network of pipe connections leading to public fountains at multiple sites, and a

---

7. Sites and services projects are designed by international organizations, such as the UN and World Bank, for the public provision of housing infrastructure for developing countries, i.e., planned plots, water, roads, sewerage, areas for schools, commercial space, etc. The scheme was designed so that the public sector could develop sites and services while private individuals could erect the housing units. It was supposed to improve employment in the building industry, improve health conditions, and raise living standards while providing governments with the possibility of reducing costs of services and housing units so as to reach the largest number of urban poor. It was also to demonstrate the extent to which self-help could be relied upon to reduce housing unit costs. Often, the allocation of plots or houses was not devoid of some type of corruption: usually, civil servants, politicians, business leaders, etc. would find poor relatives with reduced means, or persons who qualify for allocated plots, and enter into a legal contract for a negotiated amount, then transferring the plot or the house of the hungry "friend" to themselves.

water fountain was made available temporarily at a central spot in the community.

2. **Grain Mill**

The second community project was the multifunctional grain mill, and it was here that some previously unused UN funding became useful. The UNDP executive officer, who had briefed me before I started my first mission, told me that he had set aside a fund of four thousand US dollars to use for the neighborhood at my discretion. His idea was that this fund would probably be necessary to seed the community savings fund, and was intended to encourage people to save. However, I believed that the community had to put together a minimum amount of money right at the start as proof that they wanted their own self-help organization. Without this commitment, I felt the project would fail. This was why the four thousand dollars had not been used as originally planned. Now, almost a year later, we drew on that money to finance various community projects, among them the long-dreamed of grain mill. The community's collected funds were not sufficient to purchase the mill, and members wondered how they could make the purchase. After consulting with the UNDP, I decided to announce the existence of the unused money. At a general assembly, with close to two hundred members attending, I offered this sum to the gathering as a long-term loan with 0 percent interest from the UN as a reward and recognition for their efforts in creating and managing their own organization. Two-thirds of this sum was allocated to the construction of the market project, and one-third to the grain mill. Jean Bruno Ilboudo, a respected merchant and member of the central board, conducted an exhaustive investigation of the professional mills existing in the country. He recommended a generator-driven multifunctional electric grain mill made in England. Many users of this type of mill approved and backed the recommendation. We checked that it had a good guarantee, contacted the makers in England, and negotiated the buying and shipping conditions. At long last, the thousands of neighborhood women would no longer have to walk the very long distances from their neighborhoods and pay high prices for milling their diverse grains on a daily basis. The mill was delivered and installed by the end of June 1977, and after some initial management difficulties, the mill started to function normally. Soon, the mill was employing three full-time employees, and they started repaying their monthly loan reimbursements to the community savings and loan organization. By the time these two projects were underway, the three months of my second mission were over, and I once again left the community to manage their own affairs.

Project Development Analysis

It was almost a full year before I returned to assess these projects because a major conflict in Cissin provoked a six-month paralysis of the whole savings organization. It occurred when a traditional chief's authority was contested by some of his people who had begun identifying themselves more with the savings organization structure than with their chief's traditional authority. This particular traditional chief recognized how powerful and important this new savings project was for the majority of his people who supported it, and thinking of himself as all-powerful and benefiting from his traditional status, he attempted to seize control of his district's elected organization. After some unpleasant intimidation and other harassment on his part, a group of co-op members felt that their hard-won savings was threatened and brought the conflict to the interior ministry, the highest legal authority in the country. After an official inquiry that lasted six months, during which all activities were suspended, the government concluded that "given the fact that the Traditional Chiefs were fully informed and openly associated with the interests of the community savings organization, they could not under any circumstances substitute themselves to legally elected community representatives."[8] When I came back for my third mission, Jean Bruno Ilboudo had been elected to become the new president of the Cissin Caisse Populaire Central Board, and the mill was managed and functioning to everyone's satisfaction.

The next project that the community savings organization undertook was the establishment of a central market for the acquisition and exchange of goods and services. In order to finance the first phase of the

8. Burkina Faso Ministry of Interior, *December 1977 Ministry of Interior Report* (Ouagadougou: Government Printing Office, 1977).

project, the savings and loan organization negotiated a seven-year UN guaranteed fund loan. Officially, the city managed every market in town, but since the savings and loan organization was paying for its construction, the city agreed to draw up an accord enabling the savings and loan organization to run the market for a while.

The first phase of the project was the construction of 7 large shops (one for each neighborhood) and 104 smaller box-like shops. Once they were built, the shops were distributed through a lottery system because the number of applicants was much too many for what was available. A merchant's commission designated by the central board of directors defined the sizes of these two spaces (150 and 40 square feet, respectively). As the market prepared to open, we faced two problems: first, some of the beneficiaries felt that even the large shops were too small, as in the case of those selling building materials; and second, many of those who had applied for space, but had not won the lottery, wanted to start building immediately and offered to finance the costs of this second phase construction themselves. They declared that while respecting the overall plans, they wanted a box design that would be double the size of the one planned—closer to eighty square feet. Four days from the official opening of the market, these would-be merchants were authorized to build. The next day, they arrived early, with their guarantee in one hand and building tools in the other, and built the second phase in three days, keeping their promise to finish in time for the planned inauguration.

Gradually, the project expanded. At a major roundabout close to Cissin, there was an illegal market. It was filled with small merchants, mainly women, who came at dawn every day to sell their wares on the bare earth and in full sun. Cissin's board of directors decided to send a delegation to invite these merchants to their new market where they would at least have a roof to protect them from the harsh sun. At seven o'clock the next morning, which was the first day of the market inauguration, some 300 women, with merchandise bundled on top of their heads, came to take over the 150 open places planned for them. These women were attracted by the proximity of a large population, the nearness of the market to the community center, and the new and very popular grain mill, which was also very close to the school and health center. Their arrival gave instant life to the market and effectively guaranteed its success.

The number of people who flocked to the market steadily from day one made it a total and immediate success. As a result, the next phases were projected in the same way as the last one, which was by the merchants themselves. The savings and loan organization would not have to borrow from the UN anymore to build. It was the triumph of individual initiative to improve standards of living not only on a private level but also at the community level.

While the market was being planned, we organized, with the social workers' help, training programs to be given by government technicians from different ministries, such as town planning, social works, health, and education. These sessions were dedicated to the various phases of neighborhood urban restructuring, community organization, and development in this particular district area. Literacy was included in very one of the programs so that everyone would learn how to read their accounts and write their name. The broad goal of our intervention was to move the community members from being illegal rural settlers to new urban dwellers. This involved developing infrastructure—not only social and physical, but also educational. The savings program was the first important step in preparing Cissin's inhabitants both psychologically and economically for their new urban life. It enabled them to move on to neighborhood infrastructure projects after the success of the grain mill and market. These training programs prepared them to be integrated into the city life and economy and allowed them to participate fully in the UN–World Bank Habitat Project.

At about this same time, a joint UN and local government project called Habitat was parceling out close to five hundred acres of land. Their task was made easy by the existence of the various district boards of directors that helped to develop a master plan with individual lots and the localization of community facilities. This mission also helped organize the creation of a crafts center with connections to the existing and successful national craftsmen organization.

The main promoter of the crafts center was Mamoudou Traoré, a skinny young man who, paralyzed by polio, had been running on crutches with both legs dangling ever since he was born, but who had an endless, cheerful personality. Working as a traditional potter, he gave pottery classes in the house where he lived in the neighborhood and sold what he made to tourists in the capital's craft center. We met at a community meeting during my first mission, and we became friends. His dream was to create a crafts village cooperative in Cissin that would evolve into a desirable setting for the production of the various crafts specialties. More importantly, it was to serve as a place for a craft school. On the first mission, I introduced Mamoudou to a nonprofit organization, which, a few months later, offered him a hand-driven wheelchair. On my third mission, he was most happy to parade around in a new electric wheelchair!

By the end of the third mission, in March 1978, the total number of the savings association's members was reaching two thousand, and their savings were equivalent to twenty thousand US dollars. I recommended to the UN that it was time to call the Desjardins Group from Quebec to continue advising Cissin's organization on other community investments. We were about to enter a period of personal loans because there was some demand for it by members. This was outside the capacity of my mission. They were ready for professional expertise in economic development. The influence of our work was also beginning to generate demand in the other squatter areas of Ouagadougou as the government's Department of Social Works was helping new settlers organize themselves into small savings organizations similar to ours

Conclusion and Update

Some fifteen years later, on a mission in West Africa for the World Bank in 1993, I stopped by Ouagadougou with a natural and intense desire to know what had happened to the organization. I called up Jean Bruno Ilboudo, who, for some time, had been the president of the Cissin Caisse Populaire, and I was happy to receive positive news. He told me that the Cissin savings were up to the equivalent of 850,000 dollars, and, after a serious period of turmoil, the association had been advised full time by the Desjardins Group since 1989. Prior to this, in 1984, the national revolution led by Thomas Sankara and Blaise Compaoré had occurred. During a three- to four-year period, chaos reigned, and many institutions were shaken. The upheaval led to some serious theft in the savings and loan association, but the solidity of the grassroots organization led by the original leaders and backed by all of their members ensured that thieves were pursued and money returned. There was a period of instability in the association that lasted from 1985 to the end of 1988 when most of the stolen money was recovered. In 1989, the Desjardins Group, which had been working for many years in the country's rural areas, came to help the Cissin organization reorganize itself.

In November of 2005, I learned that the Cissin Caisse Populaire had grown to be a national organization with a membership of over 30,700 and savings close to 7 million dollars.[9] Today, it is a nationwide federation that includes both rural and urban savings and loan organizations, and it remains an example of a successfully integrated and self-sustained development entity. It may be worth adding that another microlending project, albeit with a different focus and modus operandi, the Grameen Bank, also took off in this same period in India, and, in 2006, the bank and its founder, Muhammad Yunus, won the Nobel Peace Prize.

I also heard from Mamoudou in 2009, some thirty-five years after the microlending project had been launched, that the original neighborhood arts cooperative had become a national arts and crafts center. I learned that he had also created a training center for the physically handicapped dedicated to helping young people with disabilities in the same way he was helped by our project. A few years earlier, he had also created his own brick-making enterprise that continued to flourish. He is just one example of the talented and dedicated people who worked hard to make the community organization succeed.

After the end of these missions in Ouagadougou, I was offered the opportunity to work with the Desjardins Group through the Canadian Council for International Cooperation. To the UN, which also offered

---

9. Adeline Zongo, the director of the Cissin *Caisse Populaire* in Burkina Faso, focused on the needs of her community. She worked with Burkina Faso's financial cooperatives for over two decades and played a leading role in the evolution and growth of these institutions. As the director of the Cissin *Caisse Populaire* in Ouagadougou since 1990, she was distinguished by her awareness of the many needs of her community. She was involved in the testing, introduction, and marketing of numerous innovative financial services and products, such as specialized loans and services for women and entrepreneurs, housing loans, insurance, etc. In addition to these innovations, she successfully introduced automated financial operations to her co-op. Under her direction, the Cissin *Caisse Populaire* underwent rapid growth and, today, can be proud of its exceptional performance. This enviable situation, combined with her outstanding qualities as the cooperative's main manager, led to Adeline Zongo being made a Chevalier de l'Ordre National in 2004 by the president of Burkina Faso.

me a full-time job, I suggested the possibility of duplicating the work I did in Ouagadougou in other major cities throughout West Africa. I thought that this would be particularly welcomed in the periphery of all major cities where rural migrations were prevalent and the populations were poor. Since the populations of West Africa have similar social structures and a relatively homogeneous culture, the problems of poverty were practically the same in this whole African region, and I was sure it was possible to develop successful organizations using the same method we had followed in Cissin. I offered to fly from capital to capital every two or three months and from town to town in the many West African nations. The goal was to help start a community savings association in the poorest neighborhoods and return to the same places six or eight months later to help consolidate each organization and its growth process until the structure of micro savings and loan institutions was established and working autonomously.

Although at first my offer was well received, the UNDP representatives consulted were concerned that the different West African countries (all former French colonies, including Mali, Ivory Coast, Senegal, Togo, Niger, Benin, and Mauritania) would not welcome the idea. These countries were all under some form of dictatorship, and it seemed unlikely that the rulers would appreciate a project promoting democracy through neighborhood autonomy and self-help.

The UN fears were not unfounded as my own missions had in fact created some tensions. During the time I was working in Cissin, Upper Volta was under a dictatorship that lasted more than twenty years. The minister of Department of Construction and Town Planning, under whom I worked, was satisfied during my first mission, but became quite angry with me during the second and third missions because the people in the communities where I worked had begun actively asking for their rights. After my second mission, I had taught them sit-in techniques, which they used in the minister's office to obtain some basic services, which was unheard of in Africa. Always concerned about their relationship with national governments, the UN did not accept my offer because it probably would have disturbed the numerous well-established dictatorships of the region. These UN officials felt that the project would foster threatening democratic ideas in countries where governments

Cissin,
Ouagadougou,
Burkina Faso,
in 2009. PHOTO
BY HTTP-//WWW
.FLICKR.COM
/PHOTOS
/KYSELAK
/2223494527
/IN/PHOTO
STREAM

would be unreceptive to them. I later learned that the UNDP would only finance and execute projects proposed and designed by the respective governments, which, unfortunately, were not always in their own people's interests. While the UN officials may have had good political reasons for their rejection of my proposal, I am convinced that from the perspective of international stability, as well as from that of the poor populations whom the savings and loan organizations could have helped directly, it was a mistake.

In November 2007, I wrote a letter of congratulations to the savings and loan organization in Cissin, suggesting that we should celebrate its thirtieth birthday. An answer soon came from the organization's new administration. All the leaders I had known seemed to have passed away, and I was brushed off. They let me know that the original organization had died in the 1980s and the organization had completely changed hands. The letter seemed to ask who I thought I was to think that I could partake in a success that was entirely theirs! This filled me with pride because it proved that the new generation was continuing to take complete ownership of the enterprise—empowerment had been slow, but had become a reality over the long term. After a few months of trying to contact some of the people I used to know, my pleasure was complete when Mamoudou Traoré contacted me. In a very touching letter, he promised to round up the few original members still alive and that they were anxious to meet again to show off their achievements. He told me that the organization had now grown to 30,700 members with an active savings of over 6 million dollars, integrating a network of over 100 urban and rural savings organizations in Burkina Faso. This project is a successful example of participatory development. It survived the cupidity and widespread corruption of the mid-1980s, and became what it is today thanks to popular will backed by the technical assistance of the Desjardins Group of Canada.

From the project's beginning, I felt it was essential to insist that the local populations become responsible and independent. Had I stayed on for a full three-year contract as originally proposed by the UN, the populations would have continued to rely on the foreign expert as they naturally did in my first three-month mission. They would have continued being dependent instead of learning early on how to make decisions for themselves. By not following the UN policy of long-term assistance, I do believe that I helped to assure Cissin's success. The UN institutional planners knew what program would best serve the ruthless rulers and dictators of the West African countries, and had just hoped that some of the international aid would in some magical way filter down to the poor of their respective countries.

As William Easterly underlines in his book, *The White Man's Burden*:

> In foreign aid, Planners announce good intentions but don't motivate anyone to carry them out . . . they raise expectations but take no responsibility for meeting them; Searchers accept responsibility for their actions. Planners determine what to supply; Searchers find out what is in demand. Planners apply global blueprints; Searchers adapt to local conditions. Planners at the top lack knowledge of the bottom. . . . Poor people die not only because of the world indifference to their poverty, but also because of ineffective efforts by those who do care.[10]

If the purpose of third world aid is to free people rather than enforce dependence, isn't it reasonable to believe that the ultimate goal of aid should be the end of aid, leading to empowerment and self-sufficiency?

---

10. Easterly, *The White Man's Burden*, 5–7.

*Cissin and
Mamoudou
Traoré's
brick-making
enterprise.*
PHOTOS BY
MAMOUDOU
TRAORÉ

Self-Help in South Africa

At the end of 1989, after I had written the first edition of *Bâtir Ensemble*, both the Ford Foundation and the US Agency for International Development (USAID) asked Ron Shiffman to visit South Africa. The two donors believed that the apartheid regime of South Africa was about to fall and were concerned with the exceedingly high expectations that once apartheid ended, people would quickly become frustrated if there was not an effective effort to address the adverse economic impact that apartheid had inflicted upon the mass of South Africans, particularly black South Africans. Because of Ron's participatory work and focus on community-based planning, he was asked to go to South Africa and assess the potential for community-initiated and self-help economic development efforts. The result of his visits and meetings with a broad range of civic organizations and antiapartheid groups was the recommendation that the Ford Foundation and USAID programs be geared toward supporting the efforts on the ground of people and civic structures established as shadow entities to the apartheid regime. He also discovered that many in South Africa belonged to savings associations for the purposes of burial and informal lending. These funds were primarily deposited in South African banks, which were anxious to accept the money, but that, in turn, refused to lend the money to black South Africans. This was, in part, due to discriminatory practices and, in part, due to the fact that under apartheid, blacks had not been allowed to own property and, therefore, had no collateral. The reaction by the foundation and USAID staff to Ron's proposals was quite favorable; however, the USAID offices in Washington, dominated by Reagan appointees, appeared to be more interested in fostering Black Capitalism than in promoting community economic development. The difference between Black Capitalism and community economic development is that in Black Capitalism, you create opportunities for a few individuals to become entrepreneurs, while in community economic development, you focus on improving the economic wherewithal of the mass of people. Frustrated by many of the recommendations being ignored and public policy being focused on the transfer of soda and beer franchises from white to black ownership,

Ron became engaged with a group of former South African divestment activists, who, during the apartheid regime, had effectively sought to bring down the apartheid government by asking investors across the world to refuse to invest in or to withdraw their investment from the repressive government. After apartheid, these activists turned their attention to creating and furthering investment in economic development activities initiated by black entrepreneurs and would-be entrepreneurs. Ron became a founding member of an organization called Shared Interest, which was established in 1994 to guarantee loans made by local South African banks to budding black organizations and entrepreneurs. The money to guarantee these loans was raised from individual, corporate, and philanthropic investors in the US. The idea was to build on local initiatives similar to those that I initiated in Upper Volta, but to adapt it to take advantage of the strong but discriminatory banking sector that existed in South Africa under apartheid.

Lessons Learned: Developing Innovations and Networks

The connection between my work in Ouagadougou and Shared Interest's efforts in South Africa is accidental, but reflects, in part, the way information gets transferred at the grassroots level. What the community leaders and I had worked at had a great impact on the microcredit activities throughout Burkina Faso. Years later, a friend of Ron's, Maria Teresa Cobelli, an Italian community development specialist, spent years working in Burkina Faso with two interrelated groups called Innovations et Réseaux pour le Développement (IRED), or Development Innovations and Networks, and Recherches et Applications de Financements Alternatifs au Développement (RAFAD), or Research Applications for Alternative Financing for Development. The latter group, RAFAD, was a Swiss-based technical assistance microfinance guarantee organization. Ron, at the invitation of Maria Teresa, had become a board member of IRED, representing North America, and while on the board, had become aware of the activities of RAFAD. When faced with the need to develop an investment strategy for South Africa to replace the disinvestment strategy used to fight apartheid, he was able to broker a relationship between Shared Interest (headed by Donna Katzin) and RAFAD.[11] Out of this relationship, Shared Interest and its local partner developed the Thembani International Guarantee Fund.

While Ron and I were friends and had worked and taught together in the 1960s, it was not the friendship, but the informal connections to grassroots networks that connected our work in different places and at different times. These naturally occurring networks are not to be ignored since they can invisibly, but critically, communicate the successes of one effort, such as that in Burkina Faso, to other places, such as in South Africa, and leverage the success of one endeavor to another.

The kind of intervention initiated by local people helped and nurtured by the kind of assistance that I was able to provide to those in Ouagadougou seeds a process that takes on a life of its own and organically begins to serve others. This was the case in Upper Volta, which later became Burkina Faso: first, the microfinance network affected the villages that I worked in and then spread throughout the country. As a result, entities like RAFAD and IRED began to learn from that experience and helped to seed other local initiatives so that the idea of microfinance began to cross borders and adapt to other environments and economic and political circumstances.

---

11. RAFAD created the International Guarantee Fund in 1996.

CASE STUDY 5

Jardies, Meudon, France

Introduction

C ase Study 5 tells the story of a housing cluster started in the late
1960s near Paris that was built and self-managed by a handful of
families. Trying to set up a new way of life, this pioneer group influenced many projects that gave birth in the last forty years to the cohousing movement, first in Denmark in the 1970s and then extending to
most of Europe, the US, New Zealand, Canada, and Australia.

Problem Identification

Meudon, which lies west of Paris on a hillside surrounding the capital
and Seine River, is a suburb whose complexity reflects its history. In
the 1960s, the Bas-Meudon, close to the Seine and industrial sites, was
largely populated by working-class families living in houses or public
housing along with a new fringe of middle-class people living in recently built half-luxury and luxury residences. In contrast, on the plateau,
Meudon-La-Forêt was a new city, welcoming people of different neighborhoods who had been evicted by renovations that had been made at
Bas-Meudon. On the hillsides, Meudon Bellevue, at the height of the old

castle, grew around the area's old bourgeois center. Older properties (formerly secondary residences of Paris inhabitants) were then sold piecemeal to developers who knew how to advertise and attract executives to the suburbs, particularly from the area west of Paris.

In this area, the luxury lay primarily in the wealth of coating materials, some modifications of detail, or in the greenery that the developer did not have to plant. But the architectural quality was lacking particular study or style, and the system of box-type apartments remained unchanged. The discourse surrounding these realizations did put the emphasis on the family space in the apartment, however, which was understood to be a place of happiness and privacy, featuring functional elements adapted to modern life where one could enjoy a healthy well-being after the long daily routine. In this type of structure, the only places to meet with neighbors were elevators or, when they existed, play areas for children. Access to equipment was calculated exclusively by car time.

The people who resided in this area belonged essentially to a social and cultural elite even if their income levels did not allow them to live in Paris—the price per square foot to build in Meudon in the 1970s was slightly cheaper than the price in Paris. For some, the concern that led to the choice not to live in Paris was education. For others, it was their critical reflection on everyday life that took them away from the capital. In these residential areas, an activist population sympathetic to leftist political parties, particularly those involved in ecological movements and environmental syndicates, was easily found.

It is in this way that the core of the residential group of Meudon managed to formulate together an idea that lead to the Jardies project. For others, expropriation or housing exiguity created an emergency situation strong enough to catalyze the desire for a different type of habitat.

Organizing and Animating People to Act on Their Behalf

The idea of building a small structure together had already germinated in the minds of a few of Meudon's residents. But in this first conception, the motives were essentially financial in nature, as well as mixed with the hope for more satisfactory accommodations. In reality, the Jardies project matured in the minds of militants and not just left-wing intellectuals. It was actually the near involvement with various civic and political groups and movements, such as the New Life Movement, school associations of parents, Socialist Party, and Municipal Action Group (MAG), which was created by those who believed that political parties were incapable of answering town planning, cultural policy, and participatory planning questions, that inspired the Jardies group to meet and to take their dissatisfactions and desires and transform them into political action. As one of the Jardies group members told me, "the meeting is not for a construction project, but for a project of life."

All adult men and women in the Jardies group worked—there were two high school teachers, a social worker, a librarian, a secretary, a laboratory worker, an architect, five engineers, a painter, an actor, a chemist, and a physicist researcher working for the French National Centre for Scientific Research. While the group had not existed before the project, each member had known at least one of the other members beforehand and had been confident enough to engage him or her with the idea.

The group was made up of ten families, and all group members lived in Meudon. It took them five years of knowledge gathering and commitment to create the cement that the project could be built on. Group members asked those interested to imagine their own apartment and plan their design with the architect; manage the construction of their apartment without a developer; manage the life of the house together without a trustee to prove that one could move against the current system, which was stiff with specialization; consider a housing cluster to break up the closed-off, single-family apartments; and find ways to engage more socially and widely with neighbors by hosting local associations.

In the minds of those who imagined it, this group would be living a level of social life hinged between family and city, but with an understanding that one could not replace the other. This integration was an important innovation in the modes of social urban relations at the time. It was called for by a deep desire of everyone, and as said by the group's charter:

> In the beginning was the desire for something else. Some had met and agreed on the way their words had imagined it precisely. Others were hesitant about words that did not describe their

desire. Nevertheless, all felt like caged bears in homes sold by merchants and decided to build a large house like a grand dress on a great desire.[1]

For this group of ten families, awareness came through a slow process of political maturation as each started wandering on their own field of engagement. It was, therefore, not surprising that when the opportunity came to make this project a concrete one, the group accepted it quickly, almost spontaneously. The Jardies project was established soon after the 1968 social upheaval.

Organization of Work Groups

The discovery by one of the group members of an available piece of land in Meudon enabled the group to be formally constituted. The first general meeting brought together some thirteen families and defined the group's determinations. Those who clung to full community life understood that this was not the way they wanted and did not stay. The group remained with nine families, which were subsequently assisted by a grandmother and a single woman.

An architect who wished to integrate the group posed as a condition of his membership to be the architect of the operation. After agreeing on this point, it was decided that the architect could not cumulate functions and that another person would be responsible for the overall administrative operation on behalf of the group.

During the whole process, the group split into three two-person teams that were responsible for different types of problems: financial, legal, and technical. Each of these three teams presented a record of its work at the weekly meetings. At the start, men performed these types of responsibilities, but soon after, the group evolved and eliminated the gender division of labor.

It is important to note that despite the division of labor during the building's construction and after, the group had always shown a strong determination in avoiding any form of organizing that could be heavy

---

1. *Jardies Project Charter* (Meudon, France: Jardies Group, 1968).

Diagram of Meudon's location in relation to Paris. ROGER KATAN

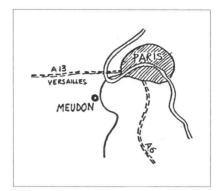

Below: Les Jardies, 2013.
PHOTO BY JEAN CLAUDE KATAN

and cumbersome. They refused to form a real estate company and preferred a structure of undivided co-ownership. These decisions were as unanimous as many of the other options taken. Without any need for a vote, decisions were made by consensus and most often by unanimity. The group cohesion and solidarity was also expressed when members came together to support one another during financial deadlines.

Establishment of the Resident-Technician

The choice of the architect was made simply. Planning and design was limited to Mr. Guislain, who had wanted to engage himself in the project with his family, and to another architect who had been contacted by some members of the group and was used as an external consultant. There was no public tender. Mr. Guislain's architectural practice focused on social housing projects that were simple, versatile, functional, and personal all at the same time. He had long valued common spaces of transition and meeting spaces in his previous work. He seemed, therefore, quite sensitive to the demands of the group. Moreover, since he was old friends with many members of the group, emotional elements unique to the history of the group's formation also played in his favor in the decision of the final choice for the architect.

Working as an architect for such a unique project, Mr. Guislain had a particularly privileged role even though he gave up part of his power. The demands of a group were often complex and ambiguous, and it was important for him to measure the degree of flexibility he could exercise over the planning and organization of the operation. His attitude was decisive in the final result.

Analysis and Outline of the Program

The first days of the group's work focused on the definition of life goals, particularly those that define the type of housing they wanted to create. Thus, the group's charter was written in a biblical language that symbolized the meaning of this realization. Its wording meant something important to the life of the group, namely, respect for individual expression:

> And one of us said that this house would be an independent project, given birth by ourselves without the help of the developer.
>
> Another said that the kids gathering around their parents was good, or at least no worse than another way, and should be retained.

The architect said that the architecture should not be a monument to his glory, but a rigorous realization of our ambition.

Another said that what we shall share tomorrow we do not know, but no barrier to sharing should today be dressed.

Another said that if someone has to leave, he shall not leave his home to the barbarians and the tribe will choose his successor.

Another said that we are tenants of this land and the right to use our apartments should not cost anyone more than it cost us.

Another said that our activities were going to scatter us at the four winds of the mountain and that the tribe needed a rallying point.

Another said that our meeting would not be mandatory except in the autumn for the selection of seeds to sow.

Another said that the doors of our common spaces should not be anything but a barrier to the wind, which would put disorder in women's hair.

Another said that each one should be responsible for the group he would invite in our walls.

Another said that we were not neutral and that we will not host any defenders of the established disorder.

Another said that children should have rights and so do their parents, and both should be reconciled.

Another said freedom to be themselves is for everyone and more so rather than less.

Another said that children are ready to become men and that the doors of the council should be open to them early.

Another said that beauty was good, but that liveliness was better and we should give it the first place.[2]

---

2. Ibid.

Having said all that, and having found in the words of others something that they could identify with, they decided to write them and accept them as a sort of rule or common law. And, as one member recalled at the whim of her memory, the last one said: "We are not yet born; we are not yet in the world. There is no world yet. Things are not made yet. The rationale is not yet found."

One of the fundamental dimensions of the project was to imagine a new habitat that would articulate social and private life without confounding them. The architecture would favor, at the same time, both the privacy of family life and the meeting of people in group activities inside or outside for any action of larger dimension. This means the development of a community spirit with an activist militancy that, at the same time, learns to live together in a group.

The clustered housing design offered a high availability of places, people, and opportunities and constituted a social core open to the outside world. Parallel to the definition of the overall project, each family independently prepared an approach to its family space needs. To specify each family's options, the architect visited each one to learn about their lifestyle and formalize criteria.

Visual Presentation and Development of the Project

At the Jardies, some families were determined to play up the domestic side of their homes, but did not want the exterior façade to reflect their interior way of life. Others did not attach importance to this, and easily imagined a cube containing a certain amount of common spaces. The architectural demand was very diverse at the beginning. Through the process established by the architect, the group progressively became aware of their latent housing desires.

Initially, the architect did not act as a technician. At the rate of one meeting per week for two months, the expression of each family was as free as possible in defining the overall program objectives. When agreement was reached on this point, the architect made a first proposal in the form of a rough clay model. This model, which acted as an overall site plan, showed the main volumes distribution and the location of the building in the land. The group studied the proposal and expressed three criticisms:

1. The garden was too divided into individual plots, and the group preferred to enjoy one common garden for all.

2. The common rooms were located too far from the site's borders. It appeared preferable to have them closer to the house's main entrance.

3. The house entrance was through a common passage for cars and pedestrians, and it seemed more practical to have two separate entrances.

After the fundamental elements of the overall program were well established, each family expressed by writing and graphics their personal apartment layout and their point of view on the common areas. Everyone got a copy of each other's draft. The architect then visited each family and talked about the precise details of their program.

At the same time, the group defined the common space's size, layout, and use. Based on these individual and group expressions, the architect built a new cardboard model of the project in which he proposed a basic structuring grid of 13.78 feet. Compared to the circle or hexagon building plans that were briefly considered, a post-and-beam system in a square shape seemed to be the best possible option for creating a flexible structure. The architect affirmed the principle of the modular volumes and of a common point between the different apartments.

In the initial model, the architect had not defined the distribution of spaces for each family. It was only after the unanimous agreement of the group on the overall volumes that each family took the pencil and specified in the model the space they wished to occupy.

It should be noted that, at this stage, the architect decided that individual choice was to be made without consultation with the group so that everyone could choose or plan their space separately. In relation to the expressed family wishes, the architect adequately provided a modular arrangement so that everyone found their place in the overall volume. This procedure proved especially important since each family got to choose a different area. It was clearly understood by all that the square foot price would be the same for everyone regardless of location.

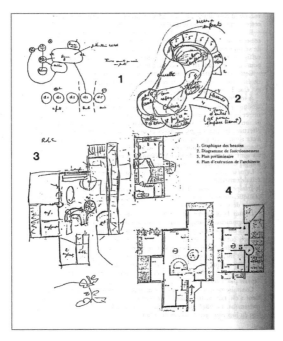

1. *Program Diagram*
2. *Function Diagram*
3. *Preliminary Layout*
4. *Final Plan*

SKETCHES AND DRAWINGS
BY THE ARCHITECT
CLAUDE GUISLAIN

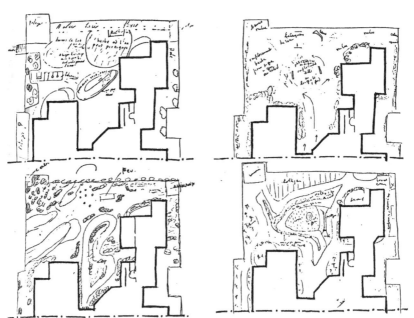

Conceptual designs for a common garden drawn by four families.

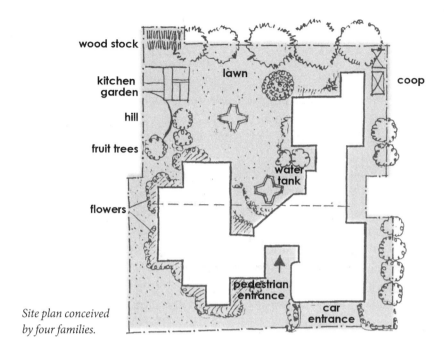

wood stock

kitchen
garden

hill

fruit trees

flowers

lawn

coop

water
tank

pedestrian
entrance

car
entrance

*Site plan conceived
by four families.*

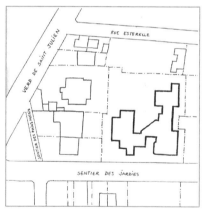

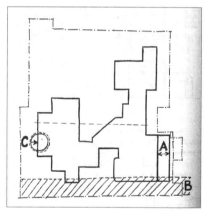

At this stage, each family was assigned a number of square modules of a prefabricated system. In this localized and concretized volume, each began to draw one or more sketches of their apartment plan. The architect then made preliminary plans for each apartment and common spaces. The plans concerning the common areas as well as each apartment were then submitted back to the group for approval. Once the last changes were made and the final plans finally drawn, a public tender to construction companies was realized.

The design method with its subsequent stages proved that this approach required a permanent back-and-forth process between each person, the group, and the technician. This was the beginning of the practical implementation of the projected lifestyle: namely, the respect for individual autonomy in constant articulation with the group.

In accordance with the first preliminary model showing the overall volumes and the steps previously described, the final draft lead to a total of ten apartments, ranging in size from 430 square feet to 1,722 square feet, and one studio at 172 square feet. The total area of apartments was 11,840 square feet with 1,615 square feet for the common areas. The complex consisted of two main buildings of uneven appearance that were interconnected by a system of walkways and winding alleyways. The final architectural style offered a variety of volumes whose total height did not exceed three stories. Contrary to what happens in luxury homes, the major investment occurred in the architectural style and not in the surfacing materials.

Design Evolution

Conceived in 1966–67 and started in March 1972, construction of the Jardies was completed in 1975. It took seven months to get the building permit, which was denied three times for regulatory reasons. Some of the issues that the original design grappled with included:

1. The proposed seven-foot high fence with a slab to protect the cars was prohibited because a recess of ten feet was mandatory.

2. While a thirteen-foot-wide area in front of the lot was required by law for a plan of small housing clusters with gardens, the irregular garden shape proposed was illegal because it spread beyond thirteen feet.

3. An individual house façade with a ground floor window was more difficult to explain and get approved by the authorities than a thirty-nine-foot high gable. (Behind this was a kind of bureaucratic inertia, which masked the mistrust of institutions who wished to protect themselves.)

Financial Framework

Each member of the group helped finance 20 percent of the project in the form of personal bridge loans and borrowing. Two banks granted the bridge loans and, having lent to the majority of the members, played a coordinating role, taking over the payment of the building contractors throughout the duration of the project. The loan was made for over a fifteen-year period, and the majority of the participants borrowed 80 percent of the necessary funds. The cost of construction amounted to 3,300 francs (740 USD) per square meter in 1975, including the collective spaces. Comparatively, the cost per square meter was reasonable in relation to the prices practiced at that time in Meudon (4,500 to 6,500 francs or close to 1,400 USD). It only shows that this group built at close to half the ongoing prices.

Type of Management

For all the purchases made during the construction period, each rider was to be signed by nine members to be honored. All members felt involved and responsible. During the operation, no individual member wanted a representative, whether from within or outside the group.

As a construction association, the group adopted a principle of solidarity in case one of its members failed on a loan at the bank. Having not yet drafted the regulation of co-ownership, members oriented themselves toward a cooperative syndicate. If one of them wanted to sell, the group prohibited speculation. It would have a right of preemption and would exert the possibility to decline if the buyer does not suit them. Since everyone was saving 30 to 40 percent on construction costs compared to the current prices, it would have been tempting to sell at market price.

Responsibilities and management tasks were shared between the families. The rotation of responsibilities was done according to the expenses amount every year or every two years. Group meetings took place in the beginning of every other week, and its presidency rotated. Children's participation was possible when they wished or when they were interested in the topic discussed. Youth aged at eighteen had the right to vote.

Neighborly relations, difficult at first, were gradually normalized. Indeed, the inhabitants of the opposite building were afraid of the noise that could result in the common space and had launched a petition against the Jardies project. The conflict eased with better understanding and mutual knowledge through several parties, such as the laying of the foundation stone, inauguration, and open house, and joint action, such as the development of a common street between the houses. Meeting rooms were also used several times a week by various associations from Meudon, and this caused no trouble.

Learning about group life was progressive, and the construction phase helped develop a strong positive step in this process. Unlike other experiments, the Jardies project did not end with the building construction. Some people began to dream about space transformation, and it was satisfying to not have generated a finished product, but a shared building flexible enough to be transformed over time with the people who lived there.

Project Evolution: Update and Lesson Learned

The Jardies is a group of people who initiated a new way to house themselves and, in so doing, have influenced multiple groups in France and Europe for the last forty years.

Meudon Bellevue, where the project was built, had always been a middle-to-upper class area belonging to a social and cultural elite that did not want to change the scale of their secluded, expensive neighborhood.

Over the years, new and somewhat more luxurious houses replaced the older, more rundown ones. No high-rise buildings exist in the area until one gets down next to the Seine River in lower Meudon, where the working-class families lived some thirty years ago. More luxurious high-rise developments have since replaced the older buildings.

Except for a couple of families that moved away from the project as time passed, the original families who have been living in Jardies for the past thirty-five years have experienced the project as a success. Today, in 2014, it looks more like an old age home because the original kids have grown up and become professionals. They have moved away and now have their own families in Paris's periphery, some even repeating their parents' experience.

The process that this group undertook led them further than any could have imagined at the outset. Indeed, the cohesion of the group (already homogeneous at the beginning) took place in the shared pursuit of a common project, and had its foundations in the trust each member had toward each other. This trust has since been woven in time: the Jardies project shows how construction technology alone is not sufficient to build a mode of living. It shows that it takes many years for a project to mature because one's relationship to space has a direct relationship to a respect of time.

This type of project focusing on the development of community life leads one to reflect on the group's role in the success of the operation. The group size was and is crucial. It should remain at around ten to fifteen families so as to retain a maximum flexibility and to preserve the group from difficulties associated with a larger, more cumbersome structure. Cultural homogeneity was also a key point in the life of this group. Regardless of the operation cost, it was critical that the motivations be common so that once the construction was completed, everyday life would not reserve any surprises. At the Jardies, the ideological level was still subject to debate, but daily practice was satisfactory and in permanent dynamism. Thus, if one wanted to talk about self-management in this project, it would be considered a learning process.

The project's concept of ownership, which did put off some of the group in the beginning, exists in a collective form as a suitable tool to create a different lifestyle. From a financial viewpoint, such self-promotion

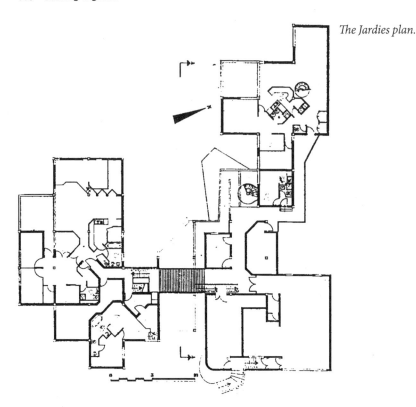

The Jardies plan.

brings some significant savings, particularly in relation to market prices. It requires that the future inhabitants be at the project initiation and lead through the legal, administrative, and financial maze, which is an occasion for real learning. This process continues and is never finished.

The relationship between the inhabitants and the architect was unique because the architect, Mr. Guislain, was also an inhabitant, an integral part of the project. This allowed him to have a better closeness and understanding of the group. Even though his fees were unrelated to the effective time spent, this aspect did directly relate to his dual status as a technician and inhabitant. The care he brought to the individuality of each family in the development of the apartments permitted a great variety of interior spaces, which allowed for the expression of the different levels of autonomy of each family. While this approach, which focuses on the emergence of differences, seems contradictory to the overall appearance of general homogeneity of the group, the finished product

The Jardies today.
PHOTOS BY
JEAN CLAUDE KATAN

demonstrates a remarkable effort on the architect's part to diversify the façades.

By putting at their disposal a broader range of tools and ideas, the architect might have encouraged each member of the group to go beyond the described limits, defining an individual expression for each apartment to correspond with each family's life, while taking into account the general constraints of the whole. The modular structure used here was flexible enough to offer various opportunities of space use for the intense life of the house to be expressed outside as well. The French authorities seemed very interested with this new approach in the housing field, but only at the level of discourse in the beginning. However, the Jardies experience was a positive demonstration. It proved that new alternatives could go from the discourse to new realizations. Since then, many groups have privately worked full time with their architects to complete similar projects.

Project Impact: Eco-Managed Habitats and the Cohousing Movement

The Jardies project has influenced countless numbers of similar participative projects in France and throughout Europe. The first six groups of self-planned and self-managed housing clusters, along with a team of architectural teachers from the University of Nantes, first met in Nantes in 1977 under the aegis of the French Ministry of Housing. They organized themselves under the 1901 nonprofit law, which allows two or more people to create a nonprofit association, so as to stimulate the idea and make possible the promotion of this type of habitat for social rental groups. They wrote a charter and formalized their movement as the "movement for self-managed group housing." The movement was quite active for more than ten years. They organized seven national conferences and published a periodical review called *Inhabitants*, and a book had been projected on the subject.

In the 1980s and 1990s, a group of professional advisers from the movement worked with French municipalities interested in the movement's objectives. As a result, they generated several operations involving future renters, which included more than ten projects started and built around Paris and others in several regions of France.

Although the movement slowed in the 1990s in France, it began to flourish in other European countries. Finland, Norway, and Sweden have an extensive cooperative movement involving all types of housing cooperatives. The movement has also spread to Switzerland, Germany, Austria, and, particularly, Belgium, where more than two dozen projects have sprung up in the past ten years.

In the Netherlands, "centraal wonen" communities have involved clusters of four to eight households usually sharing a common public space, kitchen, and dining area. At a larger scale, during the past ten years, a Dutch architect offered a solution for a housing project of 150 units in Zevenaar in the middle of a park with a small lake. With the blessing of the housing authority, he offered to design for each family their own apartment space at the equivalent cost of three months' rent. All tenants participated actively to make their space personal, and the project has been a success.

Eco-grouped habitats are housing projects conceived and managed by their inhabitants and are known today as Eco-Managed Habitats so as to take into account the actual factors of sustainability in the environment as well as in the social fields. Through self-management and community empowerment, housing clusters have become more convivial, more economical, and more ecological.

The Eco-Managed Habitat movement has recently spread widely in Denmark, where the same spirit of co-op housing has sprung and developed along with "production communes" that unite both housing and industrial programs in the same community.

In 2009, the French Eco Habitat Group (Éco Habitat Groupé), a continuation of the Movement for Self-Managed Group Housing (Mouvement pour l'Habitat Groupé Autogéré, or MHGA), adopted a charter to develop and reconcile the following orientations:

- Allow inhabitants to control the conception or the renovation of their habitat.

- Keep looking for convivial forms of habitat combining private and community spaces.

- Ensure solidarity in the social approach to urbanism and habitat. This necessitates the possibility of social mix with different

generations and different cultures. It also necessitates an opening
to the neighborhoods and the community at large.

- Build or renovate groups of ecological habitats, leading to save on
  fossil fuel through the limitations of space and energy consumption and help stop the scattering of housing projects. It should
  become an imperative of the twenty-first century.[3]

To put into practice these four objectives, the organizers set up a program with statutes to help groups at the national level through existing
local associations.

The Jardies project influenced other cooperative and collaborative housing movements as well, including the cohousing movement.
Cohousing is a type of collaborative housing in which residents actively
participate in the design and operation of their own neighborhoods and
are consciously committed to living as a community. The modern theory of cohousing originated in Denmark in the 1970s among groups
of families in semirural areas that were dissatisfied with existing housing and communities that they felt did not meet their needs. Its design
involves a clustering of dwellings near a common building, which frees
up more land for agriculture, ponds, and park-like or wild areas than
would a normal subdivision with a comparable population. The physical design encourages both social contact and individual space. Private
homes contain all the features of conventional homes, but residents also
have access to extensive common facilities, such as open space, court-
yards, a playground, and a common house.

Like in the Jardies project in Meudon, Eco-Managed Habitat and
cohousing residents generally aspire to improve the world, one neighborhood at a time.

---

3. *Eco Habitat Group Charter* (Paris: Eco Habitat Group, 2009).

Organization for Homeless People:
The Destechados, Pereira, Colombia

Introduction

The following case study on grassroots and assisted self-help planning and construction in Pereira, Colombia is included on account of its unusual qualities. The so-called informal sector in Colombia has traditionally accounted for most of its low-cost housing. This case study demonstrates the independence of a cooperative organization through a community self-help movement assisted by those with technical know-how. The success of the self-help housing movement has always depended on the outcome of individual schemes being undertaken, their degree of integration in society, and the eventual support provided by the successive governments.

This case study takes place in Pereira in 1981–82, where a motivated and organized group called the Destechados (Homeless) got together spontaneously, and independently set about to create and develop their community in an innovative and integrated way, providing an environment for their own needs.

Location of the city and municipality of Pereira in the Risaralda Department, Colombia.

MAP ADAPTA-
TION BY ISABEL
AGUIRRE

Problem Identification

Pereira is the capital of the Risaralda Department, or region, in west-central Colombia. The Destechados project is situated on the outskirts of Pereira in the township of Dosquebradas. Pereira had grown into a medium-sized town in the 1950s at a time when an armed conflict known as La Violencia (the Violence) was taking place between the Liberal and Conservative political parties of Colombia. During the conflict, Pereira was relatively calm and, as a result, attracted a large number of people fleeing from the countryside violence.

Pereira has become one of the major centers for Colombian coffee. The procedure for coffee production and harvesting has been modernized in the region to the point that hundreds of smallholders have been reduced to working as casual laborers. These workers live on the town's outskirts, including Dosquebradas.

An agricultural crisis and expansion of large plantations aggravated the rural exodus. The growth of large coffee plantations created a rise in the price of urban land, which raised the cost of construction. The working-class population solved this problem by illegally taking over areas on the edge of towns in an organized, spontaneous manner. Furthermore, politicians often provide them with subserviced land in exchange for votes—an illegal practice that is often deliberately overlooked by town administrations. In this way, huge areas of towns ended up having no basic infrastructure.

In addition, the cost of rental accommodation in the towns is very high, with some families, I was told, paying a third of their income in rent. This situation created a spurt of small home-building cooperatives on different sorts of land. In the middle 1980s, there were between twenty and thirty cooperatives of this kind on the outskirts of Pereira. The organization calling itself Destechados was one of the biggest, with three thousand members in 1982. In the new areas on the outskirts of town, politicians came at election times promising public services to get votes, but the people never got the services. The only way the people had of getting out of their predicament was to organize themselves and take control of their own community development.

Raising Awareness

On December 30, 1978, seventy-five people from a poor neighborhood of Pereira met to discuss their problems. Before this, twenty-five of them had unsuccessfully asked the City of Pereira to help them find land on which to build their homes. Rather than letting their disappointment get the better of them, they decided to create a legal organization to help resolve their housing problems in a self-help community spirit. Inspired by the goal of self-management, they establish three essential principles: unified resources, effort, and know-how.

By April 1979, 240 families had organized themselves and bought their first piece of land for building in Dosquebradas on the outskirts of Pereira. By June 1979, a second adjacent piece of land was bought. Before the end of the year, the organization boasted 1,500 members and had bought a third piece of land, bringing the total land area owned to approximately 72 acres. The rapid increase in membership had provoked an increase in the number of projects, demonstrating the success of the organization. At the same time, the group had to deal with the problems associated with construction: namely, creating a technical administration to organize training sessions and help teams working on construction to resolve financial problems to reduce building costs.

The building stages advanced with equal rapidity:

- Plan I started in June 1979, and the construction of a bridge started in January 1980.

- Plan II started in July 1980 at the same time as the first stage of Plan III.

- Plan III was composed of five zones, and a new zone was begun every three months.

The organization process for the construction of the first houses remained practically the same throughout the development of the group.

Organization of Work Teams

Right from the start, it was clear to the organizers that it was not enough to acquire land for people to build their own individual homes. It was also important to create a community. For this reason, it was necessary to think about how to get members to work together. By working together, they could save on the costs of building materials and tools and be empowered to make their own production centers.

The collective work was organized as follows: members were divided into teams in which two or three members had received prior training. The individuals with prior training provided the leadership and assisted and guided the team in the work at hand.

As this collective work was taking place, it became clear that the increased demand for accommodation meant that construction would have to be sped up. This was done by creating the position of site manager who would work with a permanent team on the project during the week and prepare the work for the cooperative team workers on the weekends. The permanent team received a salary. Made up of seven men at the beginning of 1980, by 1983, this team had grown to twenty-seven members who were scattered throughout several work sites and badly coordinated.

The activity of the work teams comprised the whole range of construction, including the following sixteen specialty teams: digging trenches, laying foundations, masonry work, installing sanitary equipment, electricity work, installing water lines, flooring work, installing beams, pouring floors, carpentry work, installing casing, roofing work, plasterwork, concrete mixing, transportation, and site cleanup. The seventeenth team was responsible for the care of the children whose parents were working at the different sites.

All the committees had a representative in the management committee and at least four members on the general assembly. The committees' roles were clearly laid out:

- The health committee was in charge of medical consultations with doctors for two hours a day. It was also in charge of two full-time nurses and a small pharmacy, as well as first aid if there were workplace accidents. It organized preventive medical workshops and the training of first aid for association members. In addition, weekly visits by specialists, such as ophthalmologists, psychologists, dentists, and psychiatrists, were set up by the committee.

- The education committee organized technical training for all areas of construction through the National Apprenticeship Service (Servicio Nacional de Aprendizaje, or SENA). It was also responsible for advanced cultural programs for the team heads and for programs on basic information, general culture, training for team research in building, and the like. The education committee also provided information bulletins so that the evolution of the operation would be known throughout the organization. This included preparing and publishing press briefings for the public integration committee and setting up workshops on audiovisual resources.

- The finance committee oversaw all areas of activity in the operations, both administrative and technical, and covered all expenses of the organization. In addition, this committee was responsible for supervising the enrollment of new members with a proof of their tax status.

- The public integration committee linked up with other public groups. Being at the heart of the organization, it was able to ensure coordination with the team heads of the organization.

- Finally, the largest committee—the technical committee—shared the following tasks among its twelve members: ensuring proper communication between architects and engineers and relaying plans to the management committee and to members of the association; supervising the ordering of materials, distributing it to the respective worksites, and checking that the formwork construction will be completed within the correct timeframes; overseeing the operation of the worksites, planning the work of the teams during the week, and preparing the collective work on Sundays; supervising those responsible for tools, drains, etc., as well as the work done by the specialized teams; and, finally, in each zone, putting someone in charge of helping coordinate any sub-projects.

Relationship between Community and Technicians

Contact between the community and technicians only took place when community groups were organized for rudimentary training in manual and technical tasks related to the building project. The technical stages preceding the involvement of the inhabitants, such as architectural design and project planning, were worked on by the technicians independently.

Traditionally, houses in the region are built either with rammed-earth construction with roofing joists of bamboo or with nonsupporting walls made of bamboo lattice plastered with a mixture of earth and whitewash. Ceilings are high in order to keep the interior areas cool, and at least two sides of the house have verandas to protect the walls from the sun and to serve as an outside living area, which is furnished with chairs, hammocks, etc. The houses introduced by the Destechados are of the "one size fits all" style, typical of the lower-middle class in both the United States and Colombia.

The membership helped in the construction of the houses, which, in their eyes, belonged to the class above their own and were, therefore, more than adequate. They also attended classes in sociopolitical and technical training, but they did not participate in the overall physical planning process of the master plan or in the planning for their own personal homes, the very place where they would live. Education and training programs could have been improved by incorporating increased awareness of the housing concept to better serve the environment, climate, culture, and wishes of the families for whom the homes were intended.

Another alternative, which recommended the construction of a basic house module of 323 square feet that would allow for expansions to accommodate different family sizes, could have been the starting point for developing methods of participation that could have adjusted to the requirements of each family. Other alternatives that could have been drawn up carefully and explained using audiovisuals with models could have incited the participants' curiosity, encouraging them to make decisions about their proper housing plan and their neighborhood as a reflection of their community.

Analysis and Development of the Program

The rapid growth of the organization, high cost of land for construction, and necessity of increasing housing density required the development of multi- or two-family groupings within the cooperative. This necessity came into conflict with the wish of some members to have a dream home that would be quite spacious and at some distance from other homes.

Home Designs

At the beginning of the project, a single house design was chosen that did not allow for changes. The inhabitants had no input on the final design of these first units. Later, another solution was suggested, introducing a certain amount of architectural variety, but still without inhabitant input on the design of their homes.

The plan for four-story buildings was eliminated. In the central area (A4 on the plan) and in zones A5, A1, and A2, the houses were modified from the basic model. These were terraced two-story homes for singles families. A diagram of the extension phases and the various combinations of interior layouts can be seen below and on the following pages. The basic cell structure occupies half of the lot surface area. It is constructed on two levels, thus permitting a vertical extension once the intermediary floor is in place.

People whose homes were built in the first phase agreed to share accommodations with a family on each of the two floors. This gave each family 710 square feet of living space. The occupants of the second phase did not want to share their two-story houses, and, therefore, decided on semidetached single-story houses rather than the duplex model. They did not want to live in high buildings. On the other hand, a series of four-story

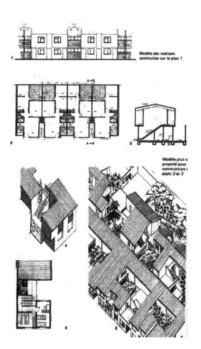

1. *Row houses in elevation.*

2. *Ground floor plan.*

3. *Section at 1/200 scale.*

4, 5, and 6. *New proposal to improve the basic original concept. Later, a horizontal extension is possible, permitting the addition of one or two 151 square foot rooms. In order to reduce pipes, water access points are coupled.*

IMAGES BY CARLOS HENAO

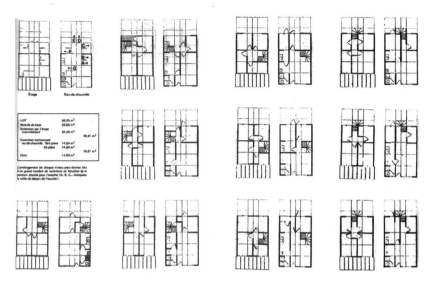

Different floor plans for individual families were drawn according to each family's needs. IMAGES BY CARLOS HENAO

towers were proposed to the occupants of the third phase. The building lot was a difficult one, and the architects wanted to introduce variation to the plan to create a new harmony. This plan was made in 1980, but was never built and has since been replaced by groups of two-story houses.

For the Destechados group members, three stages were necessary to be able to manage the housing project:

1. The totality of the construction had to be handled collectively.
2. It was necessary to participate in getting all the building components on-site.
3. The community as a whole had to be aware that the group had to work together not only on the issues related to housing but also on the many projects that affected their everyday community life.

To successfully work together, the group had to overcome the individualist tendencies that have so little to offer to the underprivileged. Collective work created solidarity among people, and it unified and involved them actively in this community project. The experience of community self-management had a special dimension because it integrated all of the political, economic, and social factors that had a bearing on the project.

Project Management

The construction process remained unchanged since the start of operations: reinforced concrete for the foundation footings and floors and concrete beams. These were made on-site, as were the staircases and the concrete blocks for the supporting walls. In addition, an on-site workshop produced wood beams for wall framing, corrugated roofing panels made of asbestos cement, and doors and windows made of galvanized metal. Some sanitary equipment was also made on-site, while other ceramic products were purchased from elsewhere.

The organization tried to produce most of its construction materials for the purpose of reducing costs and eliminating middlemen. For example, the official price of cement was 235 pesos (3.13 USD) for 110 pounds, while in some stores at the time it would have cost 450 pesos (6 USD).

The technical team was constantly involved in seeking ways to improve the speed of construction and creating further cost-cutting measures. New workshops were set up, including:

- A woodworking shop to produce beams, wall frames, and special casings. A furniture making shop was also organized.

- A metalwork shop to produce galvanized metal products, such as doors and rolling shutters with frames and grills made of cast iron.

- A workshop to produce a minimum of three thousand prefabricated concrete blocks per day. The majority of these were to be sold on the open market with the profit going to the cooperative: it cost 14 pesos (0.19 USD) to produce a block, which could be sold at 32 pesos (0.43 USD). One third of the production was to be used on-site.

- A workshop to produce beams and special U-shaped floor beams made of concrete and reinforced with the leftover metal from the metal caps produced for bottled drinks.

By the end of 1983, research was underway for producing concrete blocks reinforced with leftover ash from burning sugar cane, as well as making a mold for stackable blocks that could be mounted dry for the purpose of saving time and mortar.

Financial Resources

Starting with a capital investment of 980 pesos (13.05 USD) in December 1978, the organization invested more than 45 million pesos (600,000 USD) by 1982. The greater part of this sum was coming from the contribution of the cooperative members: the original sign-up contribution of each member was 6,000 pesos (80 USD) to help in land purchases. In addition, for 15 years, each member paid a monthly charge of 1,070 pesos (14.27 USD), of which 1,000 pesos (13.33 USD) was for construction costs and 70 pesos (0.93 USD) was for administrative costs.

Community fund-raising with various lotteries brought in 2 million pesos (26,666 USD). The only assistance from abroad came from the US, providing 4 million pesos (53,333 USD), which helped in the purchase of a cement block machine that cost 7 million pesos (93,333 USD). After a year, the 3 million pesos (40,000 USD) that had been borrowed had been paid back thanks to this well-functioning machine.

According to what I was told, the cost of the housing in the 1980s was approximately one quarter of the cost of housing on the open market. Seventy percent of the cost of manpower came from collective labor, and 30 percent was for paid employees. For a home varying in size from 710 to 904 square feet, the cost of construction was between 20,000 and 25,000 pesos (266 and 333 USD) per square foot, whereas the conventional cost was between 80,000 and 100,000 pesos (1,066 and 1,333 USD) per square foot in 1982.

Role of Training

The different aspects of building skills were combined with another kind of training: technical, sociocultural, political, and general education. This integration of practical and educational skills reflected the self-management ethos of the cooperative association.

The areas of training were as follows:

- Technical: thanks to the services of SENA, classes were given during the week in the fields of masonry, reading blueprints, electrical installation, foundations, and more.
- Sociocultural: this covered learning traditional technical skills from the region, artistic training with the purpose of integrating traditional art in the project (depending on the skills of the members), and training in various communication skills.
- Social: this covered the skills involved in organizing groups, including leadership training, the study of theoretical and practical problems, administrative organization, etc.

Assignment of Housing

In most cases (for Plan I, Plan II, and Plan III, and Zones 1, 2, and 3), the procedure used to assign completed and almost completed housing was through a lottery system and the following criteria with the teams that had worked on them:

- Those who had followed the rules of the organization, both financial (various regular monthly contributions) and technical and administrative (participation in collective labor).
- Those who had proved competent and reliable in collective work details. The leaders of work teams would recommend the best workers.
- Those who had shown particular ability in the activities outside of construction, such as educational, fund-raising, or other community activity.

After 1981, certain changes were proposed in order to encourage more families to participate in the program. Lots were distributed to groups of ten families. Each knew which one was theirs, and the houses were worked on in accordance with a lottery system. In their free time, each family was able to work on their own home. Monthly payments were 2,000 or 2,500 pesos (26.67 or 33.33 USD) rather than the 1,000 pesos

(13.33 USD) rate in order to allow the small group to defray increased costs. Another organizational alternative was the collective construction of units of 323 square feet on lots with sewage and water connections and distributing them to families so that they could, in time, fix up their own homes with technical assistance.

Sociocultural problems were due to the absence of social facilities. No social facilities were projected at the start of the town planning project because it was necessary to plan the largest possible number of homes to cater to the rapidly increasing membership. The management was aware of the problem and attempted to deal with it by planning some green areas within each project. A multiservice area to accommodate a range of activities was also planned with a health center, education center, meeting room, community hall with projection facilities, organizational offices, supermarket or cooperative store, and administrative center. Unfortunately, because of financial problems, it was unlikely that the organization would be able to invest the necessary funds for this project unless it received a loan or grant from an international foundation.

The members of the cooperative association and their families on the whole were young with several children (on average, four or five per family). For the nearly 1,700 homes that were planned, it was necessary to construct at least three or four day care centers in the different areas, as well as a primary school in the central communal area. These facilities were to be constructed in the free open space left in each of the zones.

As for the technical problems, the system of construction was literally quite heavy: concrete blocks were used for all nonsupporting interior walls, and reinforced concrete beams for the floors were extremely heavy and needed to be made lighter. Moreover, a lack of sufficient planning with regard to exterior roofing joints resulted in leaks. Research needed to be done on improving dry mounting concrete blocks, lightweight blocks, and roofing material to replace the concrete-asbestos corrugated roofing that was in use. In addition, a search for other kinds of prefabricated materials was needed. The desire of the organizers to mechanize the process and keep correcting all aspects of construction was admirable since the impact of this project and all others at the national level would be very significant.

Construction of prefabricated homes, 1982. Los Destechados, Camilo Torres.
Torres was a Colombian priest and revolutionary hero. This organization
was called The Roofless Camilo Torres. PHOTOS BY CARLOS HENAO

The association's program of 1,700 projected homes was to gather a
population of 10,200 people (at an average of 6 people per family), but
since all 3,000 members of the cooperative sought accommodation, it
brought the population to 18,000. An increase in population meant that
the project's impact would also be greater.

The seventy-two acres of Destechados property was quite undulating,
with two rivers that ran dry for two or three months of the year. These
riverbeds have embankments, but, at times, are a source of fresh air and
greenery. The town of Dosquebradas, however, had no sewage treatment
facility, no overall town plan, no regulations, and no oversight, and, as
a result, the two small rivers were polluted by the sewage that ran into
them. The organizers were conscious of the potential damage to the environment that would result if sewage continued to flow into the rivers,
along with the long-term damage to the inhabitants' health. In response
to this, a sewage treatment system was planned.

Logistical Difficulties

The rapid growth in the membership of the organization would not have been a major problem if it had been combined with a proportional increase in management. Building about 30 homes after 68 days of collective labor was encouraging. After 3.5 years, and with more than 3,000 members, the number of completed homes rose to 190. The last 20 homes were poorly done, however, and leaks in roofing and structural problems caused discontent among the occupants.

The source of the problems was essentially the poor coordination of the organization's management. For example, a site supervisor found it impossible to supervise twenty-seven men in multiple, scattered locations. On top of the difficulties in collective labor was the sheer weight of cumbersome, new materials (most had only used wood and straw construction materials in their previous campesino life) and financial concerns that often put a brake on construction goals.

The capital of the organization could not cover the high-interest payments while, at the same time, producing a greater number of prefabricated materials, researching new materials, increasing the size of workshops in order to increase production, and controlling working expenses such as materials, tools, and labor in the larger workplaces. All of these problems required continuous financial gymnastics on the part of the management. It was also necessary to overlook defective building practices. Unless a cheaper long-term loan was secured, it was likely that workmanship would continue to worsen in comparison with initial construction. If the association had been able to improve its logistics and coordination, it could have hoped that there would have been a reduction in the scale of the projects and a return to quality construction.

Lessons Learned

The Destechados experiment in cooperative home construction in Pereira has been instructive in many respects. The initial objectives of the organization were increasingly ignored as the membership increased. Financial systems and technical training could not work for three thousand families—this scale of operation required a more elaborate management structure.

Initially, the founders of the organization dreamed of a community made up of responsible citizens. To achieve this goal, they sacrificed short-term housing necessities for the political objective of a long-term participatory society.

Although it was important for families living in deprived communities to take responsibility and become more aware of the problems they faced, it must be recognized that the enormous pressures of everyday life for these people are difficult to reconcile with long-term ideals. If a family could not achieve their decent house, which was the reason why they originally signed up for the organization, then they would withdraw their membership in a context of open conflict.

New organizers later tried to resolve the urgent problems they faced with the 1,200 remaining members while keeping the initial ideals of the project in sight. This experience has been unique in Colombia and has served as a guide and an inspiration to the organization of official projects led by the Colombian National Housing Authority, the Instituto de Crédito Territorial (ICT).

Project Follow-Up:
Impact of the Project on the National Level

First of all, it is necessary to recognize that it is impossible for every public or private company to build homes intended for the lowest of income groups in Colombia. Given the state of the Colombian economy and given its government policies, the only way ordinary people could obtain reasonable housing at a reduced cost is through their own efforts and investments. The ICT recognized this, and, as a result, its directors in Pereira offered the Destechados group 4 million pesos (53,333 USD) at the end of 1981 to help with the construction of about 50 family homes.

At the national level, the regional ICT directors helped similar building organizations in more than ten towns, including Cali, Manizales, La Victoria, Barranquilla, and Bogotá. These new groups followed the example of the Pereira cooperative and also set up a national federation of cooperative homebuilding.

The year 1983 saw the official creation of a national housing federation with headquarters in Pereira. Three planning teams were created for it:

- A technical team made up of three to five professionals to identify the appropriate technologies for the region, its traditions, and its resources in order to help the technical committees in their different areas of concern—such as types of housing, plans, and technology—in accordance with the commitment made by the local cooperative associations.

- A legal team to help the federation draw up a national plan of urban reform, establish the criteria of the relationship between Destechados and the Colombian government, and build the means whereby there could be controls established over construction, land ownership, and finance markets.

- An education team to link all general education and training programs at the national level.

Four Projects from the Pacific Coast of Colombia and Tumaco

Introduction

My **work in** Colombia has mostly concentrated along its Pacific coast, from Panama to Ecuador, and particularly in Tumaco, Colombia's second major port city on the Pacific coast after Buenaventura.

My first trip to Colombia occurred in June 1980 when I helped organize a five-day seminar for the nongovernmental organization Environmental Development Action in the Third World (ENDA). The seminar's theme was on the problems of poverty and self-help. Due to a constant influx of rural poor moving toward the major cities of Colombia, and particularly around Bogotá, I discovered the difficult problems that the very poor and roofless migrants encountered while seeking safety in the outskirts of these cities. The migration was provoked by the long-existing internal war called La Violencia. People were being dispossessed from their land by the rapid increase of large capital investments in massive agricultural production. This, coupled with the government neglecting to provide even the most basic of services in the deprived areas, led to a massive exodus from the rural areas that surround Colombia's major cities in the 1970s. The following pictures depict the land invasion in the suburbs of Bogotá by those disposed from their rural communities and their forced removal by police that soon followed.

Photos pages 169–171: Birth of a squatter settlement in Bogotá, Colombia, through photo sequences taken in the 1970s by faculty members of the School of Architecture and Design, Los Andes University. Photos on this page show the first day land invasion and the beginning of the installation.

The temporary shelter installations.

The forced removal by police in the following two days.

Usually, the decision to move here or there was directly linked to the existence of a family member, friend, or anyone they knew who had some experience living in an urban area. This was followed by the problem of what to do to survive, for migrants knew full well that none of them would be able to find appropriate or useful employment in the city. Even when the family was able to generate some income, it was typically irregular, resulting in constant economic instability. When the product of the sale of their rural property permitted, it allowed survival for a few months at best or a few weeks of life in an illegal neighborhood at least. Most of the time, they joined humanitarian or religious organizations, pooled their energy and whatever resources they had, and, in the dead of the night, invaded unused tracks of land at a city's periphery. In a matter of hours, they would build light, structured shacks made of sticks of wood or bamboo dressed with rolls of tar paper and plastic sheets. These no-man's-lands instantly become "barrios piratas," or pirate neighborhoods, which were most often evacuated a few days later by a strong police force, especially when the owner of the land happened to be a politician or tied to one. Sometimes when the invasion coincided with a political election, the invaders would be able stay because it was in the best interest of the government to look the other way. In this case, the pirate neighborhood would keep growing and slowly consolidate itself to become a reality on the ground. The light structures would slowly be replaced with more solid materials as families struggling through the informal sector would find ways to earn enough money to buy one wooden wall made of regularly cut wide planks after the other and replace the tent-like tarpaper space with a real room covered with a tin roof. After a few years, the wood would often be replaced by bricks as soon as the family's economic circumstances allowed for it.

These aspects of private development, in general, occur after many long years, and are quite independent from the general community organization. They are linked with individual families' incomes while the problems of overall basic services are dependent on a solid community action. Faced with government inaction, the well-disciplined invaders unite and organize the steps toward getting basic services and consolidating their illegal settlement. The legalization process of their invasion is but one step in the long march toward the progressive development of the new community, along with the creation of small self-help enterprises through the informal economy. The most active members become organizers, training others to become leaders who seek solutions to the multiple problems encountered in the community. For practical reasons, most of the new rural migrants joined Central Nacional Provivienda (National Housing Center, or CENAPROV), a national housing organization that helps the dispossessed fight for their rights.

Chocó and Quibdó, Colombia.

MAP ADAPTATION BY ISABEL AGUIRRE

New School in the Chocó Department

History of the Pacific Region of Colombia: The Chocó Department

The Pacific region of Colombia, and especially the Chocó Department, has often been called the African Heart of Colombia.[1] The African presence in Colombia dates back to the colonial period when the Spanish began importing African slaves to Colombia as early as the first decade of the sixteenth century. Before long, Africans were steadily replacing the rapidly declining native Colombian population. African slave labor was essential in all regions of the country up until recently. African slaves were forced to work in gold mines and on sugarcane plantations, cattle ranches, and large haciendas. They were pioneers in the growing of sugarcane and in the extraction of alluvial gold deposits.

---

1. Luis Gilberto Murillo, "El Chocó: The African Heart of Colombia" (lecture, American Museum of Natural History, New York City, February 23, 2001).

Slavery was abolished in 1851, but even after emancipation, the life of the Afro-Colombian was very difficult. After 1851, the Colombian government promoted the ideology of *mestizaje*, or miscegenation. The gradual whitening of the African population was a scheme planned by the Colombian government to minimize or, if possible, eliminate any traces of African or indigenous descent among the Spanish in Colombia. In defense of their cultural traditions, many Africans and indigenous peoples went deep into the isolated jungles along the Pacific coast from Tumaco, at the border with Ecuador in the south, to the border with Panama in the north. They settled particularly in the Chocó Department in great numbers and, today, account for 90 percent of the inhabitants in the region.[2] Along with indigenous people, Afro-Colombians continue to be targets of armed drug traffickers who forcefully displace them in order to take over their lands to use for mining or wood exploitation or for sugarcane, coffee, or illicit drug plantations.[3]

Today, Colombia has the second largest population of African descent in all of Latin America, after Brazil.[4] The 2005 census reported that the Afro-Colombian population accounts for 10.5 percent of the national population, or about 4.3 million people.[5] However, because it is more advantageous to identify as white and not as black in Colombia, census data becomes problematic and a more accurate estimate may actually put the Afro-Colombian population at 26 percent, or about ten million people.[6]

The Chocó Department was created in 1945 and was the first administrative division in Colombia. In theory, Chocó, with its large population of African and black Colombians, gave them the possibility of building a territorial identity with some autonomous decision-making power. Unfortunately, powerful people in the national government, most likely for racial reasons, were determined to see the destruction of this new political-administrative unit.[7] In general, Chocó has received very little

---

2. Arlene B. Tickner, "Chapter 4: Government and Politics," in *Colombia: A Country Study*, ed. Rex A. Hudson (Washington, DC: Library of Congress Federal Research, 2010), 254.

3. Ibid., 255.

4. Murillo, "El Chocó."

5. David Bushnell and Rex A. Hudson, "Chapter 2: The Society and Its Environment," in Hudson, *Colombia: A Country Study*, 86.

6. "Afro-Colombian Factsheet," Association of Internally Displaced Afro-Colombians, accessed March 13, 2014, http://www.afrocolombians.com/pdfs/ACfactsheet.pdf.

7. Murillo, "El Chocó."

A Chocó village.

A Chocó village street. PHOTOS BY ROGER KATAN

attention from the national government, and is instead characterized by a constant pattern of displacement and natural resource exploitation, which continues to this day.[8] In the 1970s, there was a major influx of Afro-Colombians into the urban areas throughout Colombia because of an understanding that greater economic and social opportunities

8. Bushnell and Hudson, "Chapter 2," in Hudson, *Colombia: A Country Study,* 90.

could be found there for their children. This led to an even larger group of urban poor residing in the marginal areas of Colombia's cities, including Cali, Medellín, and Bogotá.

Today, most Afro-Colombians live in urban areas. Only around 25 percent, or over three million people, are based in rural areas compared to around 75 percent, or about nine million people, who live in urban zones.[9] Not until 1991, after a very strong popular struggle, did the new Colombian Constitution give Afro-Colombians the right to collective ownership of traditional Pacific coastal lands and protection for their own cultural development. Unfortunately, this important legal instrument has not been enough to fully address the social and economic needs of Afro-Colombians, of which many are still neglected and discriminated against by the government.[10]

Emergence of a New Rural School for Chocó Migrants

At the end of 1980, I joined a thirty-day investigative mission in the Chocó Department led by the Dutch Technical Cooperation. At the time, a climate of violence was beginning to touch every corner of the country. The population density in this rain forest area of the country was no more than two people per square mile, making it easy to imagine drug lords chasing poor, peaceful families from their land. When these people did not want to go peacefully, they were simply killed. At the same time, there was a steady migration of scattered families moving from their jungle isolation to the few existing small villages. As a result, the ten to fifty family villages of this region were suffering from constant population growth without basic infrastructure or any government presence. The local regional authorities were seeking financing for various socially oriented projects from the Dutch government, which had previously provided generous social involvement in the most depressed areas of the country. Our mission was to investigate the reasons for the displacement of people in the existing small villages in the three major subregions of the Chocó Department,

---

9. Murillo, "El Chocó."
10. Bushnell and Hudson, "Chapter 2," in Hudson, *Colombia: A Country Study*, 90.

Classroom in a school in the Chocó Department.

House near the school. PHOTOS BY ROGER KATAN

an area that stretches from the Pacific coast port of Buenaventura in the south up to the border with Panama in the north.

Six of us embarked on the mission in a small speedboat. Aside from the two Dutchmen, the agronomist mission chief and his companion sociologist, there was myself, a Colombian sociologist, a motorist-mechanic, and a much-needed guide who, at times, relieved the motorist during our long, intricate rides. Our guide told us the story of a governor from the Chocó who was proud to announce a few years back that he knew the region's jungle waterways so well that he did not need any guide during his visits. He had then insisted on going by himself with a guest, and had effectively gotten lost in the crisscrossing maze. Their motorboat was discovered weeks later, but they were never found—victims of the dense jungle.

It was the most no-frills mission of my entire professional career on three continents. As we moved from village to village, there were no hotels or restaurants, no showers or running water, and very little food after long days on the motorboat. Running in infinite twists between high sea and narrow streams under the densest rain forest mangroves and in the shade of an immensely impressive canopy of sky-high trees was very spectacular. We were lucky to have a good guide to lead us to the villages on time through those amazingly complex waterways. That memorable eight- to nine-hour, nonstop ride on the first day had us weaving through rough high seas into calmer wide rivers and into extremely dense mangrove passages. At times when the vegetation became too tangled, we had to go through some manmade canal. A half hour after a spectacular six o'clock sunset, our trip ended when, in total darkness, we reached the village of Nuqui, where we planned to start our investigation.

When we arrived in the village, there was no one to be seen. We discovered that after sunset, everyone retired to their home, and each house was lit by a feeble candlelight. Finally, after knocking on a few doors, we found the village leader, who then took us to the only local guest house. The two-room wooden house had red letters painted on its door that read: ¡*Aqui me quedo!* (literally, "here I stay," but which had a meaning of "nowhere else to go!" in this case). Inside, there were three bare bunk beds made of old planks and no mattresses. We asked for food, but there was none. After a long negotiation, we convinced the leader's wife to cook for us the only food that could be found: a two-pound pack of rice. She had to revive the last fading red ashes with some more wood, and one long hour later, six big hungry men crouched on the bare earth floor around a very large pot of smoking hot white rice. With no utensils to eat it with, we ate with one of our hands, and then changed hands to see if it tasted differently. We asked for salt or any kind of sauce, and when the pot was almost half empty, the woman came back with a large bottle of something I had always stayed away from: American ketchup. That rice never tasted so delicious! It was, at the same time, both meal and dessert with the sweetness of that ketchup.

We also wanted a shower or a plunge in the river to clean off, but the embankments of the large Atrato River were quite steep and the current too strong to take a chance in the deep dark night. I decided I would get up at dawn and take a fresh early morning swim. When I woke up, the sun was not up yet, but as I advanced slowly in the wide open space separating the houses from the river, I saw one and then two and then more women walking toward the river, each carrying a full chamber pot from the family's nighttime use. The women emptied their pots in the river, and as I quickly turned to walk back, totally appalled by this sight, I noticed two young village boys in the river water at belly height, who were soon joined by a few men, all bathing in a small cloud of white foam right in the middle of the floating feces. At the river's edge about an hour later, a couple of women were washing clothes amid songs and loud altercations. Life went on as usual in the village. The other thirty nights were spent stretching

Side street of Quibdó (the central major town that links the sea and all the rivers in the Choco). PHOTO BY ROGER KATAN

School kids in The Chocó. PHOTO BY ROGER KATAN

hammocks and mosquito nets between two trees after choosing with my travelling companions the least dangerous spot in the surrounding jungle. Fortunately, it rained enough for us to take some good showers.

After a few days' work, our team discovered that the reason why families were attracted to the larger villages nearby and leaving their isolated villages was that they all felt very poor and did not want their children to grow up and live a similar life to theirs. So they moved to the closest larger village because of the existence of an illusory dispensary and, at times, a one- or two-room schoolhouse—they just wanted their kids to have better health care and a basic education so that they could migrate to a city, get a job, and live better lives. We discovered that the dispensary rarely had any drugs and, at times, did not even have aspirin to fight rampant malaria. When, in rare occasions, there was a teacher in the poorly equipped school, the education was urban oriented and occidental in every respect. Nothing in the education system encouraged the local population to appreciate the beautiful richness and unique quality of their own environment, let alone possess any consciousness of their own African roots and culture.

I was struck by how little the Afro-Colombians I met knew about their African ancestry and culture. For example, one day during a door-to-door survey in a major village of the region, I encountered on the main wooden door of a house a beautiful, roughly painted image in bold red of the famous dancing mask of the Dogon tribe in Mali that represented the eternal man. I asked the owner if he could tell me the history behind this painting. He told me that the only thing he knew was that his father, his grandfather, his great grandfather, and so on had all refreshed the paint of the image and it had become a kind of family relic of an ancestry he did not know much about. I found this African trace to be very interesting.

Just as they had in the small villages, leaders in the major villages complained of their infinite poverty and total abandonment by every government agency. After hearing their self-pitying words and claims that they were the poorest of the poor on this planet, I decided to tell them about how some of their African brothers lived. One evening, I arranged to show the entire village—men, women, and children—some slides revealing how their far away brothers and sisters struggled to live in the dry, arid Sahel region. That night, everyone jammed into the small village church and sat wherever they could; all were excited and eager for a distraction they rarely enjoyed in the village. The first slides made them laugh at the African men's garb and at the painted faces of the women, but when I projected slides of naked kids with the very same swollen bellies of malnutrition as their own kids who were watching crowded in the first row, complete silence fell in the room. When they saw slides of the humble huts with very sparse trees in the middle of an immense desert of dry cracked land, they began to realize that there were regions in the world where it rains in a whole year the equivalent of what they receive in less than two weeks and how much richer they were compared to their African brothers and sisters.

After the show, we talked about the ecological richness of the Chocó region, where they only have to raise their hand to reach for a mango, a banana, or an avocado pear growing naturally around their villages, and how it was only up to them to clear land and learn to cultivate and produce. They complained that a few years back when they had cleared a big tract of land for a community rice field, a government officer had come to speak to their cooperative and convinced them that planting a coconut grove for exportation would bring more money. While they had earned some money from the coconuts for a few years, eventually, a pest had invaded the grove. When no one from the central government came to help them deal with the pest, they soon reached the point where they did not have enough money to buy their daily ration of rice. With this in mind, we talked about the benefits of self-help and the importance of diversifying their cultures and learning about pest control and other techniques for achieving successful harvests.

In my final recommendations to the Dutch Technical Cooperation in December 1980, I clearly underlined that this area should receive external help only with the condition that the Colombian government make the local educational programs more responsive to regional community cultures and to their specific environments. In parallel, these isolated regions should receive full technical assistance from the different government branches.

By the end of 1984, I was surprised to receive a call from the Colombian Ministry of National Education. The officer asked if I would be free and willing to help build the first experimental *Escuela Nueva*, or "New School." He went on to describe a new type of school as a pilot project on the Pacific coast in the heart of the Chocó Department. Puzzled, I asked the educational officer what this new school was all about. He went on to describe an educational system that would be more regionally integrated and responsive to the local culture: the very conclusion that I had written in the report to the Dutch Technical Cooperation four years earlier.

Assuming that I would be working for some international organization, the administrative officer told me that their tight budget would not include fees for my services. I explained that being a freelance professional, I usually gave my time free of charge to poor individuals or to low-income community groups, but never to governments or international organizations. However, because of the nature of the region and the community involved, I was ready in this particular case to help on the condition that my travel and basic maintenance costs were covered. My only condition was that they would hire at least one or two young Colombian architects to assist me in the process so that they would be able to reproduce this type of school in other villages of the region. They agreed to hire a young architect I had met during a series of lectures I gave at the University of Valle in Cali. Gustavo Fonseca was hired by the Ministry of Education to become my assistant in the planning and building of the first community self-help New School. Gustavo would be kept on the ministry's staff to continue organizing the self-help building of several other community schools and health care centers in the region.

Our first community meeting where the pilot project was to take place was held in the village of La Pampa, which is located at a short distance by motorboat from Guapi, a major city in the Chocó region. La Pampa had ninety families living in eighty self-built houses. Parents and children, mainly teenagers, gathered at the local church. With this first meeting, we reached the motivation needed to find the energy to work together and create a new era symbolized by the future New School education for parents and children.

Given the natural richness of the forest, it seemed natural that all construction in this region should be made with wood, which was what all the village houses were made of. With the participation of parents and children, a two-classroom school of unusually large dimensions with sanitary facilities was built after less than a month. The special dimensions of the classroom were to allow a maximum flexibility for the teachers' experimentations. The classrooms were built as an open flexible space where children of different ages, as well as parents, could meet at different times. Teacher training was to be a key element of the system. It was underlined with officials from the Ministry of Education at the start of the school planning process that the rural schoolteachers for parents and children were to be trained before coming to serve in this particular region.

We pursued community work with the clearing of a few acres of land around the New School to start an experimental farm with the help of the government's consultant-teachers. From the start, our team was joined by at least one representative from the different government agencies—agriculture and rural development, sanitation and public health, planning and housing improvement through self-help, forest and wood exploitation, and fishing and hunting. Each representative helped in his or her field during and beyond the months following the construction period.

Similar to the ones that were built later in the region, this first New School in La Pampa, finished in the first months of 1985, was the start of a new educational process for parents and children that would help develop both their immediate community and the exceptional Chocó region.

Update: The New School Movement

In 1989, the World Bank singled out the New School movement as one of the three primary school experiments in the world that had succeeded in making educational innovations and recommended that the "lessons of this experience be widely disseminated among policy-makers in developing countries."[11]

In 1999, the *UNESCO Courier* published an article by Asbel Lopez entitled "Colombia Exports Its 'New School' Blueprint." In it, Lopez writes:

> To make up for the failings of traditional rural schools, Colombia's Escuela Nueva movement offers flexible and efficient solutions which are being taken up in other countries. . . . The children, of different ages, work not at individual desks but around hexagonal tables. The teacher doesn't deliver a lecture or give orders. Each child goes and fetches a self-instructional guide and then settles down to study. The teacher doesn't demand silence in class because the school not only allows but also strongly encourages discussion and group-work. . . . Teachers have to learn to use new educational tools, which encourage both the pupils and the community to get involved. They also have to drop the teacher's traditional authoritarian role as a transmitter of knowledge. Each year teachers attend three one-week workshops, and visit a demonstration school to "learn by doing" and see the advantages of the new method with their own eyes. As well as using guides, the teacher and pupils organize "learning areas" where they collect information and objects related to class work and other aspects of daily life. For example, a natural science topic may involve having an area with sand where local plants and insects are kept. Another novelty of the New School movement is the formation of a school council that provides a practical introduction to civic and democratic life. It is made up of committees, which look after the school garden, health matters, the library, discipline, and sports, and encourages co-operation and leadership based on the interests and daily lives of the children.

---

11. Asbel Lopez, "Colombia Exports Its 'New School' Blueprint," *UNESCO Courier* 6 (June 1999): 15.

The La Niña School, for example, has a farming committee that organizes crop growing and animal breeding. "What we want is to feel proud of being country people and to learn how to use the land in a more productive way," said thirteen-year-old committee chairman David Cabal. Other principles of the New School movement are that teaching must be adapted to local conditions and lifestyles. Parents and other members of the community regularly take part in school activities, improving buildings and equipment, donating teaching materials, and helping teachers during lessons. In addition, they encourage the children to be interested in their own history and traditions. The guides suggest collecting proverbs, myths, legends and accounts of how people used to live. In this way, the school becomes a living source of knowledge about the community.[12]

In a 1997 report for the World Bank and the US Agency for International Development, Richard J. Kraft of the University of Colorado wrote: "The New School movement is perhaps the most successful educational reform that I've seen in more than 30 years' experience in almost 20 countries. . . . The boosting of teachers' skills has brought radical changes in the curriculum, in community development, in democratic behavior and in improved schooling."[13] The model has since been successfully used in Guatemala, where it was adopted in its entirety. Other countries, including Chile, Argentina, and, most recently, Nicaragua, have borrowed parts of it.

Lopez continues, writing:

The programme in Colombia has had its critics, however. Noel F. McGinn, Professor of Education at Harvard University, notes that in its early stages, the New School program "was closely monitored and nurtured by persons who were highly committed and highly talented." But as the program expanded, it "became the responsibility of people who had only received brief training [and] may not have been fully convinced about the concept."

---

12. Ibid., 14–15.
13. Ibid., 15.

... It is hard to say how many genuine New Schools there are in Colombia. Twenty years after they first appeared, many of them are "new" only in name. The Volvamos a la Gente (going back to the roots) Foundation, in Bogotá, reckons there are about 12,500 schools operating according to the original principles. ... The programme survives, despite the ups and downs of Colombian government funding, because of the tactics of the New School movement's organizers. Over the last couple of decades, every new education minister has been taken to see a "new" rural school and a traditional one.[14]

Building Technology Proposals in Bogotá

On my way back to Bogotá from the Chocó Department, in January 1984, I was asked by the French Technical Cooperation for an evaluation of the damage caused by the successive tidal waves and earthquake that had occurred on the Pacific coast in the Tumaco region. I remember receiving at the same time an urgent telex from Paris to be part of an important meeting to be arranged a few days later by the French Embassy in Bogotá at the Colombian Ministry of Housing. President Mitterrand had been elected a couple years earlier in France, and there was a great hope for change in the society, as well as a great socialist sweep in most ministries.

The French government expert, an engineer attached to the French Ministry of Construction, was then touring each of the South American capitals. He seemed to be staying barely twenty-four hours in Bogotá with the sole purpose to present, as was announced, some innovative techniques and very economical prefabricated systems in the housing construction field. Anxious and curious to know more about these new technologies, I attended the meeting at the Ministry of Housing with the ministry's chief architect, Gustavo Restrepo, with whom I had spoken with a few days earlier during a professional gathering. After the first fifteen minutes of presentation, I realized that the French envoy was trying to sell precast concrete technology for low- and middle-income housing. He was demonstrating how to quickly build cheaper and taller versions

---

14. Ibid., 16.

of the same high-rise housing projects that had been generating so many social problems in France. I could not understand why such technology was being exported while there were active discussions in France about demolishing many of the housing projects around Paris where this technology had already been used. I took advantage of an urgent call the French expert had to answer outside to discreetly tell Restrepo that his country had enough social problems and to not add to the suffering with the inhuman high-rise buildings that had cropped up around the capitals of the so-called civilized world. Once the French envoy finished his presentation, I dared to ask him in a joking tone if he would live in one of the projects he promoted.

Needless to say, after the Colombian refusal to buy this so-called miracle technology, the French ministry functionaries in Paris who dared take the initiative to invite me to that meeting were severely reprimanded. In answer to their expressed disappointment at my behavior, I simply told them that I was not a business representative, and I would gladly do away with French Technical Cooperation in the future if my role with them was to sell any enslaving technology at any price. Knowing the immense low-income housing needs in South America, France was simply trying to sell new building systems that happened to be quite innovative on the technical side, but disastrous on the social one.

While working for different United Nations offices in West Africa, I had seen the different international cooperation agencies at work. The French cooperation agency smacked of colonial times. After the following Tumaco consultation, I was relieved to find that I was never offered to work for the French Technical Cooperation again.

Tumaco Project in Colombia[15]

Tumaco Demographics

Tumaco is an island town in the Nariño Department linked with the Colombian mainland by a small bridge. The city is located at the southern tip of Colombia, close to the border with Ecuador. The Tumaco region

---

15. I have worked on the Tumaco project in its different phases over the past twenty-eight years, starting in 1982–83, then in 1995–98, and through proposals in 2005 and 2009–2011.

has roots that go back over two thousand years in the pre-Columbian era. From around 40,000 inhabitants in 1980, the city has steadily grown to reach close to an estimated 180,000 in 2010.[16] The population growth has been linked to a large wave of rural refugees fleeing from drug-related violence in Colombia's interior. As a result, there are as many illegal settlements as legal ones in the city, and urban growth remains completely uncontrolled—the population density of the island is approximately five hundred families per acre. With around 80 percent of Tumaco's urban perimeter at sea level, more than 40 percent of the city's structures are built on beaches or on stilts on the sea, and the majority of houses are dense, in disrepair, and vulnerable to flooding during high tides and other natural disasters. Due to the subsoil being essentially made up of clay and sand, the 1979 Tumaco earthquake caused the island to sink close to two feet. The economy of Tumaco is informal, and there is a great scarcity of jobs, with most being in microenterprises and tourism. Sixty percent of the total population earns less than minimum wage. The principal activity among residents is fishing.[17]

Identification of the Problems

After a severe tidal wave struck the island and the region in early 1983, I was part of a team of two professionals sent by the French Technical Cooperation to Tumaco in February of that same year. I had a two-month contract to plan a population transfer with the Colombian National Housing Authority, the Instituto de Crédito Territorial (ICT). It was two years after the December 1979 Tumaco earthquake and tsunami, which, in one night, erased several villages in the region and destroyed close to five thousand houses. I was to advise the Colombian Ministry of Housing in Bogotá to set up a self-help housing program on the mainland part of Tumaco. At the end of January 1983, a new tidal wave had left over seven hundred families homeless. Two hundred of the families were to be urgently housed in Tumaco, and the rest were to be scattered in the region's villages. Self-help cooperative building projects are, by definition, small

---

16. National Administrative Department of Statistics, *Boletín: Censo General 2005: Perfil Tumaco Nariño* (Bogotá: National Administrative Department of Statistics, 2010).

17. Information provided by Orlando Otero, surveyor at the Tumaco City Hall.

scale because as soon as the project includes more than fifty or one hundred families, the planning committee works essentially for, and rarely with, the inhabitants for reasons of efficiency, speed, and cost saving.

After Pereira's Destechados self-help experience, it was the first time that an official institution like the ICT took upon itself the planning and cooperative building of three hundred houses with the active participation of its inhabitants. The role of the ICT was to finance home building through loans to families and help them at the social and technical level in cooperative home construction. The National Apprenticeship Service (Servicio Nacional de Aprendizaje, or SENA), an administration offering technical training in carpentry, woodwork, plumbing, electricity, etc., offered its technicians to help in the project. The French Technical Cooperation helped in organizing the participation of the inhabitants at the beginning of the project. It sent a specialist to undertake a technical study of the local wood so as to use it as effectively as possible in the construction of homes. The French contribution played a key role in training project leadership.

The Ministry of Housing helped set up a town planning department in Tumaco since the town did not have one. It was made up of twenty individuals from a variety of organizations, such as unions, administration,

Tumaco Bay. PHOTO BY ORLANDO OTERO

commerce, and industry. Its first decision, made at the end of June 1983, was to prioritize the areas to be evacuated.

The Site

The 198-acre site, which is on the mainland opposite the main bridge to Tumaco Island, was originally intended for an oil refinery, and the site had a landfill for this purpose. Thanks to the donation of a semigovernmental organization called Ecopetrol, the ICT became the owner of the land for the purpose of building around 3,600 homes.

Raising Awareness

At first, the beneficiaries of the program were skeptical about constructing their houses with wood. We used photos and slides from Europe and the US to prove to them that wooden buildings can last for hundreds of years. They gradually came to accept the idea. Their fears were justified because the houses they inhabited were more rudimentary: wood rots after three to five years, so it needs continuous upkeep. The new project needed careful planning, taking into account not only the total number of families on the island but also the inevitable migration from nearby rural areas, which was already beginning.

My experience with the relocations of populations in Africa for the UN was useful here. In Mali in 1979, it appeared initially that the Sélingué hydroelectric dam would require the relocation of just twelve thousand people, but three years later, more than twenty thousand people had relocated to the new villages. The attraction of a new town or village is due to the fact that it seems to offer a new beginning for people, particularly in deprived areas, which is why it is always necessary to overestimate the initial forecast of a project.

One of my first activities was to analyze Tumaco's house typology in order to be able to design the future house plans with the displaced families in need of shelter. Most families were young, could not afford a big house, and needed some additional space as the family grew in time. For this purpose, and after visiting many of their homes, we studied together some solutions regarding a better organization and distribution

Precarious Tumaco waterfront shelters.

Tumaco street facing the bay. PHOTOS BY ROGER KATAN

of the spaces. We used sketches and a model made of a series of cubes representing rooms, and using these didactic simple models, I showed how the basic one- or two-room house could progressively grow with the family into a three-, four-, five-, six-, or even seven-room two-story house in time.

On the basis of the new adopted definitive plans, an expert carpenter in wood treatment and wood construction came from France to build a full-scale two-bedroom model home. In the building process, he trained one local engineer and a few technicians from the local housing authority, who, in turn, eventually did build some two hundred emergency wooden houses on the mainland through partial self-help in 1987. These houses were for the Tumaco families who had suffered most from the recent tidal wave and earthquake.

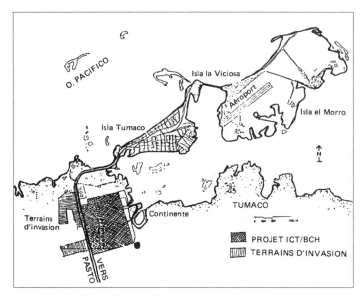

Tumaco Island as it relates to the continent. DRAWING BY ROGER KATAN

The other major problem facing these families was poverty. Their income was so low that they did not know what tomorrow would bring. For this reason, I suggested the creation of a self-managed neighborhood savings and loan cooperative. During the last three weeks of my mission, I trained a young economist appointed for a few months by the local housing authority to help and assist on a daily basis the organization of a microcredit system. This tool was to help the associates create small enterprises through microcredits that could offer them work possibilities and a better life in the future.

Brick Making in La Bocana

At about the same time as the Tumaco project, while commuting from Central America to my home base in Cali, I was offered the possibility of acquiring a piece of beach land on the Buenaventura estuary. Buenaventura is the first port of Colombia on the Pacific coast, and the land I was offered was located in the small coastal village of La Bocana at the tip of Buenaventura Bay, a two-hour drive from Cali. Very close to the Ecua-

Buenaventura.

MAP ADAPTATION
BY ISABEL AGUIRRE

dor border, this rain forest area had a great diversity of tall trees and a rainfall reaching a yearly average of nearly 20 feet (nearby Buenaventura is considered the rainiest city in the world, with approximately 22.12 feet of rain each year).[18] From Buenaventura's passengers wharf, one could reach La Bocana after a half-hour ride in one of the many small motor-boat services. Like a floating minibus system, this service links this major port to the numerous settlements spread along the estuary and the Pacific coastline region. The village of La Bocana was spread all along a generous beach of dark sand, which was often cluttered with large logs and dead branches from the tropical forest that would get cast up by the sea with each high tide. The wooden houses of the village were very modest.

Jesuits who had run a summer vacation camp for deprived kids of city slums previously owned the land. Their program had been trans-ferred a few years back to another region, and the natural tropical forest was beginning to take over the space they had cleared close to the beach. I was glad to inherit their local watchman, a man who by his looks and

---

18. Editors of *Discover* Magazine and Dean Christopher, *Discover's 20 Things You Didn't Know About Everything* (New York: HarperCollins, 2008), 317.

local knowledge could easily claim his Indian roots. His nickname was Chocoano—the nickname given to most Indians from the Chocó region of Colombia.

The land had 328 feet of beachfront and, within its two parallel borderlines, ran deep into the dense and luxurious tropical forest. The land near the sea was the only area that could be walked without the help of a machete. The deeper one walked into the property, carefully following the barefooted Chocoano moving along with his machete, the denser and more inextricable the rain forest became, with its mysterious sounds mixing with those of the hummingbirds darting through the forest. In small clearings here and there, when we were not disturbing some beautiful parrots or noble toucans, we could enjoy the surprising sight of tree-hugging orchids and bromeliads in a great variety of sizes and colors. There was also a great variety of snakes—the more multicolored one was, the more venomous it would be. After almost one-third of a mile into this fascinating jungle, which was still part of the same property, Chocoano helped me to discover a winding river that was about three to five feet wide and told me that at times of very high tides, this inlet allowed poachers in their canoes to cut timber and hunt animals to help boost their income.

From the beginning, I was set on building the house with materials found locally. The indigenous habitat was very modest and poor, and the locals built with the materials nature could give them. The average home was one or two large-sized rooms with rough plank walls, or sometimes rusted tin, and thatched roofs of palm leaves. Like the local people, I decided that the land was the place from which I would extract a good part of the wood needed for the three-story house structure I designed. I wanted the house to be high enough to catch the sea breezes.

On a small mound some 328 feet away from the beachfront is where I decided the house was going to stand. Here, I discovered, the soil was sandy, but it started to have a variety of clays that were found in the inland soil. I was intrigued by the diversity of the different colored clays for this meant the possibility of adobe construction. But why did no one seem to use adobe construction on the coast while it was used under a variety of different techniques just a few miles inland where the weather is almost the same? I was attracted to adobe building construction because it would cool the hot and humid days, and I imagined that the ground

Brick making in
La Bocana. PHOTO
BY ROGER KATAN

floor walls of the house could be built with adobe and that the second-
and third-story wood floors could be sustained with wooden posts. The
ground floor would house Chocoano and his family and have a service
and tool room. The second floor would have a very large veranda facing
the sea, a kitchen and dining room, a guest room, and a full bathroom.
The third floor would house, aside from a large water tank that would
collect the nightly rainfall from the roof, two bedrooms and a bathroom.
From there, we would be able to hear the loud village ladies who walked
daily along the beach with large pans filled with fish on their heads, selling the early morning catch.

In order for the molded adobe bricks to dry in this magic place of
endless rainy nights and sunny days, I had to first build a very large and
well-ventilated polyethylene-covered shed. There were at least two types
of clay in the land. The light grey clay resembling kaolin particularly
attracted me. There also happened to be an immense and deep kaolin
mine that crossed the land. We first tried to bake some small figures that
my wife, Julie, a potter, had sculpted with this white clay. Once dried, we
baked them the pre-Columbian way by burning wood around them for
a few hours. After a very satisfactory result, I brought a large bunch of
clay to a brick factory in Cali for an investigation at the mechanical level.
After firing, this clay became an attractive pink-to-orange professional
brick that was fit for construction.

Much later, we noticed that the molding of the natural clay left our
hands very smooth. After a scientific analysis, we discovered that this

type of kaolin had most of the oligoelements—the mineral elements necessary, in microscopic quantity, for the life of all living organisms—our body needed. So we started to take mud baths in the hole from where we extracted the clay. I knew that the mud bath treatment had been used for centuries in European spas as a way to relieve body fatigue and arthritis. Letting the clay dry in the sun, lying on the beach, and swimming in the sea were very healthy and deeply relaxing activities.

While we had easy access to building materials on the land, plain water and electricity remained a problem to be solved. The rains were so intense that one could find the phreatic level after barely digging twenty inches, but the water one could find was briny and unusable because of the closeness to the sea. Usually, the villagers had a few pans or a drum lying on the floor around their house to collect whatever rainwater ran off their roof. For the house I was building, I designed a suspended pool, similar to a basin made of wood, lined with a strong polyethylene sheet to receive the water from both sides of our large roof. It was supported by its own structure independent from the house and located under the roof on the third floor. It could contain over 141 cubic feet of rainwater, which it distributed by gravity to the kitchen and the two bathrooms. The nightly alimentation by the tropical rains insured that the pool was constantly full. Two solar panels on the roof connected to a heavy-duty truck battery supported our electricity needs for two to three hours every night.

Despite serious and repeated treatment efforts to protect the structure and all the wood of the house against invading insects and fungi, it became clear after a few years of house use that the fight was being won by the insisting pests. The rapidity with which "the best hardwoods" (according to the local population) had to be replaced because of the various types of termites that proliferate in the region was discouraging. There was much surface damage and internal deterioration of materials, and I discovered that with the major hardwood columns, the moist climate would attack any wood that came into contact with the sandy soil.

I had heard on previous missions that the Pacific coast populations repeatedly complained about wood construction, but I didn't believe them until I lived in a house there and experienced it for myself. Despite the attention I paid to molds, insects, rodents, and other small pests, I discovered that varieties of cockroaches, ants, and termites also thrive in this tropical region due to the high humidity. Sandy soils allow more moisture to be available, and consequently, termites are more prevalent and able to survive. When present in the wood, fungi will serve as another source of moisture and most probably aid in the regulation of humidity in the termite galleries. At certain times of the year, bats would also enter the house for warmth, shade, or moisture. But the big surprise came when Chocoano discovered a good-sized boa constrictor under the house, probably in search of prey or looking for mice. We kept it as a pet, just like most people do in this region, to get rid of mice. It was the type of boa that the village people would tie a leash around its neck, like a dog, to keep it from getting away and use to rid their houses of insects, rodents, frogs, birds, worms, or even stray toads.

I had been challenged by some friends to build bungalows for weekend or vacation rentals and also by local community leaders to find alternate ways for wood construction. In this special climate and underdeveloped and inaccessible region where cement and concrete blocks were prohibitive because of transportation costs, the solution was right at our doorstep. We had extended the clay mines and collected all the dead wood on the coast to use as a source of energy for firing the bricks. After the positive proof that our clay could create a good brick for construction, I decided to organize the land for making and firing our own bricks. Our beachfront was cluttered daily with all kinds of dead wood, from branches to entire logs, floating from the nearby dense forest. We had to build a shed for it to dry to be ready for use. By cleaning the beach daily, we gathered more material than needed to fire all the bricks we wanted.

Beach rentals were in great demand, and it encouraged me to think about building three or four bungalows on the part of the land closest to the beach, which would be separated from my house by trees and flowering shrubs. I decided to first start with the building of two structures, which would be all equipped with amenities and large enough to house a family of eight people each. They were designed to be built with the bricks made from the land. The roof was to be covered with homemade roman tiles while the interior floors would have special square tiles. The covered outdoor terrace floors were also to be baked from the same kaolin clay of the land. All the indoor furniture, such as the beds and the ground floor seating area, were to be natural adobe painted white while the structure and furniture of the second floor bedrooms were to be made of wood.

We started the brick production by first preparing the land. With hard-working Chocoano, along with another helper and a good chainsaw, we cleared and leveled some 360 square yards in the back of the house that was close to the existing clay pit. It was enough land to build the first of two large plastic covered sheds to house the mud brick production and drying process in this hot and humid climate. Another circular space close to this same area had to be cleaned and flattened to provide for the future brick-lined circular pit where the horse was to knead the clay.

The shed's structure was to be ample and with large overhangs. One of its two slopes was higher than the other to allow for good and constant ventilation for the raw bricks to dry. For economy, all the columns, trusses, and shoring were made of the straight, long, thin, and very hard wood trunks of the special chonta palm tree that was in profusion in our jungle. All of the wood was coated with used car oil to protect it from pests and to inhibit the shed occupancy of the numerous undesirable bats.

I hired a professional brick maker, Pablo, from the interior region around Cali where there was a long brick-making tradition. From the beginning, Pablo warned me that he was set in not kneading the clay with his feet in the old traditional way. He suggested that a horse would help best in this task, which was what most brick production centers of the interior used.

Getting the horse I bought in Buenaventura to travel to La Bocana was a serious problem. Most of the motorboats I could find for the trip were very small, and the motorists reluctant for the task. I finally found a motorist who dared take a chance. His wooden boat seemed sturdy enough and had just enough room for the length of the horse and both of us. We had to blindfold the horse and sweeten his food to have it advance slowly into place. The forty-minute ride seemed endless. I thought that we would never arrive at our destination when the restless horse started showing fear and impatience on two occasions. Fortunately, the sea was calm that day, and we made it safely, but not without intense fear. To get the horse to knead the clay, we had to prepare the special pit where the work was to be done. The area was to be circular, some twenty feet in diameter, floor lined with hard bricks, and surrounded at its edge by

Brick making in
La Bocana. PHOTO
BY ROGER KATAN

a row of standing bricks. To get those first hard bricks, we had to bake them in a country kiln.

In such isolation and starting as if the first brick ever was about to be made, we used the most economical and common method. Always under the shed's protection, we started with the raw clay, mixing it with 10 to 15 percent sand to reduce shrinkage. After being extracted from the clay pit, which maintained a constant level of water because of the continuous rains, the clay was first kneaded by foot (until we built the circular pit for the horse) and mixed with water to the desired consistency. It was then pressed by hand into molds made of fine hardwood and put to dry. As soon as we had three to four thousand dried mud bricks, we fired them in a country kiln. Our first country kilns were built by piling up the dried, raw mud bricks around two parallel tunnels and daubing the surface with mud to contain the heat. The tunnels were opened at both ends, where burning wood was shoved through from early afternoon until early morning. Since only raw bricks were used in the first firing, the ones from the outermost walls were the least burned and put to be baked again in the next firing. Later, when fired bricks were on hand to build a permanent kiln, they were used to construct the outer walls of the kiln.

Pablo the brick molder was key to the operation and head of the team. He would stand at the molding table for 12 to 14 hours a day and, with the help of his assistant, could make 3,500 to 4,000 bricks in a day. He would take a lump of clay, roll it in sand, and throw it with force into the sanded, wooden mold. The clay was pressed into the mold by hand, and the excess clay would be removed from the top with a flat stick that had been soaking in water. The excess clay was then returned to the rest of the clay to be reformed. Sand was always used to prevent the clay from sticking.

Pablo would walk up from the molding table, remove the filled mold, and take it to a drying area on a pallet, where it would be placed on a level bed of sand. He would then return the mold to the table and wet and sand it to create the next brick. The molded bricks were stacked in a herringbone pattern to dry in the air and sun during the day and always placed under the shed to protect them from the rainy nights. The molded bricks were first left to dry for two or three days, depending on the humidity level, and turned over to facilitate uniform drying and prevent warping. During this time, the assistant would also straighten the bricks and obtain a smooth surface by using tools called dressers. After four to six days of dry and hot weather, the bricks would be sufficiently hard to allow them to be stacked on end in a herringbone pattern with a finger's width between them to allow further drying. Usually, they were transported to a second shed to protect them from the rain or harsh sun before baking time. After two to three weeks, the bricks were ready to be burned.

Since the firing always started in the early afternoons and took the whole night, the kiln was protected from the regular tropical night rains under a protective structure of corrugated tin. When no fired bricks were available, the kiln was constructed entirely of green or raw bricks, which were stacked in such a way as to act as their own kiln, which are called country kilns. Dried wood collected from cleaning the beach was used for fuel. In the beginning, the fires were kept low for hours to finish the drying process. During this time, steam could be seen coming from the top of the kiln to get "the water smoke" (as Pablo called it) out. After those gases cleared, it was time to increase the intensity of the fires. If it was done too soon, the steam remaining in the bricks would cause them to explode. Intense fires were maintained in the fire tunnels around the clock for a whole night until temperatures of over 900 degrees Fahrenheit were reached.

Pablo's knowledge and experience dictated when the fire holes would be bricked over and when the heat would be allowed to slowly dissipate over the next few days. When the kiln was disassembled, the sorting process began. The bricks that were closest to the fire received a natu-

Brick house in La Bocana. PHOTO BY ROGER KATAN

ral wood ash glaze from the sand that would fall into the fires, became vaporized, and be deposited on the bricks. The best bricks were chosen for use on the exterior walls of the building. Bricks that became severely overburned and cracked or warped were occasionally used for outdoor terraces or garden paths.

The fired color of clay bricks is significantly influenced by the chemical and mineral content of the raw materials, the firing temperature, and the atmosphere in the kiln. For example, pink-colored bricks are the result of higher iron content while white or yellow bricks have higher lime content. Most bricks burn to various red hues, and if the temperature is increased, the color moves from dark red to purple and then to brown or grey at around 2,372 degrees Fahrenheit, but we never reached these temperatures with the wood we had.

Building the first wall of our home with our homemade bricks became a special event. It was a sort of religious moment that brought me back to my student days in Paris when, on several occasions, I traveled to the south of France to appreciate my studies by rediscovering eleventh- and twelfth-century Romanesque architecture. The architectural style of these churches and monasteries, built between 1000 and 1200, varied from region to region, as did their size, shape, and layout. Each building had clearly defined forms with very regular plans so that the overall appearance was one of simplicity when compared with the Gothic buildings that were to follow. Like Cistercian churches, their massive quality with thick walls, round arches, sturdy piers, groin vaults, large towers, and decorative arcading were devoid of statues or pictures. I spent hours sketching the elegant and down-to-earth proportions of these austere religious buildings, enjoying the playful decorative and sober way the monks who had built them celebrated their religious appreciation of life. Inspired by my student days, and like those monks who manufactured their own bricks one thousand years ago, I started laying our first home with bricks, using lime and sand as cement, over a foundation made of sturdy stones from a nearby rocky hill. Like those isolated monks, I started laying row after row. One course was composed of bricks laid lengthwise while the course above and below used bricks with their smaller ends showing, alternating in every row a long brick with an end out so that the wall would become not only extra sturdy but also pleasing to the eye. As a counterpoint, I laid some rows with a fish-bone style.

Just as it had felt natural and comfortable to build with adobe in the deserted region of West Africa a few years back, I felt that it was just as natural to build with baked adobe bricks under the South American tropical climate using wood from the jungle.

Teaching Brick Making in the Pacific Region

In 1988, at about the time I was in the construction process of the first two of four bungalows in La Bocana, the European Union (EU) was promoting small productive projects on the Colombian Pacific coast to help the people of this underdeveloped region economically. The project was called Pequeños Proyectos Productivos (PPP). During the bungalows' building process, the EU officer in charge of PPP, on a visit to the region, offered me the possibility to teach the brick-making technique to coastal populations. Every village had in great profusion the primary resources for this type of exploitation: clay and wood for firing it.

Transferring the brick-making technology to a small local enterprise to improve the village life of the La Bocana people was already on my agenda, but the possibility of spreading the know-how to the entire Pacific region was a proposal I welcomed. I accepted a mission to help boost the regional economy and, at the same time, improve the decrepit housing

Preparing the adobe kiln.

Preparing the adobe mix for brick making.
PHOTOS BY ROGER
KATAN

state of the various coastal settlements. Like in West Africa, people in this region were spending between one and two months each year repairing their home, constantly mending their leaking roofs and replacing columns and beams. Despite the generous continuous rains, the majority did not have enough water saved for their basic needs. Because of the rains, their cooking was done in hazardous conditions in a corner of the house, rarely with coal and often with smoky wood.

My official PPP mission took me by motorboat two hours by high sea away from Buenaventura and then almost one hour up the Cajambre River to the district town of Cajambre, where the EU project had its regional office. From there, I kept moving along the river ways from village to village, working with small groups of people and helping them

Village on the Cajam-bre River. PHOTO BY ROGER KATAN

organize small cooperatives for the production of building materials so as to improve their living conditions. The largest cooperative was called the Five Rivers Cooperative, uniting several hamlets at easy canoe distance from one another. When the associates did not have any formal education, which was often the case in the isolated villages, the project would first teach them basic reading and writing so that they could control the cooperative's accounts. For their home improvement, we taught them the necessary five steps to produce bricks for building their homes and villages with the available local clay and forest resources. They learned that the first step was mining the clay, the second step was kneading it, the third step was molding it into bricks, the fourth step was drying, and the fifth step was firing. After making enough raw bricks, they learned to dry them and fire them in a country kiln before building a permanent kiln in each of the largest villages or group of villages. To give an example, after the very first training lessons, the Five Rivers Cooperative had set up a complete installation, including a large shed construction for the drying and stocking, and after the first week, had produced over six thousand raw mud bricks. Once dried, these were baked in a temporary country kiln to be used for the building of the permanent kiln. We also helped the new co-op members increase their family water reserve by teaching them to build large plastic-lined wooden water tanks.

For the few people who had worked in the construction field in a city, the formation period was relatively easy. They knew that bricks are small and light enough to be picked up by the bricklayer for efficient handling and that the length of a brick is about twice its width, around eight or ten inches by four or five inches. When they had not lived in a city, we taught them that bricks are usually laid flat and that, as a result, the effective limit on the width of a brick set the width of the built walls.

At around the time I was building the third and fourth bungalows in La Bocana, I flew to New York City and Washington, DC for a joint World Bank–United Nations Development Programme mission interview for Africa. During my short stay in New York City, I renewed an old friendship with the engineer Vincent DeSimone, co-teacher at the Pratt Institute, who had helped me develop the Brooklyn Bridge and the other Gateway studies in the late 1960s. It was now some twenty years later, during the Reagan years. He had become a very successful engineer and could not be more encouraging, trying to convince me that I should come back to New York because traffic had worsened and that now was the time to find the money needed to build those Gateway proposals.[19] But how could I come back to restructure the impossible traffic of New York City when I was in my newfound jungle in the midst of an adventure reinventing the brick? Living anew in New York City was just unimaginable at that stage of my life.

Earthquake in Popayán

In 1991, I was sent by the EU Technical Unit for Latin America on a short project evaluation in Popayán to measure the reconstruction progress of the two hundred housing units donated by the people of Europe to the Colombian government.

On March 31, 1983, during Holy Week celebrations, an earthquake measuring 5.4 on the Richter scale hit Popayán and eleven other municipalities in the Cauca Department in Colombia. The effects of the quake were disastrous. In Popayán, 300 people were killed and about 1,500 injured while approximately 2,500 homes were completely destroyed and another 6,800 suffered major structural damage. More than 10,000 people

---

19. The Gateways proposals to New York City had been a reaction to the outraging misuse of land and the accumulation of unwanted traffic around bridges and tunnels entering into Manhattan.

were left homeless.[20] Also damaged were streets, rural roads, schools, health care facilities, shops, commercial and office buildings, rural infrastructure, and bridges.

At first, the damage made it difficult for the government to function. Public utilities needed major repairs, and the loss of electricity greatly complicated actions aimed at disaster relief. Massive operations were needed to provide emergency shelter and to build replacement housing.

The highly successful Popayán Earthquake Reconstruction Project in Colombia was financed by the World Bank and managed by the government of Colombia and the United Nations Development Programme. Three years later, in 1986, the EU sent an architect to rebuild some two hundred houses as part of a central neighborhood reconstruction effort. Immediately after the quake, and in order to take advantage of rebuilding benefits, many poor people living in shantytowns in the city's periphery saw an opportunity and invaded the most affected parts of the city center, already crowded with people living in shacks.

Close to two and a half years after the start of the project, on a one-week EU contract to evaluate this project's progress, I discovered, to my dismay, that only twenty luxurious houses had been completed during this time and had been given to families so poor that most of them could not afford a broom to keep it clean. Even the Colombian engineer in charge of construction expressed the fact that even he would have to work many years before he could afford such a house. The first thing the majority of these families did was to try and sell the house so that they could go back to living in their old shacks with enough money to live on for a while. A basic economic development program that would help boost these poor people's everyday lives while giving them a more modest shelter was much more important than a beautiful house. I could not understand why the EU technical services, knowing that the expert it had sent only had limited field experience, neglected this project and waited for such a long time to evaluate it.

My final report was a clear criticism of an EU administration that had left a project without guidance, leading to a waste of time and money. This was just after the period when Greece joined the EU, and the EU

20. Global Earthquake Model, Earthquake Consequences Database, "Popayan Colombia 1983," accessed March 14, 2014, http://gemecd.org/event/91.

had felt obligated to fill a quota by sending a young Greek architect to lead the project. My best memory of him was when he invited me for a drink at his house one evening and had played the guitar beautifully for me. He was filled with good intentions on his first difficult mission, but did not speak much Spanish and spent too much time adapting to the land and its language, as well as learning to navigate through the difficult administrative and technical maze. My report to the EU did not criticize the young inexperienced architect, but rather the EU administration that took the responsibility of sending him on this important mission and letting him work for so long without support or guidance.

My final report was not appreciated. It was received as a direct criticism of the chief officer in charge of dispatching missions in Latin America and of his follow-ups. My report questioned the reason why his staff, with their large budget, had delayed for so long in discovering the reasons for the unusual slowness of the Popayán project. They certainly were comfortable in their positions in the head office and did not seem to feel much responsibility as to the way they were managing EU tax money. The person in charge in the department was already under internal criticism, and given his tenured status, the length that he had been around, and his closeness to retirement, he could not be removed from his post.

Needless to say, after my undiplomatic report, I was barred from any official EU work. I would have to wait until 1995, close to five years later, for this "responsible" person to go into normal retirement before I could become involved in any significant mission with the EU again.

Relocating Poor Families in Tumaco

In 1991, Colombia's National System of Disaster Prevention and Response (SNPAD) requested and obtained help from the EU to displace a large number of families living in shacks on stilts built on the highly vulnerable Tumaco beaches. An internal socioeconomic survey had defined the extremely high-risk areas to be displaced and determined that 2,823 families lived illegally in the twelve neighborhoods or "barrios" facing the high seas. The Colombia–EU project's official name was the Reorientation of Tumaco Urban Growth.

In 1993, in Brussels, an agreement was made between the governments of Colombia and the EU in which the EU agreed to financially support the construction of homes and programs for social, educational, and economic development so that in four years' time, Tumaco's poorest living in illegal settlements along the beaches could be transferred inland to a safer area approximately two miles away from the island.

By the end of November 1995, the EU had named a Colombian–European codirected team. An agricultural economist and development specialist was contracted by the Colombian government and approved by the EU as the Colombian codirector for the project. In turn, I was contracted as the European codirector by the EU, and was approved by the Colombian government as an architect and community development specialist.

While the codirected team had been in place since November 1995, the first functioning funds arrived only in May 1996. The gathering of the project's technical logistics for this underdeveloped region of Colombia was difficult because of its isolation and lack of available basic services. In the 1990s, as well as today, it had very poor basic services, including erratic electricity because of defective power lines. When repaired, these power lines were often blown up by one of the guerrilla movements. This was the reason why every large or small business in town had a smelly and very noisy generator on the sidewalk. Telephone lines functioned at awkward and erratic hours when they did at all. The main water line ran from a mountain source quite a distance from the city. The villages or hamlets along the pipeline felt that they could naturally tap the water for their own use, most of the time using a machete, and patch up the hole afterwards with tape, rags, or anything they could find. This resulted in leaks, inexistent water pressure, and, more often than not, seriously polluted water in the city's supply.

I had now been in Tumaco for over two long years, and the first year of 1995–96 was entirely devoted to setting up an autonomous way for the project to function. Aside from assuring the establishment of proper water, telephone, and electric lines, we had to order the appropriate machinery for producing an average of two houses made of precast concrete components per day. At the end of the first year, we managed to be ready to start. We had built a model house with two bedrooms to be visited by everyone. The house was based on the same plans that had evolved

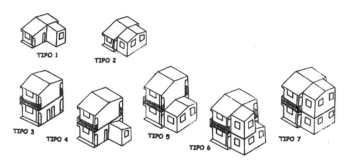

Diagrams showing the growth possibility from a simple one-bedroom house to a seven-bedroom one. FROM TUMACO PRESENTATION PREPARED BY ROGER KATAN

from a direct community consultation back when I first came to Tumaco in 1983, where the basic one-bedroom plan could grow into, at most, a seven-bedroom plan. These plans had been established after a study of the typology of the existing self-built houses and a series of extended community meetings. Fifteen years later, the same plans were reviewed and approved by almost the same community members. The only difference is that instead of wood construction, the community rightfully wanted the houses to be made of concrete. We also had to make sure that all the earthquake-resistant concrete foundations were equal in size from the start so as to allow any of the one- or two-bedroom houses to grow, in time, to become a five- six-, or seven-bedroom home without any risk. Since the basic family house was to grow and be extended in time through self-help, we had to make sure the family would be protected from any earthquake in the future.

The community leadership was composed of a series of local leaders elected from each of the neighborhoods to be displaced. They, in turn, would elect a board of directors every year during a general assembly. The elected presidents, vice presidents, and secretaries worked very closely with the two project directors, as well as with the engineers, in the organization of the community self-help aspect of the home building, such as in the installation of the windows and their frames, the bathrooms,

*Tumaco barrios before the
1997 demolition (before
the time of the transfer).*
PHOTOS BY ROGER KATAN

the staircases, the balconies, and other finishing details performed under the supervision of technicians.

We had to wait over three months to get one telephone line without ever being sure that it would work when we tried to use it, and had to constantly deal with electrical failures and a lack of running water. For these reasons, it had been necessary to open a small project antenna in Cali, the third largest city in the country and a one-hour flight away from Tumaco, to facilitate communications and administrative work—a strategy used in all other EU projects on the Colombian Pacific coast. Cali was also the home to the Colombian codirector, as well as home for most of the technical engineers.

Only when the funds were received, six months later, did we hire our project staff: a sociologist, various social workers, an economist, two engineers, and an architect. While the original budget planned in 1993 was for 2,000 houses, due to inflation, we could only manage to build no more than 1,700 homes between January 1997 and December 1999, the projected end of our mission.

The majority of the displaced population came from a very poor rural background. They all lived in shantytown-like houses suspended over the beach and sea by unreliable stilts they kept changing constantly. This caused most of the houses' floors to become slightly slanted, as well as the common walkways leading to them. These boardwalks, aside from making one seasick, often had boards missing along the shaky path to home, and there were countless stories of small children falling through them and drowning. Some of the older illegal settlements had, at rare times, the luxury of a cement boardwalk obtained through the help of some nongovernmental agency that had come after many children had died. But this was not the case for the settlements to be displaced.

The aim of the project was also to increase the economic and educational level of the beneficiary families, reinforce the formation and vocational training of the individuals in different fields, and develop community management and organizational skills. In each one of the twelve neighborhoods to be displaced, we had a small project office where our project's social workers, with the help of the local community leaders, provided information on social education and sensitized and taught families about proper hygiene and how to use a bathroom, sinks, and basic

Tumaco barrios. PHOTOS BY ROGER KATAN

kitchen equipment. Families were also taught to read and write when necessary so that they could join the new savings and loan association, allowing them to have a microcredit for whatever small project they may have or to give a boost to their existing microenterprises. The goal was to generate socioeconomic activities to improve the quality of life for these families. These small offices also had the task of recounting the number of families living in each one of these settlements and checking them against the original survey done in 1991. The aim of this survey was to make sure that no new families would want to take advantage of the project and that only the ones proven to be there for more than five years would be counted. We had several cases of new families wanting to be counted in the new survey so as to take advantage of the benefit of a new house.

Construction fieldwork started in September 1996 with the cleanup of the land to prepare it for urbanization, and the first foundations for the model homes were finished by December 1996. To diminish the earth movements and help trees and vegetable growth, the sandy soils of the site were stabilized with special sheets of vegetal earth. All foundations

*One- and two-story houses
built by our project.*
PHOTOS BY ROGER KATAN

*Bajito Tumaco
Barrio before and
after.* PHOTOS BY
ROGER KATAN

were antiseismic and a little over one foot in diameter. They were made
of driven piles fifteen to twenty feet deep and composed of round river
stones. Although the majority of the planned construction was to be
one- and two-bedroom houses, all foundations were planned for seven-
bedroom houses in projection of the fact that most families were young
and would likely wish to safely add more rooms to their house while
keeping it antiseismic.

The construction was planned at two speeds: the fast part was to
be industrial, erecting house shells of precast wall structures with roofs
done by professionals while the slower part was done by the beneficiary
families, cleaning the land and participating, always under a technician's
guidance, in the finishing details of their own houses, such as installing

Housing unit expansion being performed by beneficiaries.
PHOTOS BY ROGER KATAN

sanitary systems, doors, and windows, painting walls, and cleaning the finished product.

By December 1996, after the completion of the first pilot house, the logistics were finally in place to project building between five hundred and six hundred houses per year, which meant close to two houses per day. The budget did allow for a cost of around eight thousand dollars for a one-bedroom house and approximately twelve thousand dollars for a five-bedroom one. (I would like to underline the fact that under normal

This housing unit is also used as day care.

Families grow their own home gardens.
PHOTOS BY
ROGER KATAN

circumstances, the jump in standards from the existing shack to the new house could be reached only after at least three or four generations of social and economic progress. If it were not for the project to prevent future catastrophe, these families would never have acquired such a house without working very hard and paying for it.)

By the end of the second year, in November 1997, we had built close to 600 houses with almost 450 of them completely finished and about to be delivered to their respective beneficiaries. After this first year of construction, we were moving according to schedule and well on our way to meeting our initial goal of 1,700 houses completed within three years. At the same time, I had designed and controlled the construction of a primary school and college vocational training complex. Given the educational building deficit in the region and the number of uneducated adults and unschooled children, this educational complex was planned for 3,600 preschool, primary, and secondary students, along with a vocational training center in three shifts. The forty-two classrooms were planned in clusters of two or four, and two laboratories, an administration building, and a cafeteria, all interspersed with green areas planted with generous shade giving trees, were also to be included. Eight very spacious workshops were planned on the other side of the sports fields. Almost half of the classrooms were completed by the time of the first transfer and ready to receive the first families' children.

We decided, along with the appropriate authorities, that the first phase transfer would start with the 216 families from the El Bajito, Maria Auxiliadora, and El Triunfo neighborhoods because their location at the tip of the island left them the most vulnerable to catastrophe. Along with their numerous children, these families moved into the completed houses, and the first six primary classrooms were inaugurated.

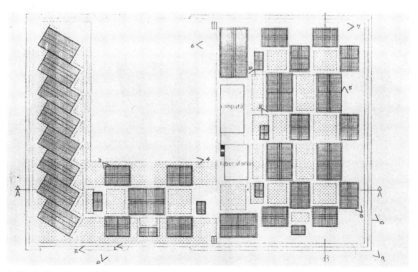

School plan: second floor and recreation area. DRAWING BY ROGER KATAN

School plan: classrooms are to be open with an extended roof to provide natural ventilation and protect from sun and heavy rain. PHOTOS BY ROGER KATAN

First Transfer of Families

Sunday, October 19, 1997 remains a memorable day for the first seventy families from El Bajito that were transferred. The first phase of completion of the catastrophe prevention program happened to come in coordination with a serious warning from the sea—two houses had been carried away two days earlier by a very strong Pacific current called El Niño, whose presence is always a warning of tidal waves to come. It all happened in the neighborhood that was chosen from the beginning to be the first to be moved because it was by far the most exposed. So the two families who had resided in the destroyed homes inaugurated the transfer when we helped them move in an emergency on October 18. We had already planned to move the seventy families of El Bajito on October 19 weeks earlier. Each family had been warned a few days earlier so they could start folding the little they had and packing their wares. They all had already worked for weeks on the finishing details of their respective houses and were all excited about the changes about to happen in their lives.

At the same time as our first transfer, we received a generous contribution from one of the project's contractors. Since October 19 was a Sunday, the contractor offered the twenty-five dump trucks that were used to carry stones, gravel, and other materials for the project during the week. At the sight of the first trucks at 7 a.m. of that beautiful day, one could sense the intense fever and excitation that grew. Aside from loading their already prepared luggage on the truck, the families could not get out without taking some pieces of their house, such as a few wall planks to make furniture, a door, a window, or pieces of their tin roof to be used by members of their families living in the nearby countryside.

Some families had a few questions and worries about the move, however. For instance, one lady needed special transport for her invalid grandmother, and we had to dispatch one of the project's cars for a 102-year-old great grandmother. Another situation arose when the owner of a little shop needed more time and help to pack her goods, as well as help to get an immediate loan to expand her house for her business. One family with nine kids did not want to unload the truck when they saw that their assigned house had only one bedroom, but this error was immediately corrected after they got their five-bedroom house.

Soldiers and local plain police officers helped us protect the area from possible invaders until the bulldozer standing by could systematically destroy each house once they were emptied. The mood was very festive. Powerful loudspeakers were rhythming the day with rap, salsa, and, at times, the local *currulao* dance music. Each of the twenty-five trucks came closer to their assigned house until each family had climbed aboard with their mattresses and packages. When he saw that his house was the only one still left standing in El Bajito, Pedro, the only head of a family that had opposed our project from the beginning and who had promised that he would never move, approached me that day when he saw his isolation. He expressed his desire to move, but on the condition that he would not be placed next to his previous neighbors. As soon as I agreed to his condition, he started to pack feverishly to be part of the transfer.

At their arrival at the project, each loaded truck was received by the project staff and several social workers who then lead the family to their assigned house. All of these families had come the previous day to wash the floors and make sure that the water and electricity services worked properly. By nighttime, the first displaced neighborhood had been transferred.

To see the first neighborhood transferred that day was cause for celebration. It was a very joyous and festive day, sparkling with happiness and much excitation. This was the day that, after years of promises, the dream that they were not really sure would ever be realized had come true. After months of social preparation, of planning and difficult construction logistics, it had finally happened, and this day was finally here to prove it.

Transfer Aftermath

One month after the first transfer, by the end of December 1997, we had succeeded in moving 216 families and clearing large areas of beaches for Tumaco residents. The results were mainly due to the active support and tenacity of the EU delegation chief in charge during the difficult project's start, Philippe Combescot. He was a young, dynamic, and dedicated person who was deeply concerned and preoccupied with the problems of poverty and underdevelopment. As the second in command at the EU delegation in Bogotá, he had been nominated as acting chief for almost two full years, replacing temporarily the former delegate who had become ill, and was waiting from the EU for a new official nomination.

Between November 1995 and June 1996, Combescot came from Bogotá on four occasions to help us solve administrative problems and several other difficult situations in Tumaco. During the two years while he was in charge of the country's delegation, he initiated some sixteen projects in Colombia—the EU chief that followed him only sponsored two new projects in four years. Combescot's last visit to the project was to introduce the new EU delegation chief to us and the local authorities. After his departure, the sustained help the project had had from the delegation in Bogotá suddenly vanished. The new chief delegate seemed tired and probably wanted to spend his last two years before retirement as quietly as possible. He doubtlessly found the amount of projects he had to manage as an overwhelming load, and he also probably did not appreciate the amount of work that his much younger and dynamic predecessor had left for him to follow-up on and develop. He seemed both cautious and troubled by my friendship with the former chief who had been sent to Central America. The new EU head was very distant and honored our project only twice in two years with a one-day visit. During his second visit, after an office briefing and a tour of our construction site in the morning, he was supposed to attend a general meeting in one of the barrios in the afternoon where community leaders had prepared a little feast to celebrate his presence in Tumaco. He declined to attend, showing more interest in the nearby beach than in these poor people's social turpitudes and endless problems. These types of gatherings didn't seem to jive with the high diplomatic image he had of his role. A week earlier, I had heard that he was spending a countless amount of time receiving luxury car dealers, inquiring about the cost of a tax free BMW or Mercedes Benz, and using the advantages of his diplomatic status, along with the reduced shipping cost to his home country of Spain, to prepare for his coming retirement while he was still in function.

The first financial irregularities by the Colombian codirector were communicated to the new delegation chief in April 1997, and a second communication followed in May. They both were left unanswered. In June 1997, during my vacation time, I asked a very competent and trustful member of our staff to serve as my replacement to the delegation. He was both a certified accountant and in charge of the savings and loan cooperative started with the project's beneficiaries. The delegation head refused my request for the replacement, asking me instead to establish a provision of expenses so that the project could go on without another in control and just the other codirector. I had to underline that the project was then employing more than 450 people and that our monthly expenses were over 600,000 euros (750,000 USD).

Upon my return from vacation, my suspicion of collusion between the Colombian codirector and our major building contractor was confirmed. After a successful year producing close to two houses per day, by the end of 1997, when the time came for the yearly accounting of what was left to be done for the 1998 budget projection, I discovered that, with the growing costs added to inflation, we would not have enough money to build the remaining 1,300 houses needed. In fact, our builders had, week after week, slowly raised their bills. I suddenly realized that if we continued on this same track, it meant leaving more than four hundred families roofless, which, to me, was unacceptable. Since these conclusions did not seem to move neither my partner in charge of the project nor our main contractors, I decided to check if I could get lower prices with other builders at the national level. After a few days' investigation, the results were positive and encouraging.

My actions aimed to renegotiate the contracts' costs with our current builders. Not only did my goal to convince them remain fruitless, but I also encountered solid resistance with my Colombian codirector. Moreover, the April and May communications to the delegation in Bogotá on the subject had remained unanswered. A few months later, I flew to Cali to attend an EU delegate lunch meeting to discuss the Pacific coast problems with our national partners. At the sight of the many attractive pictures showing the houses' construction progress, the chief delegate seemed, for the first time, excited about a possible official inauguration date for the project, where he could shine and show off a realization he seemed to be proud of. When I touched on the current problems I was facing, he seemed rather annoyed by my discourse. Sitting next to him, I discreetly recalled my different letters and faxes regarding our project's financial problems. He appeared bothered that I had brought this up, and, between two cups of wine, he discretely told me in a whisper, "we all know that there is always some theft going on in these projects. You just have to close your eyes," and, in a louder voice, he returned to the inauguration subject. From that moment, I knew I would have no support from this EU delegate.

In December 1997, the moment came to pay the monthly dues to our main contractors. Earlier, on a daily visit to our construction site, I had discovered that some heavy machinery had broken down and one rusting machine had sat idle for more than two months. In their bill, however, the contractors had added, for the second month in a row, the rental cost of these wrecks, charging them to the project. I immediately sent the contractors a note asking for a revision and correction of their prices. In the meantime, the other codirector signed a check for their total bill, which I refused to cosign. After consultation with the project legal adviser, I deducted the illegal charge from the bill and signed a check for this, but the other codirector refused to countersign. I then officially informed the delegation and also wrote to our Colombian administrative counterpart to set up an arbitration committee to help unblock the situation with an audit, joining in my letter copies of our legal adviser's opinion along with a copy of the two checks: the one including the extra charges and mine representing the real work value. I had closed my eyes the previous month on the same type of bill, but I just could not keep them shut this time around.

In the beginning of 1998, the Colombian administrative counterpart nominated an arbitration committee that concluded in March that the charges for the broken machinery were illegal, and it authorized the check I signed. Not only did the EU delegation not participate in the committee, but it kept silent, and every tentative motion to get any kind of cooperation from the administration remained fruitless. My requests ended most often with, "Do you think you are the only project we have to take care of?" The chief delegate was often in Spain visiting his reportedly ill wife and did not have much time to focus on his work.

Since our contractors wanted their contracts' costs to not only be lowered but also augmented in the year to come, they decided to stop working and threatened to take with them two of our staff engineers. In January 1998, I lined up new building contractors for interviews with the guarantee that the 1,700 houses would be completed. The approval of the start of the project remained deferred by the respective authorities despite my communications guaranteeing the completion of the project goal.

In the meantime, the director of the EU Technical Unit for Latin America came from Brussels to visit and investigate the project's problems with an officer from the EU office in Bogotá. To the proven collusion and irregularities of the Colombian codirector with the project contractors and the fact that the codirector's wife had just gotten a new car and that his house in Cali had been totally renovated by our project builders (without even speaking of the countless trips taken from his home in Cali during the second half of 1997, which his salary could not justify), the Brussels investigator answered that while he was a bit troubled by the diplomatic problems, he recommended that "it would be better to continue working as a team," leaving me to understand that I should keep closing my eyes and continue working together or I may have to leave for diplomatic reasons.

During this time, the codirector kept maintaining that the project would sink if we changed the contractors or the technical team. He kept taking as witnesses the two elected community leaders, and, together, they tried to block the annual election for community representatives for the second year in a row. As we soon discovered, the two community leaders were taking bribes from the contractors and did not want any change in the project's actual structure. To add to the confusion, these two spread rumors in the community that any change would mean the death of the project.

At about the same time, while on vacation in Colombia, Philippe Combescot invited himself to spend a weekend with us at my house. He was curious to see the advances of the project he had helped start after the hard times and problems he helped us surmount. While on this visit, he participated in a general community assembly and during a small feast in his honor, when he realized the size of the crisis and the amplitude of the obvious existing collusion, he made a speech about the project's dishonest profiteers. Knowing the animosity that existed between the previous chief delegate and the current one, the Colombian codirector felt insulted and immediately wrote a letter cosigned by the two corrupt community leaders to the chief delegate in Bogotá, asking about the official role of Combescot in Tumaco. Needless to say, his presence on the project site was not known and did not please the EU chief in Bogotá.

The two corrupt elected leaders even flew to Bogotá to visit the EU chief delegate at the contractors' expense to complain about the project's paralysis and tell him about the upsetting surprise visit by Combescot. Two weeks later, during a general assembly meeting convened in March 1998, when more members of the project's beneficiaries began to see their two leaders' game, they confounded and excluded them.

My efforts to stop the stealing met with a violent response, including death threats and a poisoned cracker that left me in a coma for five hours and three days in the local hospital. Despite interventions on my behalf by the mayor, the governor of the region, and other ministers, the EU decided to replace the two project directors. I was forced to uproot myself and moved to the south of France with my family. In so doing, I had hoped that the new management team would be able to complete the 1,700 houses.

Thanks to the EU's total inefficiency, the search for a new management team lasted close to one year, during which time the EU maintained most of the staff, costing the project to lose around one million dollars. As a result, the project ended in 2001 with only 1,060 houses completed.

Upon my return to France, I contacted national newspapers so as to report the EU's inefficiency and waste of tax money in this particular project. I was soon asked by the EU to appear for an investigation in Brussels at the European Anti-Fraud Office, or Office de Lutte Anti-Fraud (OLAF). Rather than respond to the accusation of fraud complicity (as stated by the Colombian EU representative), it allowed me to accuse the entire organization with irresponsible inefficiency. During my two days stay at OLAF, I discovered through my investigator, that my case was not isolated. I became aware of an incredible amount of problems of corruption at the international scale, which is discussed at further length at the end of this chapter.

Tumaco: Update and Proposal for 2020

Four years after the Tumaco project ended, in 2004, from my base in France, I was asked by the Tumaco municipality to do another major population transfer study. The new proposal aimed at preparing the transfer of the majority of Tumaco's twenty thousand families to about nine to twelve miles inland. An area along the main road leading to Pasto, the region's capital, could accommodate all the families and protect them from future catastrophe.

In 2005, at the initiative of the mayor's office and the municipal council, Tumaco's mayor came to meet me in France. Together, we sought financing for the project in Paris, Brussels, and Amsterdam. I was asked for a plan to move around twelve to fifteen thousand families from Tumaco to safer areas, close to where the previous EU project had been able to build 1,060 houses out of the planned 1,700 before it ended in 2001. A few months later, I proposed a plan jointly with a world-leading Dutch enterprise, which specialized in coastal protection, dykes, and landfills. The final proposal had seemed valid and acceptable at the time it was done, but did not find immediate financing.

Today's accrued knowledge about global climate change and the alarming rate at which the polar ice caps are melting, with their projected disappearance by 2040, lead me to believe that the landfill proposed in 2005 on the mainland near the coastline as an extension of the EU project would not be of any benefit over the long term. This new awareness has demanded a total revision of the previous plan.

In 2007–2008, we projected that before or by 2040, the island of Tumaco might disappear due to rising sea levels. There is now a pressing need to move the whole town from its present location on wet sandy soil to the safety of a hilly area some nine to twelve miles inland, where clay abounds and there is a tradition of brick making.

In order to avoid the catastrophic outcomes predicted as a result of global warming, I proposed using the highest, safest land area that exists at a reasonable distance from Tumaco, which happened to be along the main road leading to Pasto. I realized that the population would not easily accept a move to safety a few miles inland because, like most coastal towns of the world, fishing was crucial to the life of Tumaco. Realizing this, we proposed that a one or two hundred floating barges, protected by the numerous mangroves when at rest, could house the professional fisherman while their families could be moved a few miles inland.

This idea has been reinforced by the Colombian government's 2008 decision to build a new hospital to replace Tumaco's inadequate health facilities along the same road I proposed to move families. The new regional hospital, some twelve miles inland, was completed in 2010, and a

With global
warming, the
EU project
might disap-
pear in time,
along with
the Tumaco
Island.

FROM TUMACO
PRESENTATION
PREPARED
BY ROGER
KATAN

regular bus line now serves it. This large building has already become a point of attraction, and some of the land near it has already been bought by private investors for middle-income housing construction.

My proposal to the municipality aims at preparing a plan for the majority of Tumaco's twenty thousand families living on the island and in its immediate swampy vicinity to be transferred to the area around the new hospital. I recently advised the mayor that now was the time for the government to acquire some large tracts of land for a sites and services project before speculation takes over, making it difficult to find space for the majority of Tumaco's poorest population.

Three miles from Tumaco, all along this road, there is a tradition of brick making. As a first stage, the local government should encourage the creation of several building material cooperatives. These enterprises could start making bricks and roof tiles and stockpiling them. In the same way, carpentry shops could produce doors, window frames, and staircases while others could work on making furniture and other items.

The Colombian government should help distribute land for this new town and provide assistance for the basic master planning. In a second stage, along with a technical assistance program, the government should encourage self-help building of the houses in clusters. This could be done according to the same type of evolving house plans that we had developed during the typological studies I described in the earlier interventions and with the master plans drawn with the population during our previous engagement in the area. Along with the site and services preparation for this new town, an efficient low-cost community bus system between the new and the old Tumaco (while the island city still exists) should encourage people to slowly start building their houses through self-help. In this way, if a catastrophe occurs, the poor families know where they could run to for safety.

Parallel to this decision, SENA could provide further training and vocational courses to Colombian citizens with online, offline, and blended courses in hundreds of centers and computer labs across the country. I was told that in the beginning of 2011, SENA had announced the future construction of a training center not far from the new Tumaco hospital. On February 23, 2011, *El Espectador*, a major national newspaper, announced the planning and construction of a new branch of Colombia's national university system close to the new hospital, which would serve some thirteen thousand students who live in the Pacific coast municipalities when opened.[21]

These developments show a real interest by the government to improve the quality of life in this Pacific region by boosting its economy. Parallel to these important projects, in 2012, I was told that a private enterprise acquired a large tract of land in this same region to develop some three hundred lots for the construction of private houses and services. On this site, close to forty houses for middle-class families have already been finished by the end of 2013.

International Organizations and Problems with Corruption

The EU's aid has previously been criticized by the Eurosceptic think-tank Open Europe for being inefficient and misguided.[22] Except for a very few countries, most governments of South America are corrupt.

21. "Universidad Nacional Tendrá Sede en Tumaco," *El Espectador*, February, 23, 2011.

22. Stephen Booth and Siân Herbert, *EU External Aid: Who Is It For?* (London: Open Europe, 2011).

There have been countless projects financed in Central America, most of them involving population transfers due to a natural catastrophe, such as an earthquake or hurricane, or an armed conflict, generally a civil war. Counting on their officially acknowledged poverty, South American governments often ask for money from many different international organizations for the same projects and are sometimes able to obtain it. I was told that there have often been cases where governments have declared to one of their donors that the project has been completed with their money when it was actually financed by another donor.

For some Central American countries, drug trafficking, unemployment, and idleness are an issue. With the hundred dollars a family might receive monthly from one of its members living in the US, most of these families do not need to work, and the younger generation often reverts to mugging, violence, and drugs. This makes for the right kind of dim national statistics that attracts international organizations whenever a catastrophe happens.

During a two days stay at the European Anti-Fraud Office, or Office de Lutte Anti-Fraud (OLAF), I turned the investigation of my supposed wrongdoings into an investigation of the organization's immense and endless problems. Opening my ears to what the some of the staff had to say, I heard incredible stories. In the cases of the disappearance of 1 million euros (1.5 million USD) for the construction of houses for poor people in El Salvador and millions more in Guatemala, government ministers were apparently involved, and the EU had found it difficult to acquire sufficient proof to condemn them. A few years back, the government of Paraguay received 4 million euros (6 million USD) for an important development project, but the money disappeared before anything could be done. A national investigation took place at the demand of the EU, but how could the local ministry of justice pursue one of the closest friends of the Paraguayan president? Investigating such cases so far away from European borders becomes rather difficult for the EU, and it always ends up as a loss for the European taxpayer. This is probably the reason why OLAF was created in 1999 to replace Unité de Coordination de Lutte Anti-Fraud (UCLAF), the old anti-fraud office that was accused of covering up abuses by the disgraced Jacques Santer EU Commission. However, I was told that most of the UCLAF staff had been transferred to OLAF.[23]

---

23. Private OLAF sources.

Officially, OLAF's mission is to protect the financial interests of the EU and to fight fraud, corruption, and any other irregular activity, including misconduct within European institutions. In pursuing this mission, OLAF aims to provide a quality service to the citizens of Europe. In cooperation with its national partners (investigation services, police, legal and administrative authorities, etc.), OLAF does its best to counter criminals and fraudsters who organize their illicit activities at an international level.

In 2004, police on the order of the EU arrested a leading investigative journalist, seizing his computers, address books, and archive of files in a move that stunned European members of Parliament. Hans-Martin Tillack, the Brussels correspondent for Germany's *Stern* magazine, said the Belgian police held him for ten hours without access to a lawyer after his office and home had been raided by six officers. They asked him to tell them who his sources were, and he reported that the police said he was "lucky he wasn't in Burma or Central Africa, where journalists get the real treatment."[24] Tillack said the raid had been triggered by a complaint from OLAF because he had been one of the organization's most vocal critics, accusing it of covering up abuses within the EU system.[25]

It seems as if OLAF has become a façade behind which the EU hierarchy hides its incompetence in controlling many of the projects it finances. Today, OLAF's staff is more than four hundred functionaries with their hands tied in its Brussels headquarters, moving papers endlessly around the loss of an unknown quantity of money disbursed to projects that never saw the light of day. I was told during my two days stay that there were among them less than ninety field investigators feeding them more problems than they are equipped to solve. As a result, the losses of one million here and a few million there pileup with all of the other losses that remain hung up on investigations being buried in the underground files of the institution.

As we saw in Case Study 4 in West Africa with the UNDP and later with the EU, international organizations tend to keep their distance from local politics and often leave a project without guidance when things

---

24. Ambrose Evans-Pritchard, "Reporter Following Trial of Corruption in EU Arrested," *The Telegraph*, March 20, 2004.
25. Ibid.

become controversial in a similar manner to the Popayán and Tumaco projects, leading to a waste of time and money.

When I completed my missions in Burkina Faso (known as Upper Volta at the time), helping establish a successful savings and loan association as a tool for community development (see Case Study 4), I was offered the possibility to work full time with the UN and later with the Desjardins Group through the Canadian Council for International Cooperation. I suggested to the UN officials the possibility of duplicating the work I did in Ouagadougou in other peripheries of the major towns in West Africa, where rural migrations were as strong as they were poor. The idea I offered was to fly every three months from town to town in the many West African countries to help start community savings and loan associations in the poorest neighborhoods and then return to the same places six months later to help consolidate the organization and its growth process.

The UN officials felt that my idea could give threatening democratic ideas to those living under conditions similar those of the Middle Ages, and they could not accept my offer at that time because it probably would have disturbed the numerous well-established dictatorships of the region and their numerous corrupt ministers and officials. In fact, Burkina Faso had been under a dictatorship for more than thirty years before it was overthrown four years after my mission by a young officer who admired the Cuban revolution. It also happened that while the minister of construction and urbanism under whom I worked in Burkina Faso had been satisfied during my first mission, he became quite angry with me during my second and third missions because the people in the communities where I was working began actively asking for their rights, even going so far as staging a sit-in in his office, and he did not appreciate it. I even learned that one or two years after I had left, he had tried to steal the little money that the community had worked so hard to save. Justice was served a couple of years later when the new revolutionary government took over and he was put in jail.

Of all the West African migrations we see in Europe today, a very small percentage comes from Burkina Faso. I do believe that this is a direct consequence of the incredible national growth of the microcredit tool, which helped stabilize the population. The total savings when I last left this project in Burkina Faso was around 20,000 dollars. When I visited the project in 1993, the savings totaled around 900,000 dollars. By 2005, I was told that the project had grown nationwide and the savings had passed the 6 million dollar mark.

Several US presidents and their Cabinets, including Richard Nixon, Ronald Reagan, and George W. Bush, have also criticized the UN—in 1967, Nixon even included it in a list of old institutions that he considered to be "obsolete and inadequate."[26] The Oil-for-Food Programme, established by the UN in 1996, was one such UN program to come under heavy criticism. The program was meant to allow Iraq, which was then being prevented from rebuilding its military in the wake of the first Gulf War, to sell oil on the world market in exchange for food, medicine, and other humanitarian supplies for its Iraqi citizens affected by the international economic sanctions. While 64.2 billion dollars of Iraqi oil was sold on the world market, officially, only 39.7 billion dollars was spent on humanitarian needs.[27] Moreover, US Senate investigators concluded that the Iraqi regime under Saddam Hussein had made about 13.6 billion dollars from illegally selling oil to neighboring states and billions more through kickbacks and illegal surcharges on goods and services provided by companies contracted under the program.[28] The program was discontinued in late 2003 amidst allegations of widespread abuse and corruption. Its director, Benon Sevan, who had been suspended when the program ended, later resigned from the UN when an interim progress report of an UN-sponsored investigation recommended that his UN immunity be lifted to allow for a criminal investigation when it concluded that he had accepted bribes from the Iraqi regime.[29]

In conclusion, after my advocacy experience in East Harlem, the experience with international organizations was a shock. I had thought that these organizations' higher staff would be in some way advocates of the third world populations that they were supposed to be defending

---

26. Jussi M. Hanhimäki, "An Elusive Grand Design," in *Nixon in the World: American Foreign Relations, 1969–1977*, ed. Frederik Logevall and Andrew Preston (New York: Oxford University Press, 2008), 31.

27. "UN Facts about the United Nations Oil-for-Food Programme," accessed March 14, 2014, http://www.un.org/News/dh/iraq/oip/facts-oilforfood.htm.

28. "Q&A: Oil-for-Food Scandal," *BBC News*, September 7, 2005.

29. "Former UN Oil-for-Food Head Quits," *BBC News*, August 8, 2005.

and working for. In fact, they were stymied by their superior cadres, the super planners who bowed their heads to politicians and dictators.

As William Easterly did put it so clearly in the *White Man's Burden*:

> A planner thinks he already knows the answers. . . . A Searcher admits he doesn't know the answer in advance; he believes that poverty is a complicated tangle of political, social, historical, institutional, and technological factors. A Searcher hopes to find answers to individual problems by trial and error experimentation. A Planner believes outsiders know enough to impose solutions. A Searcher believes only insiders have enough knowledge to find solutions, and that most solutions must be homegrown.[30]

---

30. Easterly, *The White Man's Burden*, 5.

Conclusion

General Lessons Learned

Through our many experiences, we learned how to demystify the planning process and how to help people recognize the power that they had and engage in the planning of their own community and their own future. That period of exploration and innovation in advocacy and participatory planning processes was critically important in building an informed, empowered, and knowledgeable community development constituency and creating a model for effective participatory planning—one that we have since used, refined, and adapted in different contexts. Simply stated, we learned that successful participatory planning processes need to:

1. Develop a common language that can grow in complexity over time, but that should be understood by all participants.

2. Develop a level and equitable playing field for all of the participants. There needs to be a parity of power where no one actor or group has more power than another and where all of the participants know what the others in the group know.

3. Share knowledge and explore different ways of solving a given problem or achieving a proposed set of objectives. We realized

that too often communities are trapped by their own limited set of experiences and that they tended to draw solutions from what they already knew or experienced, so sharing information on how others in other places and communities addressed similar problems was important.

4. Recognize and honor what each participant can contribute to the better understanding of the issues and opportunities that need to be addressed.

5. Learn that success is dependent on the development of the community's trust in their own capacity and in the capacity of others.

6. Recognize that the community members are the leaders and decision makers, not us.

We discovered that describing a problem or opportunity, which planners and technicians were able to do with ease, was not equivalent to understanding. Understanding, we learned, was the prerequisite to action and could only be achieved after what was observed and surveyed was discussed, digested, filtered, and understood by those whose experiences, aspirations, and goals may or may not have been the same as ours.

We learned that local residents, unlike what many urban professionals typically advocate, refused to prioritize or put into separate silos important community needs such as housing, education, health, participation, and community empowerment. Residents believed that all of these needed to be addressed concurrently, and although the language they used was different, they clearly espoused a comprehensive and holistic approach to revitalization. We soon learned that the elimination of silos meant penetrating the boundaries that denied us the ability to see things synergistically and replacing them with processes that built upon porous and open edges.

Most importantly, we learned that the means and the ends were both important. That the success of the endeavor was dependent on and integrally related to the successful interplay of means and ends. The means were dependent on a critical assessment of the various modes of intervention that were necessary given the sociopolitical context on the ground and the resultant design of the participatory process.

Politics of Participation and Its Different Practices

The term "participation" varies considerably according to whether it refers to an action directed by a political body, a professional representative of power, or a militant in an urban struggle. This disparity of meaning can be equally found in Paris, Ouagadougou, a New York ghetto, or a Bogotá shantytown.

Moreover, participation is also ambivalent with respect to the specific actors involved in urban development. Maintaining a certain distance from currently prevalent technical models, participatory practices tend to be rejected, controlled, and limited when they do occur. However, they often constitute the only available means of developing local political action and, as we saw with respect to Colombia (Case Studies 6 and 7), of engaging in a politics of national development.

Each participatory process we engage in needs to be adapted to the culture, history, memory, and power of those involved and the level of organization that exists within that particular community. In pluralistic settings, this becomes more complex and, therefore, more challenging, but, again, if done appropriately, this can lead to greater social cohesion and community building. We learned that social cohesion that ignored social inclusion was fragile and lacked the moral authority to sustain itself over time.

The planning and design of the process of engagement—the means —is as important, if not more important, than the design of the end product. The process, if designed appropriately, can help build a strong sense of community—one strong enough that diversity and pluralism are not feared, but embraced.

While we were engaged on the local level, we were also in touch with other planners with similar value systems that were working regionally and nationally. What we learned locally was transmitted to our allies nationally and began to inform the development of national policy and programs that could benefit the work that we were engaged in on the local level. These included programs that dealt with the inequities and disparities that existed on a local level and sought to create places where edges were no longer borders or barriers.

From the very beginning, this holistic yet bottom-up approach to planning was coupled with a fundamental understanding that there were overriding sets of international and national principles of democracy, equality, and human rights that were inalienable—rights that cannot be taken away or denied. In today's world, be it in the United Sates, the EU, or anywhere else, how we address this overriding set of universal inalienable principles while, at the same time, allow individual and local communities to express their needs is a challenge that planners and decision makers alike must address.

I. United States

Limits of Participation for Political Administrators, Professionals, and Base Militants

Participation in the United States has been relegated to two particular sectors of activity: in urban renovation planning and in the establishment of programs intended to improve conditions in the neediest areas. However, in neither case was the notion of participation clearly defined. In the first, administrative requirements were limited to public meetings held prior to renovation plan adoption where local residents might express their support or dissent through a vote. Such votes proved to be a mere symbolic gesture rather than a genuine consultation with the public. In the second case, participation was inferred from as few as three local administrative offices being filled by local residents or their representatives.

The first phases of the urban renovation program sought to integrate middle and underprivileged classes within an improved neighborhood. The underprivileged participated because they hoped to ameliorate their community and wanted to avoid the destruction that came with dilapidated, low-rent housing and prevent the demise of their so-called ghetto culture. However, those who at first agreed to participate soon found themselves confronted with a planning process that merely compelled the acceptance of the unacceptable under the guise of a mutual decision. In the end, the urban renovation project selection process favored the most affluent families at the expense of the poorest. Popular opposition proved to have no effect even in the general assembly as votes had no probative value and any consultation measures appeared purely procedural.

It is apparently always easier and more advantageous for the middle classes than for those less privileged to engage in a regulated form of participation with respect to managing public affairs, especially at the neighborhood level of organization. When so-called advocacy planning professionals did begin working with poor communities, they did not discover the sort of environment they had been hoping to find. Instead of working with coherent groups conscious of and motivated by their neighborhoods' problems, they found themselves confronted with hostile, divided, ill-informed, and apathetic communities. But is this really so surprising?

The lower classes are constrained in their daily lives to act in the short term. Poverty confronts them with immediate problems demanding immediate solutions: food, housing, employment, and health. Their lives play out as a series of recurrent crises that use up any remaining energy they might have after tending to life's basic necessities. Thus, any sort of planning at any level necessarily implies consideration of long-term solutions only. It was, therefore, not surprising that planners found themselves in these ghettos confronted with complex situations where they had to solicit mass participation in projects whose usefulness residents, burdened by daily life, did not understand.

To participate authentically in neighborhood activity, one needs time: time to organize, time to sensitize, and time to negotiate. For the most disadvantaged, available time (and energy) is largely arrogated by day-to-day survival. A mother who has spent an entire day in an overcrowded clinic waiting room with her children is unlikely to be able to invest several further hours the same evening at a neighborhood meeting.

Faced with an apathetic community, advocacy planning leaders cannot lay blame on either laziness or stupidity. As professionals, they typically spring from the middle classes and, as such, assume justice is obtainable, expect police to behave with a minimum of respect, and even anticipate having some personal authority. However, for the disenfranchised, the world they are born into is indifferent—if not outright hostile—to their needs and interests. They are already, by and large, convinced that they cannot have a significant political or economic impact on public affairs or make those in power pay any serious attention.

Taking into account the daily insecurity that characterizes their lives, disenfranchised communities have adopted two different and apparently contradictory attitudes. On one hand, they maintain an emphasis on strong family solidarity, finding support in belonging to a group. On the other hand, their profound dissatisfaction can lead them to acts of violence both inside and outside of these groups.

Meanwhile, traditional urban planners, as a result of their training and class backgrounds, respond to their own requirements, such as the constant growth of land values and the extension of private property, and are not prepared to work within the framework of other cultures. In the final analysis, this is the main reason why, even with the help of advocacy planning, negotiations with urban planners that are attempted by disenfranchised residents rarely result in concrete results.

However, it has become impossible to ignore the rights of residents to intervene in the development of their own living environments—and this is of the utmost importance! The advocacy planning movement forced a professional community that had been previously so sure of itself to reconsider its responsibilities, and this shift is now irreversible. Residents of disenfranchised neighborhoods participated in community action programs that offered the population vital services, such as childcare, elder care, health clinics, etc., because they directly benefited, unlike urban renovation programs that only profited the middle classes.

While representatives of the central administration directed local urban renovation agencies, community action groups benefited from the status of private agencies. Once a project was approved and financing obtained, they remained independent of any administrative hierarchy. In some cases, program directors even worked together with residents to put pressure on politicians and governments to obtain important changes. Nevertheless, when participation lead to changes deemed too radical, the administration could always threaten to revoke renovation financing or even attempt to subordinate these offices to local government organizations charged with supervising them.

Community action groups typically thought that the problem being raised was not theirs, that their advice would not be taken into account as had been the case in many urban renovation programs, or that their participation would be rendered meaningless once the community action program was rejected. It is because of these fears that residents of disenfranchised neighborhoods came to reject the ideology of participation. However, even if this rejection did result in the sensitization of ghettos—and even certain lower-middle class milieus—to the potential dangers of urban renovation, it only served to increase the feelings of frustration that resulted in riots and explosions of violence. Thus, the administration put targeted groups in a difficult situation: ghettos lost when they participated and even sometimes when they did not. In these cases, participation was not only inefficient but also sometimes detrimental to the residents who agreed to it.

The inner-city residents' acceptance or refusal to participate also had consequences for the bureaucratic organizations that had created this ideological paradigm: the more residents of disenfranchised neighborhoods participated in the work of environmental planning or community action, the more things became complicated for the programs' administrators. Routine decisions were called into question, conflicts escalated, and projects took longer to finish, sometimes resulting in financial losses for the urban renovation offices. This, in turn, caused administrators to become even warier of an engaged participation—and all its consequences—than of an insufficiently developed form of participation.

On the other hand, if bureaucracies refused the principle of participation, they exposed themselves to the double risk of being reproached for being both antidemocratic and arbitrary in their actions. Neither urban renovation offices nor community action offices could dispense with these participatory rites. For, in the long term, complete contempt for residents' opinions would expose city authorities to serious pressures, as well as frighten the middle class that fears becoming the next victim of out-of-control bureaucratic programs.

Thus, the bureaucracies concerned found themselves in an ambiguous position with respect to their own ideologies. In most cases, this ambiguity manifested as acting quietly in neighborhood assemblies and choosing rather to operate amongst a very select choice of community members in order to assure a minimum of participation.

To elucidate this paradoxical situation, it suffices to pose a simple question: who is genuinely participating? From a purely functional point of view and in the social context in question, responsive participation with the government, in most cases, remained inefficient if not in direct conflict with the supposed interests of its beneficiaries.

Faced with this situation, inner-city residents despaired of achieving any sort of improvement to their living conditions, communication was cut off, and violence appeared as the ultimate recourse.

II. France

Development of Militantism

To understand the multiplicity and complexity of urban social movements in France, one must take into account the functions of the different ideological visions guiding this diversity. Some of these practices sought to encourage local associative living. Others had, as their only goal, the defense of private interests. Others still more complex had an underlying political project as their point of reference and attempted to reverse power relations in the direction of popular decision making.

Participatory movements did not call into question the hierarchical system or claimed to be situated beyond the political domain. Rather, they concerned themselves with developing associative living situations and assuring the proper management of collective teams. Their dependence on local power structures also created a liaison between administrative units and participants with very little conflict. Such participatory movements typically provide technical and administrative training to their members, thereby also producing notable speakers who might be recognized by the administration's technical services. However, to what extent do such well-known participants still speak for the realities lived by the population they are supposed to be representing? Always working within a legal framework and never questioning the norms of the right to urbanization, at best, they become new sorts of planners. In this context, such intermediaries assume a social integration function that is in perfect conformity with an official discourse valorizing participation.

At the other end of the spectrum, within the context of social movements, collective actions commonly characterized as urban struggles were also found. Such struggles are most often the product of militants in the classical sense of the term: people committed to a political or ideological project condemn the mechanisms of hierarchy and segregation. The risk run by militants is the politicization of the concrete problems posed by the residents' discontents. By behaving in this way, they chased off the insufficiently politicized masses that are nonetheless affected by the struggle's goals. As a result, many immigrants and elderly people became victims of development because those who wanted to defend them did not hear them.

Class and language differences between the politicized youth and the population exploited by the urban system present an undeniable problem that must be taken into account if we want to find forms of struggle adapted to each situation. It is through a respect for cultural difference that class alliances could become concretized. It was to the extent that militants were capable of forgetting their practical guide to demonstrations and instead borrow from popular traditions that actions could become efficient and formative.

Governmental Response: Its Concept of Participation
In 1977, recognizing that the politics of housing in France was at a crossroads, the French Ministry of Housing, the Ministère de l'Environnement et du Cadre de Vie, organized a national grassroots consultation on housing and the environment in thirteen cities. Included in its official declaration of purpose was the following guideline: "A social politics of housing cannot delegate the entirety of architectural reflection to a minority of privileged esthetes or leave decisions to the supposedly enlightened. This sort of consultation is favorable to a reflection on the past as well as the future, and can and should become everyone's affair."[1]

The first phase of consultation consisted of an inventory of all housing development completed over the past fifty years in the thirteen cities that had been selected by the minister responsible. The regions chosen ended up representing approximately 3,650,000 residents. The second phase was supposed to consist of expositions and public debates organized under the auspices of the municipalities.

The administration hoped to engage the public on housing development, and this required the will to bring the debate on architecture

---

1. French Ministry of Housing, *Declaration of Purpose* (Paris: French Ministry of Housing, 1977).

and urbanization into the schools and onto television. With respect to mass media, the administration financed three films that were shown on regional television in concert with the expositions and debates organized in each of the respective cities. However, although introducing a program into the schools was intended, it was neither defined nor put into practice.

Rather than following themes such as the worker-housing or housewife-housing relationship, the consultation group proposed seven evaluative criteria: the appropriation of space, treatment of public spaces, quality of housing, quality of nature, quality of traffic, quality of art, and quality of childhood. The materials that arose from the cities' reflections and the observations of the workings of the consultations were supposed to be elaborated in a summary document as well as presented at an exposition in Paris at the end of 1979.

To respect the personalities of the cities chosen, the consultation should have been coordinated according to the wishes of the residents in each municipality. In La Rochelle, for example, an active associative life should have facilitated the intervention of resident groups. Whereas, in Cholet, the mayor went so far as to declare: "Putting all of the steps involved in the action process into the public space would risk disturbing public opinion and encourage blockages."[2]

If the administration had really wanted this countrywide consultation to encourage residents to express their feelings about housing, they should have made four resolutions:

- Organize the free distribution of information held by the powers that be.
- Prepare work and communication tools, for example, by organizing competitions open to small projects that would then be judged by the population itself.
- Organize the basis of the consultation through resident committees rather than leaving it entirely to the administration.
- Establish a communication network connecting different neighborhoods with one another, as well as with the city and the

---

2. From *Le Monde*, February 28, 1976. Author and article unknown.

administration, so as to clearly indicate that the neighborhood is an autonomous, decentralized entity.

At the time, decentralization as understood by the central administration was limited to leaving the initiative to local city authorities. The consultation had a very elitist approach and declared that the direct integration of residents would not constitute the core of the consultation.

To illustrate the mood of the consultation, one has only to review the schedule for the city of La Baule from July 24 to August 12, 1978, which consisted of mostly small, private, and invitation-only events and just a few public debates. What could be expected from a planning consultation with a medium-sized town lasting ten hours with local residents? What should we think about the debates focused only on architecture? What could be the outcome of the themes announced for such debates? Furthermore, there was no chance of attaining anything positive unless the participants had already identified, studied, and formulated their neighborhood politics before debating at the city level. This undertaking, as put into practice, only served to exclude the majority of the population it was claiming to consult. By contrast, the New York Regional Plan Association had managed to organize an inquiry at the level of New York City of about twenty million inhabitants that had provided numerous groups a voice with the same financial means as those of the French national consultation (see Case Study 1).

In seeking to justify the democratic path, central powers claimed to encourage citizen participation in making political decisions. However, with limitations on participation never clearly defined, serious obstacles appeared when time came to put residents' proposals into practice. Government-led participation brings with it a constant ambiguity because, on the one hand, it authorizes the creation of groups with dissenting views, but, on the other hand, it wants to retain control of the operations. In the final analysis, participation as proposed by the government tends to reduce social conflict without changing any real power relations. In the housing field, the government remains preoccupied with the same social problems posed by the housing projects it had suffered previously. Taking back control of social housing continues to be of the utmost importance.

La Baule Program Table

Date	Event	Audience
July 24, 11:00 a.m.	*Vernissage* (opening)	By invitation only
July 25, 6:00–7:30 p.m.	Everyday architecture debate	Public debate
July 26, 4:00–6:00 p.m.	Promenade: Invisible La Baule	50 seats
August 7, 7:00–8:00 p.m.	Debate at the Rotary Club	Private
August 8, 2:00–4:00 p.m.	Competition: *La maison de sable* (the sand house)	30 youth between the ages of 10 and 14
August 8, 6:00–7:30 p.m.	Everyday architecture debate	Public debate
August 9, 4:00–6:00 p.m.	Promenade: Invisible La Baule	50 seats

A sample of the schedule for the city of La Baule, July 24 to August 9, 1978.
TABLE BY LA BAULE MUNICIPALITY

Since 1976, the French government has initiated programs encouraging housing project residents to participate in renovation projects. It is to this end that an interministerial commission, Housing, Health, Work, and Leisure, was charged with intervening through a national program for the renovation of housing projects called Housing and Social Life (Habitat et Vie Sociale, or HVS).

In 1981, the government appeared to increase the size of the program, which was then replaced by the National Committee for the Renovation of Social Neighborhoods, and included ten ministries that would work directly with local associations. According to their political and democratic logic, organizers and elected officials believed that if the residents had elected them, then it was so that they would make decisions on their behalf. Awakening residents and handing them responsibility would, in effect, result in sharing power and implicating them in the process, thus risking a loss of operational control.

This phenomenon perfectly illustrates my own experience. In July 1978, the secretary general of HVS made me responsible for evaluating the impact of popular participation on the renovation of a large group of housing projects in Marseille. I was invited by local officials to attend two meetings where, given the specificity of my mission, I hoped to meet with local residents, representatives of the administration, and architects.

The first meeting took place in the architects' offices and included a representative of the Marseille housing project office. These technicians decided on the location and form of the stairwells in La Grande Barre under the pretext that the president of the housing projects had just returned from a vacation in Acapulco and would enjoy round stairwells. Since I was sorry that the president would not be able to enjoy the round stairwells on a daily basis and that the residents seemed not to have been consulted on these decisions, I was invited by these officials to a meeting at the project site three days later, where they complained to me that it was difficult to get the residents to participate and that "they often contradict each other, do not know what they want, and do not know how to express themselves properly."

The second meeting took place in one of the project towers with, in addition to the same technicians present at the first meeting, only three social leaders who called themselves the buffers between the technicians and residents. I decided to leave the group even before the meeting, but not before asking to address one of the representatives of the residents' associations: "Oh yes, Mrs. X is very active in the struggle to defend her building's residents. She has three young children, so she should be home. She's on the eleventh floor, fifteenth door on the left."

Advised by the buffers, I visited Mrs. X and asked her about the experience and involvement she and the residents she represented had in the renovation's participative process requested by the HVS office. Mrs. X was blasé:

Oh, you know, they ask our opinion on the color of the hallways. We say blue, they paint them pink. It's not important. The main thing is to repair the scratches on the walls and mailboxes, and provided that they're clean, the color doesn't matter. The only problem is that the same people who smash the mailboxes, wreck the plaster on the walls, and piss in the elevators will keep doing it, even if maybe not right away. The problem is that the Turks, North Africans, and French Algerians, all piled up in the same building, insult each other and can't live together; that's he most serious thing. So, there are lots of empty apartments; people are leaving.

What cannot be brought out into the open with words is expressed by destroying the space where everyone must, nonetheless, continue to live cooped up together.

I could not manage to grasp the apathy and fatalism of Mrs. X, who had been described to me by the buffers as an important activist. Why didn't she see that with all her neighbors, it was possible to take charge of their mutual problems and try to resolve everyday concerns together?

I informed Mrs. X that the government was spending an average of 3 million francs (630,000 USD) per apartment building and that if she and her group could organize legally to take charge of and control the renovation of the 80 apartments and their exteriors in her building, they could be receiving more than 250 million francs (52 million USD). "What would you do with that money?" I asked her. "How would you proceed in managing it and deciding on its distribution? What architects would you hire and what businesses would you choose?"

She finally became animated and exclaimed: "Oh, I didn't know that! It's an interesting idea; no one ever told us. With us in control, they wouldn't be able to make so many fishy deals with businesses. So, why didn't you talk about this with the teacher and her husband? They know more about it than I do."

I left Mrs. X to make my report to the HVS office. It was obvious that the residents were not seriously involved in the participatory process and had only been given minimal information. This expensive renovation operation of about four billion francs (850 million USD) would have provided several businesses with work and allowed for superficial replastering, but it was doomed to failure because the residents had not really been consulted and the reasons for the vandalism had not been investigated.

No one could dare say that participation is expensive when compared to such waste!

The social problems created as a result of the way hundreds of thousands of housing project units were built have been a brutal reality for several years in France. One only need mention the Minguettes to reference the complexity of these inextricable problems.[3]

Piling up people from different backgrounds who are bound only by their poverty and putting them on the outskirts of the city—thus creating social and spatial isolation in massive groups of buildings—with a lack of support and services, an unreliable means of communication, and often dubious construction quality were at the very origin of the development of modern, big city ghettos. As sociologist Véronique de Rudder says: "What brings together ghetto/projects' residents is their inability to move up in the world, and this model was conceived during a period of economic expansion and a calming of the housing crisis. Housing projects are thus more of a cul-de-sac environment where families, helped along by the crisis, are becoming paupers."[4]

The degradation is cumulative. The insufficiency of funds for maintenance and repairs increases the rejection and devalorization of housing projects. The remaining families who can leave do so as soon as the vandalism worsens sufficiently. The massive majority, whether of people or buildings, is no longer agreeable. Thus, the ghettoized housing project can be defined by the inability of its residents to flee and escape a process of accelerated degradation. Violence thus gives the imagination free reign: people scratch the plaster, smash mailboxes, or destroy elevators to show they exist. They refuse to travel a path that seems to have no exit for them.

Expressed as a democratic utopia to be attained, the myth of social integration reinforces the exclusion of dominated and racial minorities. It authorizes and justifies residential segregation.

---

3. The Minguettes was a neighborhood in the Lyon periphery where, in the summer of 1981, the first violent popular unrest against the government's failure to address deep social problems took place. During the "Minguettes Hot Summer" (Été Chaud des *Minguettes),* protesters burned more than two hundred cars. This event opened the floodgates on several years of urban disorder in France.

4. Véronique de Rudder, "La Cohabitation Pluriethnique et Ses Enjeux," *Migrants–Formation,* no. 80 (March 1990). Translated by Roger Katan.

III. Colombia

Analysis of Popular Forms of Housing Production

In Colombia, as in all developing countries, we find the classic phenomena inherent to the problem of migration to the city:

- Proliferation of all sorts of illegal urbanization.
- Disorder and dispersion on the fringes and in the center of the city that are linked to overcrowding.
- Difficulty in controlling this growth and, thus, the planning of infrastructures, as well as the distribution of public services required by the spontaneous appearance of new neighborhoods. This dispersion causes an increase in operation costs that municipalities cannot afford.
- Degradation of living conditions, erosion of revenues, and inevitable social frustration soon follows.

Among the solutions to city housing problems discovered spontaneously by the population, a classic phenomenon tends to repeat itself. When rural families arrive in urban centers, they are piled up in small apartments or in furnished rooms (known in South America as *inquilinatos*). They can escape the overcrowding, lack of privacy, and high rents only by buying a small piece of land in an illegal, "pirate" (*pirata*) urban zone or by organizing illegally to invade land to build a shantytown. Pirate urbanization is illegal to the extent that the land belongs to an owner who divides and sells it without proper access to public services (water, electricity, etc.) and without permission from the municipality.[5]

The plot of land, once acquired, generally moves quite quickly from a light materials stage to a heavy self-construction (either individual or group) stage. Because of the illegal conditions linked to this sort of development and the hopes of it leading to a better life, rural people choose to adopt the city's heavy materials for construction rather than using their traditional knowledge, often resulting in technical deficiencies in structures. The cost of these buildings is very high due to the price of materials

---

5. Pirate urbanization has a decidedly legal status. An owner divides a piece of land and resells it in lots. But it is illegal to the extent that services (road, rail, and waterways networks and sewage, water, and electricity) are nonexistent on the individual lots.

sold on the city outskirts, which is generally 150 to 200 percent more than what large businesses pay wholesale. In the face of these inconveniences, larger groups are forming to build together and thereby benefit from various advantages: technical knowledge sharing, more reasonable costs for materials (through bulk purchasing), a community spirit that leads to the attainment of public and social services, etc.

Self-construction can take on two forms: it is either self-managed if launched from the base or directed if launched by an external group or institution. Self-managed associative self-construction is a group experience where each member participates in the process of community development. While the association itself can bring about a visible reduction in construction costs, its success depends on appropriate organization, available technical assistance, and the ability to obtain credit.

Self-construction is directed or assisted if official entities take charge of the group's direction; in which case, the group is provided with economic and technical resources, but is also required to follow a specific type of planning. To obtain official credit and a technical framework, several self-managed associative groups have had to transform themselves into assisted associative groups. However, in the 1960s, an alternative form of individual credit was made available to regularly employed people who could provide collateral. Then, in 1978, the beginnings of an associative credit system was created that allowed groups without sufficient income, or whose members could not provide individual collateral, to establish a group collateral. This associative credit has been functioning since 1983 to help the most impoverished groups.

To complete this aid, a network of construction material supply depots was established at the heart of self-construction zones in all major urban centers. Somewhat like cooperatives, these depots offer not only materials at a reasonable price but also technical training to ensure their proper use. There are many advantages to these projects:

- Reduction of unemployment.
- Channeling of economic and administrative resources to create technical frameworks and continued training.
- Coordination of mutual aid efforts to help legally acquire land and materials.

- Contribution to community development through the creation of associations once the housing problem is solved.

New Government Politics

The Betancur government (1982–1985) encouraged the promotion and support of grassroots initiatives by making all government resources available. The promise to solve as many housing problems as possible was one of the 1982 election campaign's most important platforms. A significant emphasis was placed upon solutions appropriate to the lowest revenues, especially those without any initial investment required by the participants. The promise was kept and many of the initiatives were partially executed. Several public organizations focused their energies on solving the housing crisis, including Colombia's National Urban Housing Authority (Instituto de Crédito Territorial, or ICT), National Apprenticeship Service (Servicio Nacional de Aprendizaje, or SENA), Department of Integration and Community Development (Dirección General de Integración y Desarrollo de la Comunidad, or DIGIDEC),[6] and Central Mortgage Bank (Banco Central Hipotecário, or BCH).[7]

Over the next ten years, the ICT applied the largest part of its resources to the construction of housing for populations earning between two and six times the minimum wage. Those earning less than two times the minimum wage—not to mention those with no regular income or earning less than the minimum wage—found themselves penalized because they could not provide the initial investment necessary to obtain access to housing. The ICT proposed a variety of solutions to these populations, including offering viable lots that left residents to construct their homes gradually and offering basic modules of differing sizes—215, 323, or 431 square feet—with the possibility for progressive development over time. However, the number of these so-called solutions[8] was clearly

---

6. DIGIDEC depended directly on the success of the Betancur presidency.

7. Initially, the BHC's main role was to invest in the development of middle- and upper-class housing, but this was later changed to focus on investing in the development of lower-middle class housing and granting associative credits to grassroots groups.

8. These can only be described as partial solutions to the housing problem because they did not provide a complete home or lodging to residents. An infrastructure where basic services need to be acquired over time cannot be considered a solution.

inferior to the demand, resulting in many people having to take charge of resolving their own housing problems.

Aware of these problems, the Betancur government decided to create a division of self-help construction at the ICT in 1983 in order to encourage the proliferation of self-constructed, self-managed housing development. The plan was to construct one hundred thousand solutions per year and, in this way, erase a housing deficit estimated by some at almost one million dollars. In December 1983, toward the end of the program's first year, the ICT projected the creation of between thirty-five and forty thousand solutions without any initial investment.[9]

For its part, SENA proclaimed 1983 the year of "popular participation as instrument of development." Conscious that resident associations and cooperatives had significant experience in such development (although often of an illegal nature), SENA was inspired by some of their projects and chose to help such groups help themselves and their communities. Between 1980 and 1982, SENA employed 42 self-construction instructors specializing in urban milieus in total with 30 full-time and 12 part-time hires. Their goal was to build 1,000 houses per year, or a yearly average of 27 houses per instructor. Contributing to this new policy, they hoped eventually to bring about 48,000 self-built solutions per year with an annual yield of 60 solutions per instructor. This required almost 800 instructors, but already, in 1983, 170 instructors had been trained to produce more than 10,000 solutions per year.[10]

In addition to the technical framework, SENA also established training programs for residents in order to increase revenues and provide jobs in the housing sector. It offered the following apprenticeship services: construction organization, business management, and public speaking, as well as specialties directly related to construction, such as masonry, sanitary practices, plumbing, etc. Moreover, these services encouraged the creation of microenterprises and the development of diverse associative structures.

Since its creation in 1968, DIGIDEC has launched more than 500 self-help projects and produced almost 38,000 houses and apartments.

---

9. Colombian National Housing Authority, *Projected National Plan* (Bogotá: Colombian National Housing Authority, 1984).

10. Colombian National Apprenticeship Service, unpublished working papers, 1983.

Thanks to a North American program, Alliance for Progress, local councils for community action networks identified by the DIGIDEC in the 1960s were developed throughout the entire country, even in the smallest villages. Official statistics indicate that more than 3,000 councils were established, suggesting an involvement of a total of more than 5 million people (Colombia's population was then 28 million).[11] Although charged with encouraging and promoting popular participation in integrated development, most of these councils advocated largely with words rather than action. As a result, their inefficiencies in achieving their original goals lead many networks to be disparaged by the general public, who saw them as tools for political control.

With the advent of the Betancur government at the end of 1982, DIGIDEC organized the first Congress for Self-Managed, Self-Constructed Housing in Pereira, the birthplace of popular self-management movements (see Case Study 6). DIGIDEC brought together public and private organizations and associations, as well as anyone else promoting this sort of housing, under one roof. This congress sought to put promoters and organizers of self-help groups into contact with public and private organizations in order to help them analyze methods and approaches to develop a new politics of housing suited to the greatest number of residents. The representatives of popular organizations emphasized the complete absence of government aid in this sector and drew up a list of the most frequently encountered problems, such as difficulties in acquiring viable building sites, the high cost of construction materials, and a lack of technical framework and financial aid. It was thus decided that (1) different statutes would be established at the national level to encourage and protect self-managed housing associations, (2) the DIGIDEC's journal would be used to inform and share various self-management experiences, and (3) university resources would be appropriated to contribute to the effort.

In addition, the government decided to expand its professional civil service with a mandate to assist in the integrated development of communities within urban shantytowns. Cadres of professionals—including engineers, architects, lawyers, and sociologists—were created when it

---

11. Colombian National Apprenticeship Service, unpublished working papers, 1983.

became a requirement to undertake such service in order to complete university studies; a condition similar to that of doctors who were already required to spend two years serving in a rural milieu.

In 1983, BCH complemented its normal assistance programs oriented toward the middle classes with a special program, the Terrasses, to help compensate for the lack of affordable housing sites in the largest cities. Intended to increase density in ground floor, self-constructed urban zones, this program encouraged the construction of one- and two-story buildings through special loans. I was told that the three biggest cities— Bogotá, Cali, and Medellín—had a combined potential total of 230,000 buildable Terrasses within their urban perimeters. Furthermore, BCH created a Financial Fund for Urban Development to assist municipalities in the definition, execution, and financing of their infrastructure and public service projects. More than 60 percent of Bogotá's population, I learned, had lived in clandestinely urbanized zones with no infrastructure in 1972, but following the BCH changes, the official legalization of these neighborhoods notably lowered this figure, though it nonetheless remained quite high.

Although the advertising brochures said that it was coming to the aid of the poorest, I was told that the BCH was not permitted financially to assist those who earned less than two minimum wages and that, therefore, more than 30 percent of the population was being excluded and forced to find help through public organizations, foundations, and other groups. All of these organizations worked together cooperatively to make their resources available to the neediest.

Thus, agreements were made between DIGIDEC, SENA, and ICT to complete diverse projects in several midsized cities. Other agreements between BCH, ICT, and savings and loan banks and more still between ICT and SENA were established to contribute both financially and technically to various other self-construction programs in the country's largest cities. These programs were all the more praiseworthy and admirable in that they placed all of the country's resources at the disposition of the people so that they might make use of the tools necessary to create homogenous, integrated communities.

The question stands: is giving responsibility to the people so that they can take charge of the creation of their own neighborhoods and cities only possible in developing countries? Even in the most enlightened of these countries, citizens are not protected from sudden shifts in political orientation, which, even if they sometimes risk calling into question new organizational structures (perhaps deemed threatening to power), can no longer threaten what has been acquired and strongly anchored in every individual involved in the formation of these groups.

IV. Burkina Faso and West Africa

Analysis of Organizing Trends and Government Politics

In the conclusion of Case Study 4, I touched upon my tense relationship with the housing and town planning minister in Ouagadougou, Burkina Faso. In West Africa, there is a strong self- help tradition at the village level, but when the community activity changes scale and becomes national, it begins to disturb the area's authoritarian regime. In dictatorships, people who meddle at the national scale become a potential threat, and this is the reason why the UN refused to repeat the Ouagadougou experience in other West African countries.

Although I worked on short missions for the UNDP between 1975 and1980 throughout West Africa, mostly in former French colonies, the longest I spent on a single project was for a whole year in Mali, where I coordinated a population transfer. In the late 1970s, I also helped some nongovernmental organizations in Senegal, and I had an experience worth describing in Benin.

Mission In Benin

In November 1977, I accompanied a medical doctor on a one-month mission for the UN Capital Development Fund in the People's Republic of Benin for the planning and future construction of 190 rural primary schools and 60 maternity and rural health care units. The mission was to propose low-cost construction methods and provide technical solutions with cost estimates. A tropical, sub-Saharan nation, Benin stretches from the Atlantic Ocean to the Sahara. At the time of my visit, the country was in the period of its acclaimed "scientific socialist" era. When we arrived, Benin's minister of health and education received us very courteously while dressed as an army general, flowering with countless multicoloured decorations. He was as short as he was wide.

In addition to the 36 upgraded existing dispensaries, 10 new rural health care units were projected to be built around the 6 provinces of the country, as well as 190 schools for the benefit of about 40,000 children. A field trip around the country allowed us to visit some 30 rural schools built either traditionally with adobe walls and thatched roofs or, more often, by conventional masonry with corrugated steel roofs. We observed that the traditional schools built with local materials were richer in natural light, cooler, and in scale with the available structural materials, such as large, local tree trunks. The so-called modern conventional schools were built with poor craftsmanship—prison-like, often very hot with the corrugated metal roof, and lacking in natural light and fresh air flow because the louvered windows had long ago stopped working. Water was found to be a severe problem in most places as well. Where reservoirs existed, they were found to be dry because their link to roof gutters had long disappeared.

Throughout Benin's three climate zones, we found that the existing traditional constructions were appropriate to each zone. They were more open with natural sunlight as we moved from the semitropical provinces of the south to the dry Sahelian provinces of the north. The ones considered to be modern were smaller and most often badly lit. In the north, I had the opportunity to see the best school of all. Both teacher and students sat under the shade of an enormous tree: a beautiful image of the very first school!

Aside from being more economical, the benefits of improved traditional construction were manifold. Moreover, apart from being familiar, they were simpler to understand for local builders. Upon the end of my mission, and in accordance with protocol, I had an appointment with the education minister. Dressed in his army outfit with plenty of medals all over his chest, the general was anxious to know about my mission's conclusions. When I began to describe my ideas for the appropriate construction technology, which aimed for not only cutting costs but also the improvement of the local population's environment, the minister stopped being diplomatic. He stood up, glaring at me from his five feet, and, gathering all of his authority, he furiously told me that I was not leaving his country until I agreed to all of the government's requests. He went on to describe his wishes: "we need the same modern schools and other big buildings that you have in Paris and New York, all made of glass and steel," and there was no reason why I should stop him from getting them. Fortunately, I had not said anything about how beautiful the simple school under "the tree of learning," as they called it, had been! The minister rang for his secretary and locked me with him until I wrote a report addressed to the UN that agreed to his government's demands. By noon, the paper was typed and signed to the general's satisfaction, and the hostage was released. At the UN headquarters in New York, I presented both reports: the professional one and the one I had signed under duress. I was soon declared a persona non grata by the general when the UN did not choose his solution.

In 1993, some fifteen years later and after the period of "socialist" confusion ended, I was back in this poor and beautiful country for a two-day international seminar on appropriate technology and popular participation in urban and rural areas. The general was no longer around, but I heard from my high-official friends from other West African countries that soon after my 1977 mission, he had warned them not to ever let me work in their countries.

Mali Experience

In January 1979, I was offered a one-year mission by the UN Office of Technical Cooperation to coordinate a population transfer in the region of Selingue, about ninety-three miles south of Bamako, the capital of Mali. The transfer I was to coordinate was due to the construction of a hydroelectric dam that would provide electricity for Bamako and the surrounding region. Started in 1971, its planned completion by 1979 meant that it would inundate around 308 square miles, including seven villages, uprooting close to 14,000 people in less than one year. My mission had been designed to prepare village residents for the move by initiating projects that would better their life economically. The villagers living east and west of the Sankarani River were generally very poor, and the little they had was the meagre land they cultivated and their precious fruit trees. We had to move them in a hurry because the timing for the flooding of the dam did not leave room for any other activity. Using as a pretext the dust and the large distance separating me from the populations to be displaced if I were to live in Bamako, I asked for and was given permission by the industrial development minister to live in the area of the dam construction site. I wanted to become the first one displaced and to build my own home amongst the villagers.

When I arrived in Selingue, I had to choose a site between two distinct worlds. On the one hand, there was the village of prefabricated houses imported from Europe, air conditioned twenty-four hours a day, where all the engineers and technicians from around the world lived apart from the indigenous population. A closed, segregated camp, it looked like a sad copy of European suburbia had been airlifted into the heart of Africa—it was so unfit that one could easily believe it to be a parody or a caricature. Fortunately, I was told that there were no empty buildings available large enough to house both a UN office and my living quarters. On the other side of this all-too-familiar scenario were the huts of the African workers made with locally found materials: adobe, straw, and bamboo. It was a strong contrast—an aggressively imposed modernity set against a traditional village know-how specific to the African rural communities. Living closer to the indigenous population meant building my own house along with a UN field office. Permission from the ministry representative was given for a piece of land right at the junction of the two cultures: just outside the limits of the expatriates' prefabricated village of engineers and specialized technicians so as to have access to running water and electricity and close to the African village of Kangare, where the Malian workers lived.

When the authorities had realized that no funds were going to be available for building conventional houses for the displaced villagers, they had asked them a few months before my arrival whether they preferred to move into the same type of traditional hut or into concrete block houses with tin roofs. More than 70 percent preferred concrete block houses. Since the peasants in these villages were very poor, their tiny huts never exceeded ten feet in diameter. I understood their wish for what they thought was a symbol of a better life— compared to their poor, small, and airless dwellings, the prefabricated expatriates' houses were dream homes. Unfortunatey, since there was no money to build such houses for the displaced villagers, the questionnaire had only served to make them believe that a new life was just waiting for them thanks to their government's national project.

I avoided any discussion about the inquest results, and I decided that I would respect local traditions when building a UN office, along with my own home, to serve as a model of a relocated house. Inspired by historic examples of Mali's traditional adobe architecture, I designed my house and UN office and built it in less than two months with the help of a handful of the best builders from each of the seven villages. By designing my house according to their traditions, they saw that the project could allow them to possess huts similar to mine, which was at least twice the size that they were used to. Construction begun with six full-time workers selected by the different village chiefs as the best in their various specialties: structuring, adobe mixing, and gathering quality roofing materials. The work team was organized, and our construction site became a two-way training program—an experimental school where they taught me their traditional ways and I taught them how to improve their traditions by incorporating an awareness of wind and the use of adobe furniture. As for the local UN office, I planned a very large, high-terraced room with a bamboo and straw-covered veranda extension to act as both a meeting and multipurpose space. During this process, the workers learned to improve and enrich their traditional ways. Because ventilation was lacking in the local huts, I taught them how to induce it by first questioning them on the direction of the major wind patterns at different times of the year. Since the UN was paying for their adobe bricks, I suggested that they could be more generous with the size of each hut. We hired a helicopter to take aerial photos, allowing us to have exact plans for each village. We then proceeded to draw the plans for each new village in the image of the old one, but, this time, with a larger land area for each family, allowing them to plant a small garden to grow vegetables, build a chicken coop, or do whatever project they wished. With only five or six months left before the start of the inundation, it was essential to have at least one large, comfortable hut with a small annex to store belongings ready for each family.

Mali's minister of industrial development, who controlled the more than four-hundred-million dollar cost of this national project, was known to be taking a tax for each contract conceded in the multiple techni-

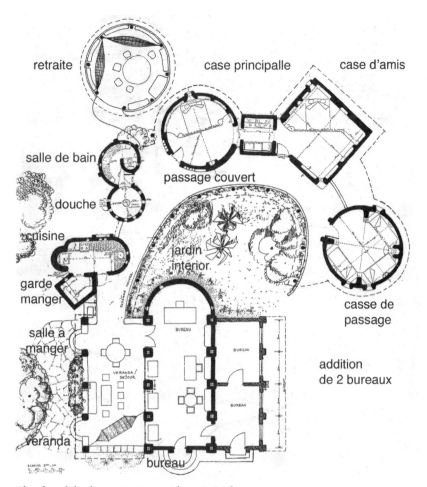

retraite

case principalle

case d'amis

salle de bain

passage couvert

douche

cuisine

jardin interior

garde manger

casse de passage

salle à manger

addition de 2 bureaux

veranda

bureau

Plan for adobe demonstration residence in Mali. DRAWING BY ROGER KATAN

cal fields tied into the hydroelectric dam construction process. As a result, the lucky international contractors selected in the final short-list of their particular specialties would discretely include the minister's share in their final submission proposal. Moreover, the minister had been in power in this dictatorial government for over twenty years, owned countless properties, and was known to have a very comfortable life. When it came to who would manage the very low UN budget (less than one million USD) to displace around fourteen thousand people in one year,

Adobe house in Mali, facade view of the kitchen.

View of the guestroom (square hut): bed, shelves, and lighting are made in adobe.

View of the guestroom: bed, shelves, and lighting are made in adobe.

View of the main bedroom (round hut).

View of square and round huts.

View of the passageway leading to the traditional rooms.

PHOTOS BY
ROGER KATAN

the minister had made clear that he wanted his administration to manage it. While I wanted to compensate each family by at least paying them for the work of extracting clay to make their own adobe bricks for their huts, his idea was to rent or borrow heavy machinery from his many contractor friends in the nearby construction site and have his administration extract mounds of clay soil and dump them at the new village sites, hence avoiding any form of aid to the displaced. Since these villagers were being forced out of their homes with less than eight months warning before the inundation of their villages and with no compensation whatsoever for their forced move, I thought that the minimum the project should do was to pay them for making their own adobe bricks and the other materials necessary to build their own huts. Since the minister was quite sure that the UN was inclined to my approach, he kept creating problems to stall the transfer and its related programs. His executive director had the audacity to tell me at one of our tense meetings: "don't you know that if you and your UN were not around, we would know how to move our people much faster than you: by showing a hard stick and an open truck, and by ordering them by force to get in or be drowned! We would drive them away and dump them in some wasteland far away from here . . . the interest of our nation comes first."

Our team was constantly blocked by Mali's central administration regarding the social workers and other professionals necessary to help move the population. I was condemned to spend my time writing reports and justifications for the additional staff needed. Most of the programs for community development for which I was supposed to be supporting had to be put off until after the transfer. The mere presence of my house was an annoyance to the minister—especially when engineers and other visitors referred to it and asked him why there were not more like it around. He became even more annoyed after a full-page article about the project was published in the German newspaper *Frankfurter Rundschau* in February 1980.[12] The journalist had come to investigate how well European and German funds were being spent on this big hydroelectric dam. He had been sent by the UN to stay for a couple of days, and during his

---

12. Pierre Simonitsch, "Malis Aufbruch ins Industriezeitalter," *Frankfurter Rundschau*, February 20, 1980.

investigation, he stayed in the guestroom of my house. One month later, a full-page spread of his article had two photos: the dam and my house. The photo's caption—"What Is Development?"—incited the minister to believe, and apparently even to say, that I was sabotaging his project.

The transfer was in dire need of personnel to handle the logistics and help with the many desperate families who were increasingly falling into a state of great anguish and tension. An antagonism was also building up between the populations and the minister's office to the point where I received a delegation of a dozen representatives from the seven villages who came to ask me to go with them to see the president and to tell him about the carelessness of his local administration and the fact that the villagers were suffering as a result. I simply told them that as a foreigner, I had no right to meddle in national matters and that I would be expelled if I did so. However, I encouraged them to go speak with their president. He spoke Bambara like them, and he would probably hear their compelling plea. I also told them that I could not stand by and be a witness to any accident or drowning, and, for that reason, I had made the heartbreaking decision to renounce my contract. They were disturbed when they learned that I was about to leave the project because the authorities were doing all they could to stall the transfer. I just could not bear to be present the day innocent people would be drowned because of the callous indifference of their corrupt government. A few days later, a small group of village leaders with two traditional chiefs came and told me that contrary to their usual respect for higher authorities, they had the local sorcerers place all kinds of fetish objects on the main roads taken by the Minister on his regular visits to the dam construction site to have him disappear and for me to stay. Unfortunately, those fetishes were not going to do their job properly or on time.

I decided to write a letter of exasperation to the UN, resigning from my mission. Since I had close to two months left before the end of my one-year contract, the UN representative in Bamako did not accept my letter of resignation. He suggested that I develop the idea of a Center of Appropriate Technology, something which I had proposed one day at a meeting in his office during an informal seminar with a couple of the more forward-looking ministers. In this way, the national construction standards in Mali could change from being French (ever since French colonization) to becoming nationally and traditionally oriented. Once the written proposal was completed, I flew to Nairobi, Kenya, where the United Nation's Habitat headquarters was located in order to present my proposal with an estimated budget. Eight months later, a message from the United Nation's headquarters in New York reached me in Colombia, inviting me to go for a short mission to Bamako to create a Center of Appropriate Technology.

I had no idea of what had happened in Selingue after my departure. Trying to get some news of Africa while in South America was, in the 1980s, as difficult as getting news from another planet. Flying from South America to Africa at that time necessitated changing planes in Paris. It was with a certain apprehension that I embarked on the flight to Bamako. An engineer I had met in Selingue was on board and gave me some news of the project that calmed my anxieties. My departure apparently had a direct effect on the population transfer organization. Less than three months after I tore myself away from the project, the industrial development minister was finally removed by the president after twenty years of absolute power. From the beginning, he had considered the transfer like any other ordinary business—a technical contract linked with the mechanics of the hydroelectric machine. The unfortunate consequences of the transfer delays he had probably intended for me to endorse had finally turned against him. That was what had been predicted by another sympathetic young minister who had advised me to leave the project. And I also learned that the new minister's right-hand man and executive director of the Selingue hydroelectric works was the young engineer who had taught me to speak Bambara. All this was good news as far as the new direction was concerned, but I did not find the same good news in the newly self-built villages where the population was left struggling to survive.

In conclusion, the Selingue dam, which was built to produce electricity for the capital of Bamako and the surrounding region as well as spur economic growth, had a direct negative impact on the economy of the Inner Niger Delta and the livelihoods of its one million inhabitants, who lost out completely. The displaced 13,500 Selingue people living in the valley of the Sankarani lost their homes, grazing lands, orchards, and other agricultural lands according to a recent evaluation study.[13] In turn, the very large but slow-starting irrigation project around the newly created 308 square mile lake that was put in place, along with the fisheries and other lake activities, seemed to have only profited the few privileged friends of the powerful rather than the needy, displaced population that it was intended for. Furthermore, although the new villages had only wanted to have at least one light bulb per concession, they were not given access to electricity from the nearby dam until 2000, twenty years later. Only after blocking the roads leading to Selingue, did the villages finally get one miserable light bulb for each concession that sheltered between six to fifteen people.

The Center of Appropriate Technology, for which I returned to Mali in mid-1981 to help start and structure in Bamako for three months with a UNDP contract, lasted close to twenty years and helped to build some major structures thanks to a helpful and democratically elected president. During its existence, the center had had several objectives:

- Underline and encourage the use of local traditional materials to reduce construction costs and improve the housing quality of the majority of the population.

- Improve the quality of life and housing conditions through the exploitation and the development of natural resources such as clay, lime, etc., the use of renewable energies such as solar, biogas, wind, and compost, the mobilization of human resources, and the participatory process.

- Encourage the development and expansion of the country's energy, human, and mining resources. For example, lime quarries were spread all over Mali's territory and were hardly exploited. A good earth stabilizer for construction, lime has been traditionally used in mortar and plaster because of its superior plasticity, workability, and other qualities. Today, lime's dominant construction use is in soil stabilization for roads, airfields, building

---

13. World Bank, *Africa—Reversing Land and Water Degradation Trends in the Niger River Basin Project* (Washington, DC: World Bank, 2011).

foundations, and earthen dams, where it upgrades low quality soils into usable base materials.

Limits and Requirements of Participation

In the western world, the individual is increasingly dependent on the inextricable web woven by the techno-bureaucracy that is meant to protect and assist all. Completely dependent on the established order, with its ever more excessive organizational system, individuals are increasingly less able to act without the assistance of those who claim to know how to help. They can only behave by bending themselves to standardized, uniform norms, tastes, and values at the risk of being treated as deviant if they do not. Progressively losing their social identities, they allow their status as citizens to be dispossessed of, finding themselves mere users. Responsible, motivated, and concerned citizens have become conditioned to acquire an assisted mentality, relinquishing all of their rights—except the right to consume.

It is not surprising that after three decades of such practices, many governments have begun to paper over the damages at enormous costs, walling off and, most often, destroying a large number of the projects that ultimately failed to solve the problems. In the face of displacement, disinformation, media hype, and the almost total delegation of power to the system's elected officials, who are themselves often subordinate to a greater techno-bureaucracy, more and more groups and individuals have joined together to confront a distant and anonymous power base. These associations, themselves barometers of popular opinion, have often transformed into mobilization groups and information networks of their own. Each of these associations and action groups, in their own way, has attempted to invent another way of doing and being within this creative disorder, something which is doubtlessly disturbing to an order that has been constructed over centuries of centralism and delegated democracy.

It is, therefore, not surprising that the principle of participation first appeared in highly centralized countries. On account of their complex administrations, decision making in centralized governments become increasingly removed from those concerned. Moreover, under the guise of technical rationality, centralized institutions are quick to brandish the sacrosanct principle of "general interest" without ever entirely explaining it. This general interest principle often runs contrary to the interests of local groups, breaking their dynamic, because it effectively silences them.

A Lived Example of the General Interest Principle in Action

In the El Barrio neighborhood of East Harlem, public administration sought to integrate large groups where the population had organized solid social structures within a dilapidated urban fabric. With the consent of public powers, the population, by means of associations, presented a counterproject, and several meetings were scheduled. However, when there were disputes, the administration blocked discussion, claiming to defend the general interest that the discussion was meant to symbolize as opposed to the particular interests defended by the neighborhood associations. Claiming rationality, the administration deemed itself uniquely capable of carrying out neighborhood development.

This phenomenon of centralization quite often leads to authoritarianism with consequent blockages in the system. The multiplication of serious social problems in the urban milieu, including mental illness in the individual, is, in large part, due to the impotence, resignation, and diversity of the populations concerned. And these populations can then only demonstrate their vitality and significance by means that are analogical to the symptoms of a social or mental pathological state in an individual. In *The Myth of the Machine*, Lewis Mumford writes: "If man had originally inhabited a world as blankly uniform as a housing development, as featureless as a parking lot, as destitute of life as an automated factory, it is doubtful if he would have had a sufficiently varied sensory experience to retain images, mold language, or acquire ideas."[14] In fact, centralized bureaucratic systems depersonalize relations and devitalize situations, for when social problems are analyzed abstractly and solutions expressed on paper, all personal and familial substance disappears.

---

14. Lewis Mumford, *Technics and Human Development*, vol. 1 of *The Myth of the Machine* (New York: Harcourt Brace Jovanovich, 1967), page?.

To avoid direct confrontation, the administration is prepared to make enormous detours. Refusing conflict, it resists innovative solutions and hides behind obsolete legislation with what can be characterized as the avoidance model. At the local level, municipalities can halt participation to the extent that officials have been elected and perceive any attempted autonomy as calling their prerogatives into question. This reluctance on the part of municipalities is all the more marked when their own power is limited and dependent on regional and governmental authorities.

A Lived Example of the Avoidance Model in Action

The New York State Bridge and Tunnel Commission projected in 1968 to create an access ramp from one of the bridges linking East Harlem to the airports so as to decrease traffic congestion at the intersection of 125th Street and 2nd Avenue. This project was about to cut a neighborhood in two: on one side was a public housing project and on the other was a dilapidated but still very vibrant urban neighborhood. With respect to the construction of this access ramp, the administration neither confirmed nor denied circulating rumors. After a discrete inquiry, neighborhood leaders realized that the study of the access ramp was already well underway. Tangible proof reinforced their conviction when they saw drilling equipment arrive at the project site. This single-handed administrative action perfectly illustrates the avoidance model approach: a public administration will prefer a secret action over a frank discussion that might involve opposition and conflict.

Municipalities close to the Groups for Municipal Action (GAM) movement knew what the administration was doing and felt obliged to act on two levels: one directed toward the public administration and the other toward the population. This is why it is important not to dupe residents with respect to the extent of the powers at play, a phenomenon we have seen in many of the case studies discussed in this book. On the other hand, it is important to see clearly the arbitrariness and contradictions inherent in such power mechanisms.

Our representative democracies come under heavy fire because elected officials cannot possibly represent the multiple positions that brought them into power, especially those that opposed them in their election. In fact, elected officials are prisoners of a political game and represent only their own personal interests and those of a small number of individuals constituting their clientele. This is why a huge gap often separates decision making and the diversity of local expression. However, to put into place new political modes founded on direct contact would mean to fight against many powerful people and their discourses.

Any form of social innovation carries with it a condemnation of all or part of the existing social system and, to some extent, its abolition. If, in 1968, people chanted "power to the imagination!" in the streets of France, it was because this exclamation expressed the conviction that what could be conceived was not limited to the functional laws that lead to segregation in terms of usage, space, and class. Today, it is not merely irresponsible individuals calling for the right to open experimentation as some might have us believe. Community movements, whatever their past, present, and future setbacks, bear witness to the need to create links and to seek out the symbolic dimension excluded by a purely functional, commercial system of relations laying claim to normalcy.

We have seen throughout this book, innovation always comes up against an arsenal of norms and regulations that hold back or rule out experimentation. In effect, the judicial system is so constrictive that it defines the way we should work, teach, heal, live, and die. The individual is denied any relationship with those responsible for the norm and can only suffer the effects. Thus, one can only effectively oppose this stifling system with a thoughtful popular force. To a certain extent, one must dare to act illegally through civil disobedience in order to locally modify power relations in society. For example, without the risks taken by certain squatters, many old neighborhoods would have definitely been razed to the ground: it was the illegal occupation of a building in East Harlem initiated by the Renegades that inspired the city of New York in 1965 to launch a program encouraging community management of disused buildings in poor neighborhoods controlled by the city. And was it not also the creativity of shantytown residents and self-help groups, often working illegally, that inspired the Colombian government to establish a new kind of politics (see Case Study 6)?

Another limit to development lies in the systematic division of labor: specialization brings about a loss of general knowledge and know-how.

With respect to urbanization, in a society where decisions are made by those who supposedly know best, residents are no longer masters of their own work. They are expected to pay for and consume their housing and shut up, just as architects are expected to draw, managers are to manage, and leaders are to lead—this is what is normal.

Today's tendency toward de-specialization is accompanied by a rapid decline in the number of professionals, including doctors, mechanics, architects, etc. If one wants to play the role rightfully expected of one today within the context of current transformations, an architect will have to stop adopting a single position behind the power of financial organizations and effectively engage the very people these projects will affect. In order to listen to the people, he or she will have to develop communicative techniques to help and stimulate groups and individuals to imagine the places where they want to live, work, and play. To give people back their multidimensionality, they must be treated as active, responsible, and conscious individuals engaged in society. It is only on this condition that they will take charge of the future of their communities.

However, current governments often talk about creating a new kind of citizenship while continuing to treat citizens as consumers. Is this not a contradiction? Or is it rather a continuation of the same politics they are denouncing?

Fortunately, it is clear to many people today that development grounded in such rationality, along with the profit obsession with functionality and efficiency, can only lead to individualism, apathy, and, in the end, disorder and violence. Governments have begun to recognize these malfunctions, which, in reality, are contradictions inherent to the system they represent. This is why we see them taking up numerous grassroots demands at times and brandishing the word "participation" at every opportunity.

An Example of Deprofessionalization

In medical care, more and more people are taking their health and illness into their own hands, preferring self-diagnosis over those of experts. Prevention has become one of the most popular subjects of magazines in the US. Furthermore, numerous groups of people suffering various illnesses have formed in order to benefit from each other's experiences and treatments, especially in Anglo-Saxon countries.

The development of deprofessionalization is not limited to medicine, as such mutual assistance and self-help has extended to plumbing, electricity, construction, car repair, etc. For years already, do-it-yourself television shows on home repairs have earned some of the highest ratings.

It is, therefore, important to fight against extreme specialization and get back to a diversified, artisanal sort of know-how. At the collective level, for example, it is essential to call on different capacities of different people and, thus, create networks of solidarity in the community. It is necessary to move beyond the residents' supposed incompetence.

I have been told that apartments finished by residents have numbered as much as 25 to 50 percent of those finished by specialized businesses in urban zones in both France and the US—not counting the fact that this investment of time and work reinforces an affective personal attachment to the living spaces involved. Furthermore, as we have seen in Case Study 6, in Pereira, Colombia, a self-constructed house costs one quarter of that of a conventional structure of a comparable sort. The official ICT administration recognized this by giving a self-managing group, the Destechados, an order for the production of fifty houses.

It is also important to rethink the information flow in society and community, and it is necessary to recognize that every resident has the capacity to express important facts. We have demonstrated that situations in which the resident-technician relationship was efficient were precisely those where the technicians were conscious of their own limits and were favorable to the expression and capacities of the residents. Whether it be in Meudon, Harlem, or Ouagadougou, it is because local communication networks were put into place that groups were able to imagine housing developments corresponding to their cultural, economic, and social realities of place.

Thus, it is necessary to grasp what will motivate individuals and move them into action, and for this, it is necessary to listen to what is being expressed and, at times, what cannot find expression. Finding out what motivates individuals or groups to mobilize them is the main key to participation.

Motivation: The Key that Unlocks Action

I was sent to Mali in 1980 by the United Nations to coordinate a population transfer of twelve thousand people spread over seven villages. Among certain villagers, there was a rumor that the government was going to build small sturdy houses made out of cement cinder blocks with sheet metal roofs (which was ridiculous for a climate of 104 degrees Fahrenheit almost all year) to compensate the villagers for the loss of their traditional village huts made of sun-dried adobe bricks with grass roofs. With the help of local, traditional masons, I decided to install myself at the heart of the displacement site by building an adobe house, which then served as a workshop-school. Thanks to this action, after two months, it was no longer a question of sturdy houses, but rather of reconstructing new villages out of improved traditional materials along with their appropriate equipment and social services. The psychological effect on the local residents was effective, and the traditional chiefs were, thus, still able to control the growth of their villages, which would have been infinitely more difficult in an environment reflective of another culture.

Four years earlier, at the heart of the UN's Habitat Project in Ouagadougou, I was given the task to create a habitat cooperative to help the residents of Cissin rebuild their neighborhood (see Case Study 4). Previous such UN missions lead by so-called experts, who were actually economist-bankers, had failed because they thought the residents were much too poor. These experts typically based their conclusions only on official statistics that judged populations without fixed or regular incomes to be incapable of saving. It was, thus, necessary to find the needed motivation in the residents themselves so that they would take charge of their own project. Inspired by the traditional village system of solidarity called *tontine*, which is a kind of loose association where families pool their resources under their traditional chief to pay for village needs, I put together a successful microcredit system. This offered poor people who were systematically turned down by banks the means to obtain loans to improve their home and their community. We organized a membership drive, and within the first four weeks, we had close to two hundred members. An autonomously controlled credit union was established in each of the six neighborhoods, and, in close association with one another, savings were pooled and loans dealt out.

The sensation created by a popular credit union allowed representatives of diverse, established neighborhoods to adopt a very new perspective. First, they had an official recognition of their identity, which reinforced their right to exist in their neighborhoods. In contrast, populations on the peripheries of large West African cities had previously not been counted in a formal census, and they were never immune from bulldozers driving them out of their homes on any day. Belonging to a credit union had, thus, empowered them as full-fledged citizens. Moreover, training in accounting and management opened the way to the functional literacy of a large number of the credit union's members since they had to be able to control what was written in their bank statements. All of these elements contributed to helping residents take charge of their neighborhoods' future.

During the first of my three assignments, Upper Volta's minister of Housing and Development was satisfied with the success of our action. During my second assignment, he was barely polite, but by my third and last mission, he was angry because he was receiving repetitive and insistent demands from the community. When not heard, community members had resorted (as I had encouraged them) to sit-in techniques in his office! This was previously unheard of in the prevalent West African dictatorships. As a result, the UN refused my suggestion to establish community credit unions in other West African countries that were plagued with the same type of government. This definitely caused me to stop working with the UN in Africa.

From Sit-In to Occupy

The sit-in movement of the 1960s was an integral part of the nonviolent strategy of civil disobedience and mass protests that eventually led to passage of the Civil Rights Act of 1964. It is, by definition, an organized protest in which a group of people peacefully occupy and refuse to leave a location.

Today, the sit-in has led to the international Occupy movement against social and economic inequality. Its primary concern is the belief that large corporations and the global financial system control the world in a way that disproportionately benefits a minority and undermines the future of democracy.

Among the diverse, citable examples in the US and in Harlem, more specifically, I will return to East Harlem and the plan to build an access ramp from one of the bridges linking East Harlem to the airports. The survival of this neighborhood depended solely on the tenacity with which the residents defended themselves against the plan imposed by the city. Almost illiterate mothers—usually confined to their kitchens to feed their children—used small car counters at their neighborhood's biggest intersections in order to establish a counterplan to the one proposed by the New York State Bridge and Tunnel Commission. The residents' plan was finally accepted by the officials, but this was only a slim victory for them.

In France, within the framework of the housing project renovation program in Marseille, I was able to awaken an active interest that shifted residents from fatalistic apathy to decisive militantism merely by providing them a little economic information about the amount and the way the administration was spending its investment capital.

In South America, in Tumaco, Colombia (Case Study 7), it was necessary to demonstrate the economic importance, at both the regional and individual levels, of a center that could produce wood components in order to obtain the population's support for the self-construction of their houses.

These examples and others taken up in the case studies developed in this book show that it is neither more difficult nor more important to find the key to motivation in France than it is in West Africa, North America, or South America. Motivating local populations results from informing them, exchanging and sharing ideas, and, in many cases, simply listening to better understand and create the climate of confidence necessary for residents to take charge of their future.

Also, any work of this kind requires time. Each of the experiences recounted here demonstrated that significant time was necessary for the participatory process to succeed. In general, this time is not considered work time, but rather time taken from family life, social interaction, and leisure. Neighborhood meetings often took place in the evening, and between meetings, it was the unemployed, stay-at-home mothers, and the marginalized who put these plans into action. However, in the eyes of authorities, the proposals made by such groups did not carry the same weight as those of the specialists paid to plan and develop—professional time is, therefore, the only socially valorized time. Yet, is the only kind of work, salaried work? Can unemployment not take on a creative dimension? Can it not to be the contrary; that it is fragmented, salaried work—disconnected from the community—that destroys independence and creativity?

As long as professional work is the only valued work, as long as the home is only a refuge against the aggressions of the external world, and as long as leisure remains a consumer good, no creative perspective can emerge in the lives of a people who are doomed to remain prisoners of a system that reduces them to passive dependence and apathy. In some cases, this system provides a year's sabbatical that allows for a certain rupture and distance from day-to-day work. The image of unemployment presented by administrations and unions remains purely negative. The time has come to acknowledge the idea of creative unemployment. If its definition were broadened, the development of soft technologies would favor individual initiative and bring back another notion of time. While production time is evaluated in terms of profit, creative time follows another logic, that of personal fulfillment. The stakes are political and will determine much about our civilization.

In *Les Chemins du Paradis,* André Gorz cites the work of the sociologist Nathan Ackerman with regard to an exchange system originating in Quebec and introduced in Sweden several years ago:

The union of associations bringing together an increasingly larger range of productions and services gives each member the right to receive, in the form of goods or services, the equivalent of the number of hours given to the collectivity. This cooperative union could provide, for example, credit for vacations, the services of a team of painters or plasterers, consumer products, or equipment in exchange for a predetermined number of hours working for the cooperative or developing the neighborhood. An isolated individual, a group, or a family could provide these hours intermittently, as necessary in function of respective needs and possibilities. The exchanges and work provided also take on a nonmarket form of each according to his abilities, to each

according to his needs. . . . Thus, any community project no longer depends on unpredictable public or private financing. The
back and forth between group work, optional micro-social activities, and autonomous personal activities guarantees everyone's
balance and freedom. Complexity, indecision, and overlapping
maintain open spaces where initiative and imagination can be
exercised.[15]

This complexity is life's richness, and, when encouraged by the ministry, it should be instituted to assure a real process of dialogue. In the same
way, texts on neighborhood projects speak effectively about the greatest
amount of information to be passed on to residents. However, they do
so without providing the material means, without extensive technical
participation, and without a substantial diffusion of information—i.e.,
the establishment of a budget for information and exchange. The potential dynamic of these ideas might inevitably lead to failure despite initial
good intentions.

In the end, the decentralization undertaken by an administration
marks the realization that centralized power cannot and should not or-
chestrate and control everything, especially neighborhood life. A degree
of autonomy for municipalities and a certain confidence in local, grassroots politics are highly desirable. It is, at long last, necessary to recognize
the neighborhood or village as the smallest and most homogenous unit,
which best understands the most fundamental aspects of daily, social
life. The neighborhood, like the village, has a specific, irreplaceable, and
evocative power that makes it a necessary political and creative interloc-
utor, notably for the initiatives it alone can undertake.

How can populations as different and made fragile by socioeconomic
criteria as the abandoned shantytowns of Bogotá, Cissin in Ouagadougou, or East Harlem be considered the most dynamic and creative? In all
of these cases, success means multiplying initiatives to reinforce social
life as a magnifier of creativity, independence, and influence on the outside world. Cissin and its credit union and the Renegades in New York
with their occupation and renovation of a building have succeeded in
spreading their versions of action to other neighborhoods, both locally

---

15. André Gorz, *Les Chemins du Paradis* (Paris: Galilée, 1983), 3. Translated by Roger Katan.

and globally. Through their dynamism, they succeeded in contaminating other populations and inciting them to action. Was it not the Destechados in Pereira and similar groups elsewhere that inspired a politics of national aid to grassroots groups in Colombia (Case Study 6)? At a more local level, there are even more examples. Did the city of Lille not recently invite one of the members of the grassroots Roubaix APU to create a program to organize its subway?

It is important to remove taboos linked to the phenomenon of participation. It is true that this can be expensive because it requires huge amounts of time and enormous social costs that are a result of the large groups constructed over the past twenty years. The issues were elaborated earlier in this chapter in the section on the housing renovation problem in the United States.

Any participation in the conception of a large project requires direct contact with the populations concerned and not only with traditional representative structures. Otherwise, dissent will inevitably arise in the course of its completion. Participation does not mean opting for simplistic solutions, but requires the creation of a new language along with new tools to express another way of doing things. This act is linked by its very nature to the universal history of the development of human institutions. If we recognize residents' rights to determine the way they want to live, a new architecture and a new urbanization that integrates every facet of life can take place. Without a permanent dialogue between researchers-technicians and residents, it will not be possible to dislodge this new way—where the groundwork is only just being laid—from the inertial habits of yesteryear. To conclude, participation provokes fear, and those who criticize it are frightened by the dangers implied by it.

It is true that all of these burgeoning tendencies carry with them a protest against the system of the established order. It is also true, as Alain Touraine said, that it is not enough to criticize bureaucratic excess: "Our society's vitality and its future possibilities depend on its ability to replace the social organization model of the last three centuries—the construction of order—by another: The management of change in complex situations."[16]

---

16. Alain Touraine, "L'enjeu d'un débat sur la bureaucratie," *L'Express*, October 7–13, 1983, 56.

It is, therefore, necessary to call for permanently decentralized information that is available to everyone so that the line separating institutor and instituted does not remain static. We will then have a mobile, open, and diversified society: mobile because it will no longer be fixed by definitive models, open because it will be receptive to the diversity of social relations and the management of change, and diversified because the intensity of the forms of experimentation can be highly variable according to the groups concerned. There is a possibility for our society to behave as a living organism in a continuous process of experimentation.

However, it is still necessary to temper this desire for experimentation with an observation: human affective capacities have been so limited by our institutions that people can no longer undergo the emotional charge created by situations that are too weakly structured. For this reason, it will be necessary to foresee stabilization phases in our society's evolution that provide all of us the needed time to reflect and appreciate the progress accomplished, as a function of our history's cultural values, in order to better understand the future.

In conclusion, it will be less a question of knowing whether we can adapt to a particular type of social organization than one of knowing whether this type of organization can effectively contribute to the development of humanity's potential for intelligence, inspiration, and free creativity.

All of these experiences led us over the years to refine the process of participatory and advocacy planning that we practiced. Based on those experiences, the definition of "good planning" that we would offer is one that is predicated on the integration of vision, reason, and democracy. Planning is the result of the critical tension between vision—the ability to envision and develop alternative approaches to problems and opportunities; reason—the trust in the capacity of the mind to understand nature and society; and democracy—the trust in the capacity of people for self-governance. Vision is dependent on ingenuity and creativity; reason is dependent on a rational systemic analysis; and democracy is dependent on the empowerment and participation of the people directly and indirectly impacted. As long as the interests of minorities, the less powerful, and future generations are taken into consideration and respected, successful planning is possible.

Appendix

Case Study 1: RPA and Listening to the City

Organization of Choices for '76 at the Operational Stage:
A Metropolitan Experiment in Resident Education and Communications

Role of Television

The issues and arguments for and against Choices for '76 were presented in five films, which were all shown on each of the television channels in New York and its region.

Having the eighteen television stations in the region show the films helped to secure the participation of newspapers and get the financial assistance needed. Through the wide range of programing schedules on television, a larger number of viewers were able to watch the films.

Throughout its time presented on television, Choices for '76 recorded a stable 5 to 8 percent of families watching, which is a record when these percentages are compared with general programing. The total audience could have been even greater, especially in certain segments of the population, but it is difficult to capture interest if there is not enough intense advertising.

An average of 26,500 ballots were filled out and returned after each of the five programs. Three-quarters of the ballots were from people who watched the program on television.

Nearly twenty thousand people participated in a panel discussion on the topics raised by the television programing and during breakout sessions at home, churches, or offices.

Role of Other Media

Nearly one hundred thousand copies of the paperback *How to Save Urban America* were distributed, but only one ballot in eight came from people who read the book first.

The forty-six daily newspapers in the area published information about the project: thirty-six of them included, at least, an article and an editorial on Choices for '76 per week for an average of thirteen weeks before and during the project. For seventeen daily newspapers, there was an article per week.

Newspapers certainly brought the most generous contribution to the project. They published numerous articles and editorials and distributed the ballots at their own expense. Four-fifths of the ballots were distributed through these newspapers as a public service. Thirteen daily newspapers published the data and the issues involved before people were called to vote. The massive participation of newspapers was due to their enthusiasm for this project and a long relationship of trust with Regional Plan Association (RPA).

Unfortunately, a study on the newspapers' impact has not been completed very accurately.

Financing the Transaction

Almost two million dollars was donated to the project either in money or in service: one-third by private foundations, one-third by large companies, and one-third by the state.

The project had a day-to-day budget without a known total budget and used each achievement accomplished as leverage to receive more financial support.

Development of Choice

In order to reach a wider audience than just those interested in regional planning, it was important to distribute relevant, clear, comprehensive, and attractive information.

A first draft was discussed by the RPA team and submitted to the nine largest regional institutions of planning for review. It was written by the RPA and included basic information on the themes of housing, transportation, environment, poverty, city, and suburbs. These written documents were then subjected to expert analysis by the public institutions participating in the project. On some issues, the opinion of specialists and private organizations were requested.

After several revisions, the documents were submitted for the opinion of the Citizens-Councilors Committee, which changed the wording and the number of choices. The revised document was then handed to the film's producer, the publisher of the paperback, and, finally, the Gallup polling organization for test preparation and final editing.

Focus Groups

More than twenty thousand participated at least once in a newsgroup. It seems that through these meetings, several objectives were met. These focus groups served to:

- Provide more complete information than given on television.
- Enable the application of general ideas developed on television and through personal circumstances so that people could
  think more concretely about the challenges.
- Demonstrate that planning decisions are a combination of different views.
- Get people to understand the need for collective action for achieving certain goals.

References

Arnstein, Sherry R. "A Ladder of Citizen Participation." *Journal of the American Planning Association* 35, no. 4 (July 1969): 216–224.

Association of Internally Displaced Afro-Colombians. "Afro-Colombian Factsheet." Accessed March 13, 2014. http://www.afrocolombians.com/pdfs/ACfactsheet.pdf.

Booth, Stephen, and Siân Herbert. *EU External Aid: Who Is It For?* London: Open Europe, 2011.

Breasted, Mary. "Tenants Evicted in Brooklyn as Demolition Begins." *New York Times*, September 13, 1973.

"Burkina Faso." In *Encyclopaedia Britannica Online*. Accessed March 10, 2014. http://www.britannica.com/EBchecked/topic/85420/Burkina-Faso.

Burkina Faso Ministry of Interior. *December 1977 Ministry of Interior Report*. Ouagadougou: Government Printing Office, 1977.

Bushnell, David, and Rex A. Hudson. "Chapter 2: The Society and Its Environment." In *Colombia: A Country Study*, edited by Rex A. Hudson, 63–140. Washington, DC: Library of Congress Federal Research, 2010.

Caldwell, William A., ed. *How to Save Urban America: Choices for '76, Key Issues Confronting Cities and Suburbs*. New York: A Signet Special/New American Library, 1973.

Carson, Rachel. *Silent Spring*. New York: Houghton Mifflin Company, 1962.

Citron, Christiane, ed. *A Search for Solutions: Poughkeepsie and the Model Cities Program*. Poughkeepsie, NY: Vassar College, 1969.

_____. "Students Complete Seminar, Stress Community Awareness." *Vassar Miscellany News* 53, no. 22 (May 1969): 1, 7.

_____. "Students Organize Seminar, Plan Study of Urban Issues." *Vassar Miscellany News* 53, no. 12 (January 1969): 1–4.

_____. "Students Sit in Dean's Office to Demand Katan's Rehiring." *Vassar Miscellany News* 53, no. 11 (December 1968): 1.

Civic Alliance to Rebuild Downtown New York. *Listening to the City: Report of Proceedings*. New York: Civic Alliance to Rebuild Downtown New York, 2002.

_____. *A Planning Framework to Rebuild Downtown New York*. New York: Civic Alliance to Rebuild Downtown New York, 2002.

Colombian National Housing Authority. *Projected National Plan*. Bo-gotá: Colombian National Housing Authority, 1984.

Davidoff, Paul. "Advocacy and Pluralism in Planning." *Journal of the American Planning Association* 31, no. 4 (November 1965): 331–338.

de Rudder, Véronique. "La Cohabitation Pluriethnique et Ses Enjeux," *Migrants-Formation*, no. 80 (March 1990): 68–89.

Discover Magazine, Editors of, and Dean Christopher. *Discover's 20 Things You Didn't Know About Everything.* New York: HarperCollins, 2008.

Easterly, William. *The White Man's Burden: Why the West's Efforts to Aid the Rest Have Done So Much Ill and So Little Good.* New York: Oxford University Press, 2006.

Eco Habitat Group Charter. Paris: Eco Habitat Group, 2009.

Evans-Pritchard, Ambrose. "Reporter Following Trial of Corruption in EU Arrested." *The Telegraph*, March 20, 2004.

Fiscal Policy Institute. *World Trade Center Job Impacts Take a Heavy Toll on Low-Wage Workers: Occupational and Wage Implications of Job Losses Related to the September 11 Wrold Trade Center Attack.* New York: Fiscal Policy Institute, 2001.

"Former UN Oil-for-Food Head Quits." *BBC News*, August 8, 2005.

French Ministry of Housing. *Declaration of Purpose.* Paris: French Ministry of Housing, 1977.

Gans, Herbert J. *Urban Villagers: Group and Class in the Life of Italian-Americans.* New York: Simon and Schuster, 1962.

Glazer, Nathan, and Daniel P. Moynihan. *Beyond the Melting Pot: The Negroes, Puerto Ricans, Jews, Italians, and Irish of New York City.* Cambridge, MA: MIT Press, 1963.

Global Earthquake Model, Earthquake Consequences Database. "Popayan Colombia 1983." Accessed March 14, 2014. http://gemecd.org/event/91.

Gorz, André. *Les Chemins du Paradis.* Paris: Galilée, 1983.

Group of 35. *Preparing for the Future: A Commercial Development Strategy for New York: Final Report.* New York: Group of 35, 2001.

Hanhimäki, Jussi M. "An Elusive Grand Design." In *Nixon in the World: American Foreign Relations, 1969–1977*, edited by Frederik Logevall and Andrew Preston, 25–44. New York: Oxford University Press, 2008.

Harrington, Michael. *The Other America: Poverty in the United States.* New York: Simon and Schuster, 1962.

Jacobs, Jane. *The Death and Life of Great American Cities.* New York: Random House, 1961.

Jardies Project Charter. Meudon, France: Jardies Group, 1968.

Katan, Roger. *Bâtir Ensemble.* Paris: International Council for French Language in partnership with the International Institute of Mediterranean Architecture, 1988.

———. *Manhattan State Hospital Evaluation.* 2 vols. New York: published by author, 1968–1971.

Kliesen, Kevin L., and Daniel L. Thornton. "Tax Rates and Revenues since the 1970s." *Economic Synopses* 2011, no. 24 (2011): 1–2.

Labor Community Advocacy Network. *Labor Community Advocacy Network to Rebuild New York Policy Statement.* New York: Labor Community Advocacy Network, 2002.

Lopez, Asbel. "Colombia Exports Its 'New School' Blueprint." *UNESCO Courier* 6 (June 1999): 14–16.

Lyndon B. Johnson. "Annual State of the Union Address." Speech delivered before a joint session of Congress, Washington, DC, January 8, 1964.

Mays, Jeff. "East Harlem Zoning Plan Envisions Commercial Corridor, Affordable Housing." *DNAinfo New York*, January 30, 2013.

Mumford, Lewis. *The Myth of the Machine.* 2 vols. New York: Harcourt Brace Jovanovich, 1967–1970.

Murillo, Luis Gilberto. "El Chocó: The African Heart of Colombia." Lecture at the American Museum of Natural History, New York City, February 23, 2001.

National Administrative Department of Statistics. *Boletín: Censo General 2005: Perfil Tumaco Nariño.* Bogotá: National Administrative Department of Statistics, 2010.

New York State Assembly. *The Lower Manhattan Economy after September 11th.* New York: New York State, 2005.

Partnership for New York and Chamber of Commerce. *Working Together to Accelerate New York's Recovery: Economic Impact Analysis of the September 11th Attack on New York City.* New York: Partnership for New York and Chamber of Commerce, 2001.

Pratt Institute Center for Community and Environmental Development. *Making It in New York: The Manufacturing Land Use and Zoning Initiative: Vol. I: Report.* Brooklyn, NY: Pratt Institute Center for Community and Environmental Development, 2001

Pushkarev, Boris S. "The Town Meeting on Cities and Suburbs." In *How to Save Urban America: Choices for '76, Key Issues Confronting Cities and Suburbs,* edited by William A. Caldwell, 185–230. New York: A Signet Special/New American Library, 1973.

―――――. "The Town Meeting on Poverty." In *How to Save Urban America: Choices for '76, Key Issues Confronting Cities and Suburbs,* edited by William A. Caldwell, 135–183. New York: A Signet Special/New American Library, 1973.

"Q&A: Oil-for-Food Scandal." *BBC News*, September 7, 2005.

Seifer, Nancy. "Northside: Another Corona: The New Ethnocide." *Village Voice*, February 15, 1973.

Shore, William B. "Choices for '76: The Results and the Lessons." *National Civic Review*, 64, no. 1 (2007): 6–20.

―――――. "The Town Meeting on Housing." In *How to Save Urban America: Choices for '76, Key Issues Confronting Cities and Suburbs,* edited by William A. Caldwell, 13–44. New York: A Signet Special/New American Library, 1973.

Simonitsch, Pierre. "Malis Aufbruch ins Industriezeitalter." *Frankfurter Rundschau*, February 20, 1980.

The Architects' Resistance. *Architecture and Racism.* New York: The Architects' Resistance, 1968.

Tickner, Arlene B. "Chapter 4: Government and Politics." In *Colombia: A Country Study*, edited by Rex A. Hudson, 213–282. Washington, DC: Library of Congress Federal Research, 2010.

Touraine, Alain. "L'enjeu d'un débat sur la bureaucratie." *L'Express*, October 7–13, 1983.

United Nations. "UN Facts about the United Nations Oil-for-Food Programme." Accessed March 14, 2014. http://www.un.org/News/dh/iraq/oip/facts-oilforfood htm.

United Nations Development Programme. *Report on the Sahel Drought.* New York: United Nations Development Programme, 1975.

————. *Sahel Region Report.* New York: United Nations Development Programme, 1970.

United States Census Bureau. *2008-2010 American Community Survey.* Washington, Government Printing Office, 2001.

World Bank. *Africa - Reversing Land and Water Degradation Trends in the Niger River Basin Project.* Washington, DC: World Bank, 2011.

————. *Current Economic Position and Development Prospects of Upper Volta.* Report no. 564a–UV. Washington, DC: World Bank, 1975.

————. *Main Report.* Vol. 1 of *The Economic Development of Upper Volta.* Western Africa series, no. AW–19. Washington, DC: World Bank, 1970.

Index

Page references followed by *fig* indicate an illustrated figure or photograph.

accountability demands, 11
Ackerman, Nathan, 277–278
ACSA's Distinguished Professor (New Jersey Institute of Technology), 8
"Advocacy and Pluralism in Planning" (Davidoff), 10
advocacy planning movement: first community development corporation (CDC) launched in the US, 16; Groups for Municipal Action (GAM) ideology driving the, 14–15, 270; Mobile Local Aid Service (MLAS) [later TAG] created during the, 15; public workshops in France and Europe during the, 13–16. *See also* participatory (advocacy) planning
Afro-Colombians (Colombia): emergence of a new rural school for Chocó Department, 176–183; *mestizaje* ideology marginalizing, 174–176; slavery and early history of, 173–174; traces of Africa found among, 180–181
AIA New York City Chapter, 43–59
Alfred P. Murrah Federal Building bombing (Oklahoma City), 43
Allende, Salvador, 74, 78
American Association of University Women, 33
American Institute of Architects (AIA), 8
America*Speaks*, 48-49, 52-57
Anglo-American Corporation of South Africa, 8
Another East Harlem Project: Minimum Standards vs. Minimum Decent (Architecture Record), 87*fig*
Architectural Magazine, 89
Arnstein, Sherry, 10
Association of Collegiate Schools of Architecture (ACSA), 6
avoidance model, 270–272

Banco Central Hipotecário (BCH) [Colombia], 252, 255

Bâtir Ensemble (1988), 84
Bedford-Stuyvesant neighborhood (Brooklyn): CDC (community development corporation) launched in 1965, 16; demographics of the, 4; Pratt Center's continuing involvement in the, 63–64
Benin. *See* People's Republic of Benin
Berkeley's Free Speech Movement (1960s), 6–7
Beunaventura map (Colombia), 193*fig*
Beyond the Melting Pot (Glazer and Moynihan), 94
bill of rights, 9
Black Capitalism, 128
Bogotá (Colombia): building technology proposals in, 186–187; forced removal of squatters by, 171*fig*; French Technical Cooperation proposals for, 186–187; ICT housing organization helping dispossessed migrants in, 172; Ministry of Housing in, 188; potential Terrasses housing program in, 255; squatter settlements or "barrios piratas" by migrants to, 168–170*fig*, 171–172; Volvamos a la Gente Foundation in, 186
Breasted, Mary, 78
brick making projects (Colombia): La Bocana, 192–202; Pequeños Proyectos Productivos (PPP) project for teaching, 202–205
Brooklyn-Queens Expressway (BQE) funeral protest, 68–69, 72
Burkina Faso Microcredit Case Study: birth of neighborhood committees to support, 112–114; examining community engagement through the, 104–105; first information flyer about community savings associations handed out to residents, 111*fig*; grain mill community investment, 118–119; on the Habitat Project, 106–107, 116; improved financial stability due to the, 231–232; lessons learned on developing innovations and networks, 129–130; Mamoudou Traoré successful brick-making enterprise during the, 121–122, 123*fig*, 124; outcomes and update on the, 122–127; problem identification in, 108–112; project development analysis, 115–116, 119–122; reflections on self-help in South Africa, 128–129; relation between inhabitants and technical experts, 114–115; self-help through microcredit system, 105–112; structure for the micro savings and loan organization, 112–114; summary of, 19; *tontine* (traditional village system of solidarity) functioning as motivation in, 274–275;

between Katan and, 4–5; influences on career of, 11; New York City-based urban planning work by, 1; *Report of Proceedings* cover photograph taken by, 49*fig*; speaking at the Northside Housing dedication, 83*fig*; wide professional experience of, 2

Shore, William B., 39

Silent Spring (Carson), 33

sit-in protest: international Occupy movement evolving from the, 275–276; as part of the 1960s civil disobedience strategy, 275

Skidmore, Owings & Merrill LLP (SOM), 8

Socialist Party (France), 133

social organization model: social upheavals (1960s) changing the, 3, 7–10, 275; society's vitality as requiring change in, 279–280

social problems: associated with poorly developed housing projects, 89, 249; East Harlem Multiservice Center to address poverty and, 18, 93–97; East Harlem's continued problems with health disparities and poverty, 102; federal income tax debate as part of discussion about, 37–38; how housing authority housing projects can generate, 89; New York RPA discussion and strategies to address poverty and, 37–38; of South and Central American governments, 229; urban architecture students awareness of neighborhood poverty and, 63–64. *See also* corruption

social upheavals (US, 1960s): description of, 3; disparities being addressed during the, 9–10; student protests during the, 7–9, 275

South Africa: Anglo-American Corporation of South Africa in, 8; Burkina Faso Microcredit Case Study in, 104–127; lessons learned on developing innovations and networks, 129–130; racism of "White, Colored, and Black" bathrooms projects in, 8; reflections on self-help in, 128–129. *See also* West Africa

Spanish Harlem neighborhood (NYC): *Another East Harlem Project: Minimum Standards vs. Minimum Decent* (Architecture Record) on, 87*fig*; changing demographics of, 4, 85–86, 101; New York State Housing Authority role in settlement house project in, 85, 87–89; settlement house for the elderly project in, 3–5, 18, 86–89. *See also* East Harlem Projects/Vassar College Case Study

S&S Corrugated Paper Machinery Company (Northside), 65, 70–71, 73–74, 79

St. Nicholas Church (Brooklyn), 81

St. Nicholas Neighborhood Preservation and Rehabilitation Corporation (St. Nicks Alliance) [Brooklyn], 80–83

Stern, Nikki, 56–57

Stern magazine (Germany), 230

Stobierski, Rudy, 65, 68

Street: Magazine of the Urban Environment (Winter 1973–74) [Pratt Center], 66*fig*–67*fig*, 69*fig*

Sullivan, Brian, 81–82

Surdna Foundation, 44

Sweden exchange system, 27–278

TAR (The Architects' Resistance): condemning "White, Colored, and Black" bathrooms projects, 8; origins and mission of, 8; treatise written by, 7–8

Technical Action Groups (TAG) workshops, 15

technical experts: Burkina Faso Microcredit Case Study relations between inhabitants and, 114–115; establishment of a preliminary outline by, 25; Jardies self-managed habitat's resident-technician, 136–144, 146–148; lessons learned about relationship between residents and, 23; relationship between Destechados (Homeless) and the, 156–157; training provided to the Destechados (Homeless) by, 161–162. *See also* urban planners

Tillack, Hans-Martin, 230

Touraine, Alain, 279

transportation issue (New York), 36

Traoré, Mamoudou, 121–122, 123*fig*, 124

Tuareg people (Burkina Faso), 105

Tumaco earthquake (1979), 188

Tumaco Island (Colombia): demographics of, 187–188; global warming impact on the, 226, 227*fig*; map showing how it relates to the continent, 192*fig*; new hospital completed in 2010 on, 226–227; photograph of Tumaco Bay, 189*fig*; photographs of waterfront shelters and streets in, 191*fig*; Reorientation of Tumaco Urban Growth project relocating poor families in, 207–225; update and new proposals for 2020 on, 225–228

Tumaco Self-Help Assisted Project Case Study: French Technical Cooperation role in the, 189; identifying problem and setting up a self-help housing program, 188–190; raising awareness among residents, 190–192; selecting the housing project site, 190; summary of the, 20–21

About the Authors

Roger Katan is a French American architect, artist, and educator known as a proponent of the community-based design practices of participatory architecture and advocacy planning. He has been a university instructor, international consultant, lecturer, activist, and author. *Building Together* is his third book on participatory design practice.

After architecture studies at the Ecole des Beaux Arts and MIT, Katan worked for Louis Kahn in Philadelphia in the early 1960s. During 1964 to 1975 in East Harlem, New York, Katan created one of the first community design centers. Working with Pratt Institute and City College graduate students, he provided free technical assistance to neighborhood organizations. In 1968, he obtained US citizenship. He taught architecture at Pratt Institute, New York City College, and Pratt Graduate School of Tropical Architecture for ten years, with one year at Vassar College, teaching and practicing advocacy planning in the community. From 1976 to 1980, Katan was consultant to the French government on participatory practice. From 1976 to 2006, Katan worked on missions with the UN, World Bank, and European Union serving uprooted communities in West Africa, South and Central America. Katan currently lives in Sauve, France, and continues to be a consultant to the Municipality of Tumaco, on the Pacific coast of Colombia.

Ronald Shiffman FAICP, Hon. AIA, is Professor Emeritus at Pratt Institute's Programs for Sustainable Planning and Development. He is founding director of the Pratt Institute Center for Community and Environmental Development, which grew out of joint work with his mentor George M. Raymond. Trained as an architect and urban planner, Shiffman is an expert in community-based planning, housing, and sustainable development. He is recognized as one of the founders of the community design and community development movement in America. He has authored a number of articles on urban planning, social justice, and community economic development and was the lead editor of the book, *Beyond Zuccotti Park*.

Professor Shiffman has received awards from community-based organizations: Architects, Designers and Planners for Social Responsibility, the local chapters of the American Institute of Architects and American Institute of Certified Planners, and the Municipal Art Society. In 2012, he was awarded the Jane Jacobs Medal for Lifetime Leadership for his work to promote community-based activism over the last fifty years. He is also the recipient of the American Planning Society's prestigious 2013 Planning Pioneer Award.

newvillagePRESS

New Village Press specializes in books about grassroots community building. If you appreciated *Building Together*, you will enjoy other titles from our press.

Ronald Shiffman was the lead editor of **Beyond Zuccotti Park: Freedom of Assembly and the Occupation of Public Space** and a contributing author to **What We See: Advancing the Observations of Jane Jacobs**, both of which were listed as Ten Best Books in Urban Planning, Design, and Development by *Planetizen*.

Other recent New Village titles offer practical insight into healing distressed neighborhoods—**Urban Alchemy: Restoring Joy in America's Sorted-Out Cities** by Mindy Thompson Fullilove, MD, and **From Foreclosure to Fair Lending: Advocacy, Organizing, Occupy, and the Pursuit of Equitable Credit**, edited by Chester Hartman and Gregory D. Squires.

Those seeking exemplary case studies by design educators engaged in community-based learning will want **Service-Learning in Design and Planning: Educating at the Boundaries**, edited by Tom Angotti, Cheryl Doble, and Paula Horrigan. And **Building Commons and Community** by Karl Linn is a classic work that documents half a century of citizens working together with design professionals and educators to build shared spaces in low-income neighborhoods.

Two international books about revitalizing communities through their school environments are **Awakening Creativity: Dandelion School Blossoms** by Lily Yeh and **Asphalt to Ecosystems: Design Ideas for Schoolyard Transformation** by Sharon Gamson Danks.

Learn more about our books and authors at **NEWVILLAGEPRESS.NET**